GLASGOW'S BLACK HEART

Douglas Skelton is a Glasgow-born journalist and author
who has been chronicling crime for 20 years. He lives in Ayrshire.

Also by Douglas Skelton

Blood on the Thistle
Frightener (with Lisa Brownlie)
No Final Solution
A Time to Kill
Devil's Gallop
Deadlier than the Male
Bloody Valentine
Indian Peter
Scotland's Most Wanted
Dark Heart

GLASGOW'S BLACK HEART

A CITY'S LIFE OF CRIME

DOUGLAS SKELTON

MAINSTREAM
PUBLISHING

EDINBURGH AND LONDON

First published in Great Britain in 2009 by
MAINSTREAM PUBLISHING COMPANY
(EDINBURGH) LTD
7 Albany Street
Edinburgh EH1 3UG

ISBN 9781845964894

A catalogue record for this book is available
from the British Library

Typeset in Caslon and DirtyEgo

Printed in Great Britain by
Clays Ltd, St Ives plc

This book is dedicated to the memory of wee Dan Broon frae Pertick, who started me on my life of crime by sending me round the cop shops.

ACKNOWLEDGEMENTS

A number of people helped keep me right on certain things and/ or provided me with info. Thanks are due to Joe and Kate Jackson, Jim Steele, Karin Stewart, her mum and dad Anne and Kenny, Katie Bell, Stephen Wilkie and May Mitchell of the Strathclyde Police Museum.

Mark Sweeney of the Scottish *Sun* and Gary McLaughlin helped me with the photographs.

Meanwhile, Margaret kept me supplied with coffee during the long, l-o-n-g writing period. Thanks are also due to Bill Campbell, Graeme Blaikie and the staff at Mainstream for once again putting up with me, particularly editor Claire Rose.

CONTENTS

CHAPTER ONE

THE FIRST GREAT BANK ROBBERY

Glasgow, 13 July 1811. It was the Saturday of Glasgow's annual fair, a holiday that has the reputation of being forever wet and cold but which this year had dawned warm and sunny. The fair ran for eight days then and its focal point was Glasgow Green, where entertainment of all forms was presented to thousands of revellers from across the west of Scotland. Meanwhile, a profit was made as trades were plied and goods were hawked from the variety of stalls set up on the Green. There was food, of course, and craftware and patent medicines, while all around tumblers, acrobats, singers and dancers vied for attention alongside bizarre freak shows and animal acts. The crowds attracted other, more secretive, individuals to the revels – pickpockets, conmen, whores and pimps, for such an event was one of the highlights of their year, too. And there was the noise – the blaring of trumpets, the braying of beasts, the cries of hawkers, the beating of drums, the tolling of bells, even the rattle of gunfire from the penny theatricals as they presented the stories of blood and death that the masses loved so much.

However, the fun of the fair was of little interest to three men lodging in the house of Mrs Stewart at the bottom of the Broomielaw. Using the names Moffat, Stone and Down, they had been in the

11

city since May. They had told their landlady that they were in town on business connected to the Union Canal and had remained with her until Fair Saturday, even at one point moving with her to a new house. They had arrived with a single trunk and a portmanteau, and one morning Mr Moffat, who appeared to be their leader, had carried in a coarse wooden box about eight to ten inches long, which was nailed shut and thought by Mrs Stewart to contain papers.

But Moffat, Stone and Down were not what they seemed. Their business was not with the Union Canal but with the Paisley Union Bank. During their three-month sojourn in Glasgow, they visited the bank's premises in Ingram Street both during the day and, more surreptitiously, by night. They had somehow managed to make wax impressions of vital keys – suggesting an inside man – and from those impressions they had made copies.

On Saturday, 13 July, they were ready to stage what may well be the first recorded bank raid in British criminal history.

It was the bank's custom to take possession of large sums of cash on weekends from its Edinburgh agents, James Hunter & Company. The money was collected by a porter from the coach at the Black Bull Inn in Argyle Street and carried to the Ingram Street premises. On this particular week, there was a considerable amount and the porter hefted it to the bank with some difficulty. Once in the office, the money was lodged in a strong iron safe. The building was locked up and the keys taken into the safe keeping of the manager, Andrew Templeton, who was also a magistrate, at his home in St Enoch Square. The porter, who doubled as caretaker, then accompanied his wife to sample the attractions of the fair on the Green. The building remained empty until Monday morning, when it was discovered that robbers had relieved it not only of the Saturday morning deposit of gold guineas but also of a substantial wedge of the bank's own notes. Some accounts say the haul was £20,000 – the equivalent of well over a million today – but others place it as high as £45,000. However, the bank was unwilling to confirm exactly how much had been taken.

Mrs Stewart had become suspicious of her three English lodgers, who had quit their rooms on the day of the robbery, supposedly heading for Bristol. She told investigators that she had seen them with skeleton keys and plans, which she had presumed to be part of their business. She had also sent a box to London for them, addressed to Mr Little, c/o Scoltop, a blacksmith.

Coachmaster Alexander Leith, well known in the city partly because most of his nose had been bitten off by one of his own horses, reported that three men had come to his stable at around 5 a.m. that Sunday wishing to hire a carriage to take them to Edinburgh. There was some haste, they said, for one of them had received a letter saying his brother was lying seriously ill. Ever hospitable, he invited them into his home and offered them two gills of rum and two bowls of milk. While they waited for the carriage to be readied, old Sandy Leith had plenty of time to size up his customers – and was able to provide a fairly detailed description to Procurator Fiscal Bennet.

The first was a stout man, about 5 ft 7 or 8 in. tall, full-faced with a ruddy complexion and a nose inclining to purple. He had large black eyes, short black hair and was dressed in a long dark-coloured coat, bluish striped trousers or pantaloons and boots. He was aged at least 40 and had with him a greatcoat under which he had a large parcel tied up in a handkerchief or shawl. This man appeared to be their leader. He said his name was Moffat and he was something of a gentleman, as was the second man, who was roughly the same height and had a similar coat and trousers or pantaloons. The third, though, was in appearance much like a tradesman. He was taller than his companions by an inch, was slender in build and wore a long dark coat similar to theirs. The post-chaise they hired, old Sandy said, had dropped them off in Edinburgh's West End.

The chase was now on. Two representatives of the bank took a coach to Edinburgh, where they joined forces with a 'most active city officer', Archibald Campbell, to track the men down. They picked up the trail at Drysdale's Hotel, where they learned that the three men had hired another post-chaise to take them to Haddington. There, they had stopped at the Blue Bell Inn, where they had passed a £10 Paisley Union Bank note. They had changed a further £20 note at the town's Press Inn before moving on to Berwick.

And so it went on. Mr Campbell, clearly something of a human bloodhound, tracked them to England, following a trail of notes and matching descriptions. In Darlington, a waiter recognised their descriptions and produced a £20 note. He accompanied Campbell and Robert Walkinshaw, representing the bank, south towards London, sometimes travelling on the very same post coaches that had carried the three men ahead of them, meeting more innkeepers along the way who recognised their quarry. Many of these witnesses recalled the same bundles that had been seen in Glasgow, Edinburgh and points south, while at Welwyn, two staging posts from London, the men had been spotted dividing banknotes between them 'in a most public manner'. Here they left a portmanteau, identical to the one Mrs Stewart had seen, to be forwarded to an address in Tottenham Court Road.

Once in London, Campbell and Walkinshaw made contact with the famed Bow Street Runners. Formed in the mid-eighteenth century by magistrate Henry Fielding, the author of *Tom Jones*, and later strengthened by his half-brother, 'Blind John' Fielding, they became, in the words of author and lawyer James Morton, 'the small private army of the senior magistrate at Bow Street'. They did not have a uniform – their badge of office was a baton with gilt crown – but they were the forerunners of the Metropolitan Police and the obvious point of contact for the two out-of-town investigators.

They met up with officers Stephen Lavender and John Vickery, who took them to Tottenham Court Road and the smithy of John Scoltock, to where Mrs Stewart had sent the box – the man's surname had been misspelled – and which had also been the forwarding address for the portmanteau left at Welwyn. Scoltock was known to Lavender and Vickery. They also knew that he was associated with some of the most daring crooks in the city. In his smithy they found a number of lockpicks, skeleton keys and 'various other implements for housebreaking'. The portmanteau was later found to contain dirty shirts and linen, two with the initials JM embroidered on them. Scoltock was under the supervision of the courts – having lost a lawsuit – and living in St George's Fields. There the officers found another familiar face, Houghton, or 'Huffey', White.

White was an accomplished housebreaker who had been found guilty at the Chester Assizes for 'being at large before his sentence of transportation had expired' and duly received a second banishment, this time for life. However, he escaped from the Woolwich hulks – rotting old ships at permanent dock in the Thames – before he could sample the delights of Botany Bay. White was later identified as one of the three men who had travelled south from Edinburgh. The officers also arrested Scoltock, his wife and Mrs White. It seemed that they had just missed another of their targets – James MacKoull, alias Moffat, who had left the house shortly before they arrived.

* * *

The name James MacKoull, or MacCoul, is little known today but he was something of a criminal celebrity. He was born in 1763, the second son of a respectable London pocketbook maker and a mother who was described as 'a female of abandoned habits, and long known as a shoplifter and thief of the lowest grade'. He received some education – his ability to read and write put him head and shoulders above most men of his background – and his father had him apprenticed to a leather-stainer. His early years, though, were characterised by a struggle as to whose genes would come out on top, those of his hard-working, honest father or of his larcenous mother. In the end, the maternal influence won the day – he was forever stealing from his friends and eventually his more dissolute habits saw him sacked by his employer. By then, he had grown into an intelligent young man with a reputation for being somewhat fleet of foot – handy attributes for the criminal he was to become. He was also something of a pugilist, another skill that would stand him in good stead, for the shoulders with which he would rub throughout his life did not belong to the gentlest of creatures.

However, when he and two accomplices robbed a well-known and well-connected retired undertaker in a park in broad daylight, things became too hot. Although they got away, they had been seen by a number of people and MacKoull feared that the heavy hand of the law would shortly be feeling his collar. He appealed to his father for help and it was arranged that he would join His Majesty's Navy, serving on the *Apollo* as an officer's servant, a function he also performed on the *Centurion*. A life on the ocean wave seemed to agree with him, for he stayed in the service for nine years, serving in the West Indies and along the North American coast. When he returned home in 1785, he was loaded down with wages, prize money and presents for his two brothers and three sisters. His younger brother, Ben, would not enjoy his company for long; he was executed for robbery the following year. His older brother, John, was the best educated of them all but he too had fallen under his mother's malignant influence and was 'well known to Bow Street'.

Once back in his old haunts, MacKoull's real nature swam to the surface again and he gave himself up to every type of debauchery his funds would allow. He attended bull-baiting, cockfights and boxing matches – gentleman's pursuits all, but also places of interest to the faces of the eighteenth-century underworld. He developed an adroitness at the gaming tables that bolstered his funds for a time but soon the inevitable happened – he found himself broke. Unwilling to take up an honest trade, he instead transformed himself into a gentleman pickpocket. His time abroad had taught him a number of tricks. His speech and manner were sufficiently polished to allow him to pose as a respectable man and he was able to tell a good story well. He was no longer James, or Jem, MacKoull, the disreputable son of a pocketbook maker, but Captain Moffat, the former master of a West Indiaman, who was fond of a game of chance. He cosied up to the often aristocratic card players beside him and plied them with liquor before relieving them of their well-lined purses and watches.

Then, at the age of 28, he met a woman and fell in love. Depending on which account you read, she was the owner of a respectable lodging house for swells or a woman who 'kept a house of certain description' – in other words, a whorehouse. By now very well known to the runners of Bow Street and other magistrates, MacKoull decided it was time for him to lay low for a while. He avoided his previous haunts and friends, living instead off the largesse of his new wife, while also keeping his hand – and fists – in with some amateur pugilism. However, he did not fully abandon his criminal habits, for he became a receiver of stolen goods, storing them first with his mother and sister, then in his wife's home, in an alcove created by the bricking up of a window to avoid payment of the window tax, a storage facility known as a 'Pitt's Picture' after the prime minister who brought in the tax. This new phase in his career did not last long, for the goods were discovered and he fled to Germany, where he posed as a merchant while picking up his old trade of fleecing gambling partners. When things became too hot for him there, he briefly touched down in London before heading north, where he was unknown to the authorities.

In September 1805, he landed in Leith, where he stayed for a time at the Ship Tavern before finding lodgings in New Street, Canongate. His ability to tell a tale stood him in good stead in the dockland inns and taverns, while his dexterity at lifting wallets kept him in spending cash. However, he botched the dipping of a gentleman's pocket at a theatre and was pursued by a town officer named Campbell – perhaps the same Campbell who would so doggedly follow the trail south after the Glasgow job. In a close, the officer struck his quarry on the back of the head with his baton and MacKoull tumbled headlong down some stairs to lie still at the bottom. It seems Campbell may have panicked then, thinking he had killed the man, for he left him lying where he was. MacKoull, though, had only been knocked senseless and he dragged himself to his rooms in the Canongate, where he laid low for a time to recuperate, telling everyone he had been waylaid by some drunken sailors. Forever after he had a deep scar on his forehead where he had struck the stairs.

In November 1806, he decided to leave Edinburgh – the reason why would not be suspected for a number of years – and crossed the Irish Sea to Dublin, where he narrowly avoided a lengthy period in jail when another dipping went wrong. By October 1807 he was back again in Edinburgh, where he was arrested for picking a man's pocket. He talked himself out of that charge and took off to London. But in 1809, he was back in Scotland, facing a charge of passing false notes in Stirling. Again, his luck held, for he was cleared. That luck ran out in Chester in 1810, when he was picked up for being 'a rogue and a vagabond' and set to six months' hard labour in Chester Castle.

On his release, he returned to London, where he took up with Huffey White and a lockpick specialist named Harry French. MacKoull was down on his luck. His pickpocketing days were over; his once nimble fingers were now considerably fatter than before and he had botched too many of his jobs. He had another notion, and White and French were just the boys to help him out. He had learned of the vast amounts kept in the Glasgow bank at the weekend, again suggestive of some inside information. All it needed was three brave, cunning and skilful lads to relieve the bankers of that booty. So, after French had sold off his household goods to finance the expedition, the three set out for Glasgow.

* * *

It's not clear just when MacKoull decided he was going to gull his confederates out of their cut but it is generally accepted that such was his plan. Huffey White's wife, for one, did not trust him. After the job, she had met MacKoull on the stairs as she was entering Scoltock's house in Tower Street. She confessed to her husband that she had 'fears for his safety in such a place, the more especially as she had seen Jem MacKoull coming out of the door'.

'It's all very well,' Huffey reassured her. 'We've nothing to fear from him.'

It was shortly after that, just as they were to sit down to a supper of roast goose and green peas, that the Bow Street officers raided the place. MacKoull had been due to return for the meal but failed to show – which was either another example of his great good fortune, or he knew the raid was in the offing and so kept his distance.

Whatever the case, MacKoull was talked into returning the stolen money to save Huffey from the hangman's noose and in return for no further proceedings being taken against himself and French. An approach was made through an intermediary – a Bow Street officer and acquaintance of Mrs MacKoull named Sayers, then on protection duty for George III – and, amazingly, an agreement was reached. MacKoull had given £13,000 to a boxer friend named William Gibbons, who had hidden it up a chimney in a back room of his premises. Gibbons later said that it was Mrs MacKoull who came to collect it.

However, MacKoull had a trick up his sleeve, for only £11,941 was returned to the bank. Although company representatives went away satisfied, Huffey White was unhappy with the situation. Saved from the gibbet he may have been, but he still faced the prospect of going back to the hulks and then transportation to the colonies.

'Does the gallows villain mean to do us out of the rest of the money?' he raged in his cell when his wife told him what had happened. 'Go and tell him that I won't stand it: had all the money been restored I might have got a free pardon.'

Harry French was also far from pleased with MacKoull's finagling. A lawyer who knew all three later said that French had told him that he would shoot MacKoull on sight for cheating him out of what he believed was rightfully his. French never followed through on his threat, for he vanished from the city soon afterwards. Some have it that he was turned in by MacKoull and transported to New South Wales, others that MacKoull had him killed.

Huffey White most certainly did not reach New South Wales. He once again escaped and within a few months was arrested trying to rob the Leeds mail coach. He was hanged in Northampton. When asked if he had any last requests, he suggested that someone might take his place.

In 1815 or 1816, William Gibbons met MacKoull at a 'ringmatch' and was told that the criminal fraternity 'were all down upon him for bucketing his pells [concealing part of the haul]' and doing White and French out of their piece of the action. It was MacKoull's opinion that 'it was nobody's business'.

After he had returned the money, MacKoull went into hiding, for his holding back of the rest of the cash was seen by the authorities as breaking the terms of the agreement. He was known to be living with a prostitute named Reynolds and it was while he was hiding in her Hatton Garden rooms that he was arrested. Denying all knowledge of the robbery – the repayment had been made through a circuitous chain of intermediaries and could not be directly linked to him at this stage – he was hauled back to Edinburgh. However, once again, it seemed he was living a charmed life. There was a flaw in the warrant and he applied to 'run his letters' – that is, be brought to trial within a reasonable period of time. On 12 June 1812, he was released by the Lords of Justiciary.

The following year, he was back in Edinburgh, spreading money about. He even opened an account with the British Linen Bank, lodging over £2,600 in notes, £800 being Paisley Union Bank script. This attracted the attention of Mr F.G. Denovan, a former Bow Street Runner and now master of police at Leith. MacKoull was pulled in but continued to deny any involvement in the 1811 robbery. As none of the notes could be linked to the haul, he was allowed to go.

In return, MacKoull gave the bank £1,000, a decision he soon thought better of, launching a court action for the money's return. Criminal justice may have moved swiftly in those days but civil actions, then as now, could run for years. And so it was with his suit against the Paisley Union Bank. He, on one side, claimed that the money was his and told everyone who would listen that the company executives were the real robbers, while the courts were 'corrupt and abandoned, for delaying to grant him justice'. On the other side, the bank's directors were certain that he was the man behind the robbery and that the notes, still in their possession, were part of the haul.

Unfortunately, they could not prove it. Delay followed delay and MacKoull, hesitantly it must be said, agreed to a judicial examination, which he sailed through with his now usual aplomb.

Finally, towards the close of 1819, the matter could be delayed no further and it was referred to a jury court. It was time for the bank to put up or shut up – they must either prove their claim that MacKoull was a master criminal or return the money, and more besides. As the *Edinburgh Annual Register* of 1820 put it, 'they must refund £1,000 with six years' interest, and £800 expenses, and have the mortification of being braved and mastered by a common London thief and pickpocket'. They refused to go down without a fight, so they hired Mr Denovan to investigate the matter for them. He retraced the steps taken by Archibald Campbell in 1811 and found many of the original witnesses. Denovan also managed to convince Huffey White's wife, John Scoltock, William Gibbons and others to give evidence on the bank's behalf.

The hearing began on 11 May 1820. Such was the fame of the case that the outer passageway and the court itself were packed with spectators. So densely packed was the courtroom that when John Scoltock's name was called, MacKoull tried to leave but was prevented by the press of bodies. 'The instant he saw [Scoltock],' reported the *Edinburgh Annual Register*, 'he changed colour, and sunk by the side of the wall in a kind of faint. He was assisted out of court, and did not again make his appearance for some time.'

Scoltock confirmed he had made the keys used in the robbery to MacKoull's specifications and that while the plotters were in Glasgow all correspondence was with MacKoull, as neither White nor French could write. Some of the keys were contained in the coarse wooden box mentioned by their landlady, Mrs Stewart. He pointed out that the address label on the box had misspelled his name as 'Scoltop', which was a mistake MacKoull often made. On their return from Glasgow, MacKoull told him, 'You would hardly credit what a precious lot we've grabb'd, and what sort of notes they are – like dirty, coarse brown paper, and damned heavy.'

Then MacKoull turned to White and said, 'Huffey, we shan't sell 'em, but go down into the country and smash 'em [pass them].'

Huffey, though, was unhappy with this plan. 'Jem, we're doing wrong. You or me should go to the other man.' This other man, Scoltock believed, was French. MacKoull agreed and said he would go to see him then and there.

A short time later, the Bow Street officers arrived and made their arrests. Scoltock admitted that after the money had been repaid to the bank, he had approached MacKoull for a promised payment, pointing out that as he had kept so much of the booty back he could afford to pay him. 'Well, little one,' MacKoull had said, 'have patience. I must go into the country and smash them first, and that is not such an easy job, as they are eyeing me in all quarters. But when I get them smashed, you shall be satisfied.'

William Gibbons' testimony also proved damning. He was the boxer and coachmaster who had hidden some of the cash for MacKoull. In court, he was asked if he knew a James Moffat, the name under which MacKoull was pursuing the case.

'No,' said the boxer, 'I do not know any person of that name.'

The bank's counsel then demanded that the defendant be brought forward. MacKoull was found hiding among the crowd and escorted to the side of the witness box, where he stood with his head hung low so that Gibbons could not see his face.

'Witness,' said his lawyer, 'do you know that man?'

Gibbons strained forward and then said in a stage whisper, 'Jem, hold your head up, I can't see you.' Then, when he looked up, Gibbons affirmed, 'Yes, this is James MacKoull – I never know'd him by any other name.' He went on to confirm that MacKoull had given him the money and that Mrs MacKoull had later collected it so that it could be returned to the bank to save Huffey's life.

The civil case went badly for MacKoull. In the end, the jury found in favour of the bank, leaving the Crown no option but to serve him with a criminal indictment. The trial was fixed for 12 June and again the parade of witnesses was wheeled in. MacKoull's brother did his best to prevent some of them from appearing. Gibbons, for instance, was threatened but the old boxer was not a man to be fearful of such things. He duly turned up and repeated his evidence. Scoltock, though, was not made of such stern stuff and took flight. However, he was found and dragged back to Edinburgh to tell his story in a criminal court. Again, the case was the talk of Edinburgh and the courtroom was filled to capacity. The corridors outside were crammed with people waiting to get in and every bit of space was taken up. The spectators were so boisterous that their noise constantly interrupted the proceedings and finally the judge ordered that the hallways be cleared.

Throughout the case, MacKoull appeared confident, even cocky, as if he knew something the others did not. For some witnesses, he reserved a malignant look that was said to make the blood run cold. Henry Cockburn, later a judge, was on the prosecution side and he felt the full force of MacKoull's evil eye, which some said was 'full, clear and piercing – so much so that a single glare was exceedingly disagreeable'. In his *Memorials*, Cockburn noted that he was 'a very peculiar looking scoundrel, both in face and figure' but does not mention that he was so unnerved by the man's close attention that he complained to the court.

MacKoull's luck had finally run out, for he was found guilty of the robbery and sentenced to death. As he heard his 'melancholy fate', the *Glasgow Herald* reported, 'his countenance turned pale, and he appeared confused, as if he had not anticipated the result'.

'However secretly the crime had been perpetrated,' the judge said, 'and however dextrously planned, it was seen by an eye above.'

MacKoull couldn't help but agree. He later told the governor of Edinburgh's Calton jail, 'The hand of God is certainly against me, else such a connective chain of evidence could not have been brought forward at so great a distance of time.'

His wife, from whom he was estranged, visited him in jail and vowed to use whatever means she had at her disposal to have his sentence reviewed. The strings she pulled certainly worked, for his execution was put off three times and then postponed subject to His Majesty's pleasure. This news astounded anyone familiar with the case and raises questions about the possibility of interference in the case. It was said that at some point in his criminal career MacKoull had relayed certain information to the authorities and that this service was like a 'get out of jail free' card. Certainly, it would appear that he had no compunction about ratting on colleagues but was that enough to save his life? Or if his wife was a powerful madam, did she have some dirt on someone in authority that she could use to help her former lover?

Whatever the case, the experience took its toll on MacKoull. He began to have nightmares, 'his cries and imprecations were so horrific as greatly to annoy the inmates in the adjoining cells'. Weight dropped off him alarmingly and his black hair turned to grey. His deterioration was such that it was claimed that no one who had known him before his conviction would have recognised him.

It was during his time in prison that the story took one final twist – and it harked back to the 1806 murder of Edinburgh bank porter William Begbie, found stabbed to death in Tweeddale Close, with £4,000 of notes gone. It was known now that MacKoull was in Edinburgh at the time and that he had left hurriedly for Dublin soon after the killing. It was also known that he had been back in the city for a short time when some of the stolen notes were discovered in a wall. The description of a man observed by a witness stalking the porter up Leith Walk matched MacKoull. His lodging house was near the murder scene. Mr Denovan, the Leith police officer, was certain that MacKoull was the killer and resolved to visit him in prison to interview him about it. When asked about his lodgings in New Street in November 1806, MacKoull seemed to guess where the questions were going and, Denovan wrote later, 'rolled his eyes, and, as if falling into convulsion, threw himself back upon his bed'. Eventually, he denied being in Edinburgh at the time. 'I was then in the East Indies – in the West Indies. What do you mean?'

'I mean no harm, MacKoull,' Denovan replied. 'I merely asked the question for my own curiosity, for I think when you left these lodgings you went to Dublin. Is it not so?'

'Yes, yes, I went to Dublin – and I wish I remained there still.'

Denovan was in no doubt that MacKoull had murdered Begbie and lost much of the stolen money at the Irish gaming tables. But no one can ever be certain, for MacKoull said no more about it. On 22 December 1820, his mysterious illness finished him off. According to Glasgow writer and reformer Peter Mackenzie's *Reminiscences* and Douglas Grant in *The Thin Blue Line*, someone smuggled poison to him and he killed himself. Whatever the cause of death, his wife had him buried in Calton Graveyard, beside the jail.

Many years later, the remainder of the stolen money was returned to the bank. It has been hinted that the trail led to a man of some wealth and influence and that not only was Mrs MacKoull up to her neck in the caper but so was her pal Sayers, the former Bow Street Runner. However, there were no further prosecutions and just how far up the social register the crime climbed is open only to speculation.

What is certain is that the Paisley Union Bank robbery of 1811 was the case that put Glasgow on the criminal map. The fact that such a provincial financial institution had the kind of money that would attract the attentions of crooks like MacKoull, White and French is a perverse example of how prosperous the city had become. However, even though Glasgow had come of age, its police force was yet little more than a toddler. It had been formed in 1800 but even 11 years later it was not deemed worthy to investigate a crime of such magnitude. That was left to the city's procurator fiscal, Edinburgh town officers and London's Bow Street Runners. Glasgow's finest were not much more than nightwatchmen and the investigation of major crimes would remain out of their hands for many years.

CHAPTER TWO

THE EYES OF GLASGOW POLICE ARE UPON YOU

They came from the outlying villages of Gorbals, Govan and Anderston. They moved south from the Highlands, some voluntarily, others having been forcibly cleared from their homes to make way for sheep and accommodate the gentry's love of hunting. They crossed the water from the islands and from Ireland to escape poverty and famine.

And they settled in the city on the River Clyde, where they found work in the mills and factories that had grown out of the Industrial Revolution. But the homes in which they found themselves, clustered around Glasgow Cross and down towards the river, soon became slums and spawning places of disease and crime.

From 1765 to 1800, the population increased from 28,000 to 77,000. Daniel Defoe might once have written of Glasgow "tis the cleanest and beautifullest, and best built city in Britain, London excepted', but it now had its dark side. The Molendinar Burn that St Mungo had crossed with his oxen was now a sewer. The rich merchants and industrialists swaggered in their red cloaks on the covered and flagstoned piazza beside the Tontine Hotel at the Cross and kept the great unwashed at bay with a sharp blow from their walking sticks. But beyond what had become the civic centre, around the Tolbooth, the main thoroughfares were, according to industrialist turned chronicler of times past Robert Reid (writing as 'Senex' in the mid-nineteenth century), 'allowed to remain in a state of great filth'. He continued:

> In many of them were deep ruts filled with mire, and their gutters were made the receptacles of putrid accumulations. The streets were seldom swept or cleaned, except when the heavens kindly sent down a pelting shower of rain, which acted as the gratis scavenger-general of the city. Often a heap of dung was formed by individuals on the public streets, and allowed to remain there till it suited the proprietor to use it for manure, and sell it to others for that purpose.

Wherever there are people trying to make an honest coin, there are others more than willing to steal it from them. Robbery, rape and murder were fairly common in the dark, muck-caked highways and byways of the old town, and the Tolbooth jail was seldom short of customers. Even in the eighteenth century, the blame for much of the crime was placed at the door of a breakdown of family values, although the term had yet to be coined. 'Wickedness, it seems, has got a loose rein,' observed the writer of a broadsheet (a single-page publication recording such sensational events, also known as a broadside) in 1773. 'Swearing, debauchery, insulting and Sabbath-breaking goes on without a check, the fathers have forgot the correction of their children, and many, too many, mothers idolize their daughters even to their own destruction.'

What the city needed was a police force to keep the rising tide of lawlessness in check. The sheriff and his officers were responsible for the investigation and enforcement of laws but there was only so much they could do. The 'Charlies', the watchmen who patrolled the streets after dark, were simply not up to the job. They were expected to call out the hour, ignite what little street lighting there was and clear the streets of dung. This last duty at least brought some income, for it could be sold on as manure. These old men, fond of a tot of rum or two and often found asleep in their guardhouse, were the butt of many a joke played by the young dandies of the day.

On one momentous occasion, in February 1793, members of the notorious Hellfire Club lived up to their name when they circumvented what security there was and accidentally set fire to the watchmen's headquarters in the Session House of the Tron Kirk near the Tolbooth.

There had been attempts at creating a municipal police force before, notably in 1778 and 1788, but these had foundered. The rich merchants who ran the town recognised the need for a crime-busting body of men but were just not happy with the idea of having to pay for it. Although the force would be under the control of the local authority, the taxpayers of the city were to have a say in its running, even to the election of the master of police. By 1800, the Session House and church had been rebuilt and Parliament had agreed that a new force be established, at public expense, to police the city streets.

So, on 15 November 1800, the first police force in Britain mustered in the newly rebuilt Session House on the Trongate.

The watchmen were still needed and could be recognised by their greatcoats with a number in white on the back and their 4-ft-long staves. Now, though, there were two sergeants and six constables above them, resplendent in their vests, breeches and new blue coats – the very first boys in blue. And much was expected of them. Dr John Aitken, one of the police commissioners appointed to oversee them, said after the first gathering, 'Our first impression was that the force was so large and overwhelming that it would drive iniquity out of the city as though by a hurricane.'

The watchmen continued to patrol the night-dark streets of the town and call out the hour. As an added extra, they updated the inhabitants on the weather. They still had to sweep the streets of all the muck that had gathered during the day (and there are police officers today who'd say they are doing the same thing). At first, they walked those mean streets in large squads but very soon a system of beat patrols was devised and each watchman was given a lantern and candles to light his way. The men, still largely elderly, tried to use these candles as little as possible in order to sell them and supplement their ten-shilling weekly wage. They were also issued with a rattle to alert other watchmen and the two uniformed constables also on patrol (of the remaining four, two were on duty in the Session House and two would be off). This rattle, very like the kind of thing later used by football fans, was the first method of communication issued to the fledgling force. But in the narrow warren of streets that formed the city, a rattle croaking in the still of the night was all that was needed to have colleagues running – whether it was towards or away from the flashpoint depended on their character and devotion to duty. It may also be the source of the term 'rattled nerves'.

Even though the watchmen still spent too much of their time dozing in the various guardboxes on each beat, they did have an effect on Glasgow's night people. As arrests increased, the Session House became too cramped, so the headquarters was moved across the Trongate to the north-west corner of Bell Street and Candleriggs. There, one storey up, the force had a large room and two 'walled presses or closets' for prisoners. They also had a large room on the ground floor with a further seven cells. Within two years, they had to move again and a former joiner's yard in South Albion Street became police headquarters.

After three years, the first master of police, John Stenhouse, resigned and publican Walter Graham took his place. His lofty manner, both in attitude and in bearing, for he was over 6 ft tall, soon brought him the nickname 'the General'. It was his nature that saw him removed from his post two years later when he refused to go out on night patrol. His successor was the equally tall James Mitchell, a former officer of the Lanarkshire Militia and a stickler for discipline.

Although he worked hard to hone his men into a tight unit, they still had a long way to go before they would be much more than the nightwatchmen of old. As we have seen, when the Paisley Union Bank was robbed in 1811, it was not to the police that the bank turned but to the procurator fiscal. The police force was not designed to be an investigative body, even though magistrates at the police court often intoned to those before them, 'The eye of Almighty God and the Glasgow Police will be on you, so be careful of your future conduct.'

* * *

Apart from the few cells in police headquarters, Glasgow's prison provision comprised the Tolbooth and a 'Bridewell' – a house of correction – in Duke Street. In addition to crooks, the jails also had to cater for vagabonds and debtors. The Tolbooth jailer was also expected to supply coals for the council and court meetings but in addition to his salary he received monies from the prisoners themselves, particularly the debtors. However, not every jailer profited from the arrangement. In 1661, the city treasurer was ordered by the council to give jailer Charles McCleane twenty Scots pounds or one pound, thirteen shillings and fourpence sterling 'for his extraordinary pains in keeping the Tolbooth and getting no profit thereby, having only thieves and lounes [insane persons] as prisoners'.

Prisoners, meanwhile, were allowed to supplement their funds by begging from the windows. They did this by lowering a bag or a basket on a length of rope to the street in the hope that a friend, relative or kind-hearted stranger would drop in a few pennies. On one occasion, an inmate thrust his head out to see if anyone was making a deposit to his jail fund and ended up wedged between the bars on the window. As a punishment, the jailer left him in that position for some time before he sent someone to cut him free.

Naturally, other implements could also be placed in these makeshift hoists, implements that may well have been used in furthering the many escape attempts. In October 1791, convicted thief James

Plunkett escaped from the Tolbooth. He was rearrested on 25 November when he tried to steal four pairs of silk stockings from a shop on the Trongate. He was chased into the Saltmarket, where he was caught when he stumbled over a bag of stones that was to be used for building a causeway. Determined not to be returned to the jail, he tried to pull his pistol but his pursuers managed to disarm him. He knew the jig was up when someone in the crowd recognised him as the prisoner who had fled the jail the month before, although he had tried to disguise himself by cutting his hair.

The Tolbooth buildings were erected in 1626. All that is left of them now is the 113-ft-high steeple with its four-dial clock. It is imposing enough today, sited in the centre of the confluence of High Street, Trongate, Gallowgate and Saltmarket, but in the seventeenth to nineteenth centuries it must have been a most impressive sight. And it needed to be, for it was not only the centre of civic authority but also a symbol of judicial power. The sheriff court met once a week at the Tolbooth and, along with the police court, dealt with relatively minor offences. Often the sheriff or the magistrate presiding sat on the bench reading a newspaper or even drinking, paying little heed to the proceedings and only looking up to pass sentence, generally guilty. It was left to a clerk to make sure everything ran smoothly.

There was no permanent High Court of Justiciary sitting in Glasgow, so more serious cases were dealt with by the West Circuit Court, which arrived in the city every April and September, amid great pomp and ceremony, and situated itself in a room that formed part of the Tolbooth complex. The old judges, more used to the comforts and splendour of Edinburgh, found coming to Glasgow something of a chore. The building was somewhat cramped, what with the burgeoning civic authority and legal hierarchy all sharing the same ground with an ever-growing band of miscreants.

By 1807, there were just under 2,000 criminal cases being heard each and every year. Punishments were swift and hard and not every sentence entailed prison for any length of time. Convictions in serious cases, and even some petty thefts, meant death by hanging (from the Tolbooth condemned cell, those who were about to die could salute the gallows paraphernalia dangling from the steeple). Whipping was also common – a record from 1575 states that the common hangman was paid five shillings 'for scourging of ane hussy throw the town'. Men could be punished by being nailed by the ear to a post. A few took the opportunity to wrench their heads clear and escape. Others had their liberty removed for periods of time – and that was the cause of serious overcrowding.

By 1807, the old jail was deemed insufficient for purpose. The prison population had exploded to four times the number it could comfortably house and its thirty-two cells were crammed with criminals and debtors awaiting trial. The conditions were near intolerable, even in those days when the most basic sanitation was something akin to luxury. Just over a century later, a speaker at the Old Glasgow Club told his audience, 'Innocent and guilty, young and old, diseased and infirm were confined together, without courtyards for exercise, chapel or infirmary. No wonder that jail fever [typhus] was a scourge, and incarceration was not only punishment but a direct cause of degradation to those who were convicted of a first offence and not beyond redemption.'

The gentlemen of the town council approached Parliament for the funds to build a new prison but were refused, so the magistrates and bailies resolved to go it alone. They had grand plans: the new facility would house not only a jail but a courthouse, for the increase in the number of arrests obviously had had a knock-on effect on the business of trials and sentencing. And a site had been selected that was thought ideal, although as crime writer Bill Knox observed, 'their choice was hardly a beauty spot'.

The stretch of land at the foot of the Saltmarket was an isolated spot, approved of by prison reformer John Howard because it had ample space looking towards Glasgow Green and the river to the south. However, it was the site of the town's slaughterhouse and on a portion of land known as the Skinner's Green the tradesmen dried the freshly skinned fleeces and hides of the slaughtered beasts.

For years, dung and unused animal guts had been piled onto the ground here and allowed to rot until they were totally putrefied. Houses in the area were occupied by 'scullions and tripe cleaners', while the watchmen used the banks of the river near to the old bridge 'as a receptacle for the filth from the streets'. In 1810, a new slaughterhouse with seventy-seven killing rooms and two cattle yards was opened on an acre of land south of the Bridgegate. The associated industries moved with it.

Two years later, the first part of the new courthouse was opened. As the town's treasury had to cough up for the new building, some parts of the grand design – including a great dome – had to be scaled down to keep the costs to only £34,811. However, the court building was still impressive, with grand Doric columns rising from an impressive stepped entranceway facing onto the Saltmarket. Now the visiting judges, the juries (made up at that time of property owners – gentlemen, farmers and merchants) and the lawyers had a proper courthouse in which to decide the fate of accused persons from Glasgow, Lanarkshire, Renfrewshire and Dunbartonshire. Even so, many cases continued to be heard in Edinburgh, much to the chagrin of local officials.

Then, on 14 February 1814, 35 of the town's prisoners received a grand Valentine from the council – for they were the first to be moved to the brand-new jail. Half of what was initially known as the Glasgow Burgh Prison, later the South Prison, was given over to debtors. Their cells had fireplaces and windows, while those of the 'delinquents' had neither. Unlike the Tolbooth, the new jail had large rooms to allow the prisoners to associate with each other and galleries for fresh air and exercise. Each of these galleries had a water closet (a toilet) and an unlimited source of fresh water. This was handy for the daily washing down of the courtroom, if not for the cleanliness of the inmates, many of whom were almost total strangers to soap, unless, like condemned thief Robert Hunter Guthrie, they had stolen it. Criminals were expected to work while in jail and what money they earned was used to pay prison expenses.

Those confined to the four condemned cells, of course, were not allowed to avail themselves of the galleries or communal rooms. If contemporary reports are to be believed, they generally spent what little time they had left in contemplation and prayer.

The prison was thought to be large enough to hold the city's criminals comfortably. But it was a case of 'if you build it, they will come', for within five years of opening, the 35 inmates had increased to 158 – 100 of whom were 'delinquents', and 16 of them female. The remaining 58 were debtors, who were not so much being punished for their debts as coerced into paying up. At the time, debtors could be jailed in Scotland even for small amounts and remain imprisoned until the debt was cleared. After 1835, a debt had to be over one hundred Scots pounds, or eight pounds, six shillings and fourpence sterling before imprisonment was an option. By that time, debtors were no longer placed in the South Prison but would find themselves in the extended Bridewell in Duke Street, by then known as the North Prison (some sources refer to it as the Bridgewall).

After 30 years, the council offices moved from the South Prison site to the new county buildings on the north side of Wilson Street. The smaller courts went with them. In 1888, the municipal authority established its grand City Chambers headquarters in George Square, where it still sits. In 1856, a second court added to the Saltmarket site took up part of the cell areas and one of the exercise yards of the prison. By 1870, the South Prison was all but closed, a few cells only being used as an overflow for remand prisoners awaiting trial when the spaces under the courthouse were full. Its function had by then been taken up by the expanded Duke Street prison, and in 1882, the new Barlinnie Prison was constructed. The land for it had been bought in 1879 from the Barlinnie Farm Estate for £9,750.

But the area around the foot of the Saltmarket that housed the courts and the prison can lay another claim to being the black heart of Glasgow. Today there stands on Glasgow Green an archway that was originally erected in Ingram Street as part of the Assembly Rooms. Partly designed by Robert and James Adam and built in

1796, the Assembly Rooms were the centre of Glasgow's social life for half a century (superseding the old Tontine Hotel) until they were demolished to make way for the city's main post office. The central archway was retained and eventually rebuilt on the Green.

Its current situation bore very little relation to the colour and gaiety of the Assembly Rooms, however, for it was here, between 1814 and 1865, that Glasgow staged its public executions. 'You will die facing the monument' became a well-known Glasgow expression during this time, for one of the last things a condemned man would see would be Nelson's Monument reaching to the heavens from Glasgow Green. In 1819, murderer John Buchanan sought to confound the prophecy that had been laid on him by a friend. He had vowed he would never die facing the monument and when he found himself on the scaffold he kept his word by turning to the side.

CHAPTER THREE

YOU WILL DIE FACING
THE MONUMENT

For Lanarkshire miner Matthew Clydesdale, alone among those executed on Glasgow Green, the monument may not have been the last thing he saw.

He had killed an 80-year-old man with a pickaxe and was sentenced to hang on 4 November 1818, with his body to be donated to Dr James Jeffrey, professor of anatomy at the University of Glasgow, for public dissection. Trainee doctors and surgeons needed cadavers for research purposes and society at large frowned on the opening up of anyone other than convicted murderers or unbaptised foundlings. Clydesdale's execution went without a hitch, courtesy of Glasgow hangman Thomas Young, and the body was placed in a cart to be escorted by soldiers to the college dissecting rooms at the top of the High Street. Dissections could be viewed not just by students and medical men but by any member of the general public interested in such a grisly spectacle. Grisly spectacles being a great draw in those days, there were generally a number of curious laymen packed into the seating area. This time, though, they were in for a shock.

Clydesdale's body, the face still covered by the white hood that had been hauled over it by the hangman, the hands and feet still tied, was laid on the table. But then, instead of Dr Jeffrey slicing and dicing his way through the corpse, it was lifted again, placed in an armchair and the bindings cut away. Into one nostril was placed an air tube; the other end of the tube was attached to a bellows and the corpse wired up to an early form of electric battery known as a voltaic pile. The object of the exercise about to be carried out by Jeffrey's colleague Dr Andrew Ure, professor of natural philosophy, was galvanism, a test of the nervous system that saw newfangled electricity being used seemingly to reanimate dead tissue. That same year, Mary Shelley used the theory to enable Dr Frankenstein to create his famed monster.

When the bellows were blown, Clydesdale's chest appeared to heave until the corpse seemed to breathe on its own. Then when the battery was activated, a leg shot out with such force that it almost knocked over a student standing nearby. The dead man's face began to contort and twitch; some swore that it flashed them a ghastly grin. Some accounts state that the eyes opened and the arms and legs moved until finally the cadaver began to rise from the chair – but this was a tale that grew in the telling.

Nevertheless, what they did see terrified many of the spectators. Dr Ure later wrote that many of them attempted to flee. 'One gentleman fainted,' he noted wryly. The exhibition came to an end when, reports state, Dr Jeffrey seized a lancet (a long surgical needle) and plunged it into Clydesdale's jugular vein. The creature fell to the floor 'like a slaughtered ox on the blow of a butcher'. Apparently – and perhaps not surprisingly – such shocking, not to mention blasphemous, scenes ensured that it was the last time the Glasgow magistrates allowed a felon's corpse to be sent to the dissecting table. The anatomists in search of knowledge would have to find other means of obtaining their raw materials.

Soon afterwards, the murderous acts of Burke and Hare in Edinburgh in 1820 led to a relaxation of the rules regarding cadavers for the dissection tables, but in 1894 Andrew Aird recalled in his

Glimpses of Old Glasgow fears that there remained 'cruel men' in the city's 'dark and lonely places':

> [They] lay lurking about supplied with plasters which they stuck over the mouths of such persons as came near them, and whom they put to death . . . carrying the dead bodies to the dissecting rooms of hospitals or giving them to doctors as 'subjects' for dissection. I recollect it was the custom for timorous people when passing the wynds to put their hands upon their mouths, so as to ward off the death-dealing plaster.

* * *

Hangman Tam Young was something of a legend in what was a tight little noose of executioners. He became well known in the city for the calm, dispassionate way in which he sent his customers to their doom, always wearing his uniform of a yellow-buttoned blue coat and a blood-red collar. Other hangmen had worn it before him, but not his curiously shaped predecessor, Archibald McArthur, known as 'Buffy'. McArthur was just over 5 ft tall, stout and bandy-legged with a 'big bullet-shaped head'. He was said to have been 'a good-natured, inoffensive creature', despite his unhappy home life – his wife was known to enjoy a good drink, while his hunchbacked son died young in the Royal Infirmary. The council provided his family with a home in South Montrose Street, near the Ramshorn Kirk, but the post of 'hangie', or 'finisher of the law', was not one calculated to make a man popular, even though it was his job to dispatch rogues into eternity. Mobs took to attacking McArthur's home, so he moved to an almshouse in the High Street. He died aged 40 in the same hospital as his son.

Lanky Tam Young was a Borderer who was an unemployed labourer in the Calton area when, in 1814, he spotted a newspaper advertisement for the post of Glasgow hangman. Tam took up the position at a salary of £52 per year, plus a guinea for every execution.

In addition to a house – within the grounds of the prison, to keep him safe from the ire of the mob – the council also agreed to provide him with two new pairs of shoes every year, as well as coal and candles. As extra protection against assault, Tam kept two dogs by his side, one a giant Newfoundland he named Hero. Over the next 23 years, he sent 56 people in Glasgow and a further 14 in other parts of the country to their deaths. He was also responsible for administering public floggings, events possibly even more horrendous to witness than the hangings.

In 1822, Edward Hand was sentenced to be whipped through the streets of Glasgow, having been found guilty of an assault in Greenock. He was to receive 80 strokes: 20 at the prison, 20 at Stockwell Street, 20 at Glassford Street and the final 20 at the Cross. If he survived this brutal treatment, he was to be banished for life. Tam might have been a quiet soul but he was not slow in coming forward when he thought he was not receiving his due or being treated with disrespect. In this instance, he disputed with the magistrates over who should carry out the task of tying Hand to the cart that would wheel him around the town. His duties included performing labouring work around the jail but this, Young believed, was beneath his station as public executioner. He also queried who would be carrying the spare cat-o'-nine-tails. The two issues were resolved: Hand was finally bound to the cart by someone else and the whip was tied to the end of the vehicle. Satisfied, Young carried out his office, watched by a large crowd. His naked back lacerated by the 80 strokes, Hand survived and was duly banished. Flogging was thankfully phased out by the mid-nineteenth century but its bastard son, birching, was practised well into the mid-twentieth century.

Tam Young died in 1837 following a long illness. The city never appointed an official executioner after that, although there were hangings aplenty.

John Murdoch had been assistant to both Young and McArthur, as well as others, for 30 years when he became the go-to guy for towns needing someone 'topped'. A baker to trade, he performed his official duties on a piecework basis. He was around 70 years old when Young died; rheumatism had stricken his legs and he could walk only with the aid of a stick. Newspapers commented on the sight of him tottering up the steps to the platform and in 1849 one reporter opined that it was perhaps time that he gave up the work altogether. But old Murdoch grimly hung on – the £30–40 fee for a topping was not something he was eager to do without – and at the age of 84 he almost botched what was to be his last service for Glasgow.

On 2 October 1851, Archibald Hare, a man said to be of 'repulsive and dogged aspect', was sentenced to death for the stabbing of a man in Blantyre. Murdoch may well have been in the courtroom to hear the verdict, for it was his habit to attend the circuit court whenever a capital case was to be heard. Hare, whom legend wrongly states was the nephew of bodysnatcher William Hare, was to die on 24 October. The hangman laboriously hauled himself up the gallows steps and fixed the rope around Hare's neck. In addition to being repulsive and dogged, Hare was a very slight man and when he was turned off he merely twisted on the end of the rope, trying desperately to free his bound hands in order to clutch at the hemp biting into his throat. Murdoch had to speed the man's end by grabbing hold of his legs and swinging on them until the struggles eased and finally ceased. The authorities concluded that this particular finisher was too old to continue and allowed him a pension out of the public purse. He died aged 89 in Bothwell.

After his retirement, Glasgow hired hangmen from other parts of Britain to 'get their business done' as Tam Young used to say.

It would have been Tam who did the honours at the first quadruple hanging in Glasgow – during which two of the men facing their doom publicly displayed their affection for one another.

Robert McKinlay (also known as 'Rough Rob'), William Buchanan, Robert Hunter Guthrie (the man who stole soap from the Paisley soap works) and Alexander Forbes were led to the scaffold on the Green on 8 November 1819. They had each been found guilty of various counts of housebreaking. McKinlay and Buchanan had been audacious enough to break into Bothwell Castle, near Hamilton, and make off with a gold watch, a silver snuffbox, a silver spoon, a silver candlestick, a silver bread toaster 'and several articles of wearing apparel'. They had forced open a window and crept around the castle while the owner, the Right Honourable Lord Douglas, slept.

Glasgow-born McKinlay was a 23-year-old former cotton spinner who had, a broadsheet said, 'long given up the sober pursuits of industry' to set about 'gaining a livelihood by fraud and theft', taking up a 'more dangerous way of living by preying on the property of the public'. At the time of his arrest, he was also wanted for a variety of other burglaries. He had broken out of Greenock jail and avoided recapture by going to sea for eight months. He was caught 'in the Green asleep' with some of the stolen items on him and 'his Lordship's neckcloth about his neck'. He was destined to have something less pleasant around his throat.

He had perhaps been fingered by his accomplice, who had been arrested earlier. Buchanan was only 18 years old and was also a cotton spinner to trade but was of a 'very unsettled disposition, and much addicted to pilfering', a state of mind that had already seen him do a twelvemonth in the Bridewell. Lord Douglas appears to have been a very forgiving man, for he did what he could to have the men's lives saved, although he failed.

Guthrie, a Paisley weaver, and Forbes, from Glasgow, had been found guilty of a housebreaking in Kilmarnock, during which they had taken a silver watch, five shirts, two pairs of shoes, cloth, food and cakes. A police officer spotted them near Barrhead two days later and, with the aid of a ploughman, managed to arrest them, finding some of the stolen articles on them. When condemned to death, Guthrie stated that he thought the sentence 'very hard'. Guthrie, at 25 years, was by trade a wright but was a known criminal who had also previously tried to break jail, in his case the prison at Ayr, while 18-year-old Forbes was of 'honest industrious parents' but had 'given himself up to idleness and drunkenness'. He, too, had escaped from prison, having busted out of Paisley. He continued with his life of crime, almost being caught in the Gallowgate once, until he was arrested. Again, unsuccessful efforts were made to have their sentences commuted. In the eyes of the law, they were all menaces that had to be eradicated.

All four were described by a broadsheet of the day as 'good-looking young men'. The writer went on to say, 'Never did the inhabitants of Glasgow, and the surrounding countryside, witness a more awesome and disturbing spectacle.' Another broadsheet commented:

> The melancholy scene we have this day witnessed must have the effect of touching with anguish the heart of every friend of humanity – every lover of our species; four young men (a sight never before witnessed in Glasgow) suffering ignominiously, shamelessly, and ingloriously on the scaffold, for breaking the laws of their country, whom, had the ability they evidently possessed, been directed aright, might have been an honour to themselves, a happiness to their families, and made them useful members of society.

This writer hoped that the 'heartrending spectacle' the public witnessed would make anyone tempted to follow in their footsteps by 'preying on the property of the public' think twice. What the spectators thought of McKinlay kissing Buchanan farewell as the nooses were draped around their necks can only be surmised. Obviously, there was something more than just friendship between the two young men, who continued to hold hands, made difficult by their being bound, until Guthrie gave the signal to the hangman. The four men 'struggled very much' before they were finally still.

The following year saw another quadruple execution. On a Sunday in December 1819, a gang invaded the home of the late Dr Robert Watt in Crossmyloof. Watt, a well-known doctor, had died seven months before. His widow, her young children and their servants were in the mansion at the time and the men, their faces blackened, proceeded to ransack every cupboard and drawer before making off with all the cash and silver plate they could find. One held a loaded pistol to the head of the widow while another wrenched the rings from her fingers.

Four men by the name of Grant, Crosbie, O'Connor and McColgin were arrested the following October and tried in Glasgow in November. When they were condemned to death, the lawyer and social campaigner Peter Mackenzie noted, all 'broke out into a loud volley of curses and swearing, and actually attempted to kick some of the witnesses and officers of justice near to them'. At just after 3 p.m. on Wednesday, 8 November 1820, they were turned off together by Tam Young. According to one report, the four men struggled dreadfully before they died and their bodies hung for forty minutes before being cut down.

Mackenzie went on to detail the tragic life of Mrs Watt after the event. She lost much of her fortune through bankruptcy and all but one of her children died before her. Only the youngest girl survived but tragedy hit her, too. Just before she was due to marry a distinguished surgeon, he died of typhoid fever.

The following year, Young officiated at a triple execution. On 24 October, Michael Macintyre, William Paterson and Wardrope Dyer were brought from the prison and marched across the road and onto the scaffold. Macintyre and Paterson had been found guilty of breaking into a house and stealing 'various articles of wearing apparel'. Macintyre was a 20-year-old Irishman whose parents had 'endeavoured to gain a livelihood by hawking earthenware through this country'. Their son was left to his own devices and tried to make a living by selling gingerbread in the streets but during this time 'became acquainted with idle and dissolute company'. He soon drifted into crime and was 'well known to the keeper of the Bridewell'. He enlisted in the army but his larcenous nature led him to be found 'several times guilty of plundering his comrades' so he was punished – no doubt by flogging – and then drummed out of the regiment. He obviously did not learn from the experience, for he was arrested fairly soon after returning to Glasgow. His accomplice,

Paterson, born in Manchester of Scottish parentage, came to Glasgow after his father died in the East Indies. His upbringing was such that he very early on 'fell a prey to every species of vice with which every large city abounds'.

Dyer was a native Glaswegian, having been born to reputable parents in the Drygate. He became a weaver but 'got acquainted with women of very questionable characters, took up with gamblers, boxers and bullies who were always the first to point out the object of plunder, and ever ready to partake of the booty, but too wary to share in the danger'. Dyer, though, was all too willing to take the risks and that brought him to the platform where he would die facing the monument. He was only 22 years of age.

In the jail, before they were led out, Dyer had been moved by the preaching of the minister but Macintyre and Paterson were made of sterner stuff and warned other prisoners within earshot that if they ever wished to avoid hanging, they should plead guilty. After the execution, it was revealed that Dyer had pointed out the haunts of 'questionable characters' to the authorities and that the eye of the Glasgow Police was now upon them.

The final declarations of the condemned on the platform were generally of a religious nature – warnings against drink, keeping bad company, fornication and so on. On 12 November 1823, Paisley weaver turned housebreaker David Wylie warned the crowds to beware of gangs of thieves. He urged onlookers to avoid 'bad company, especially resetters [fences], who haunt young men in their houses; who give them meat and drink for the pilfer which they prompt them to take in a clandestine manner; little money is given to the depredators, and what is gained by these destroyers of youth, who sell the property of honest people, is spent in debauchery, drunkenness and every thing which degrades human nature'. He considered 'bad women and sabbath breaking' two of the worst evils, in addition to the one for which he was convicted. Wylie died aged 17.

Perhaps the strangest of all declarations on the scaffold came in 1853, when Hans Smith McFarlane and Helen Blackwood were executed for murder. They had lured ship's carpenter Alexander Boyd to a house in the New Vennel. There they had drugged him with a mixture of whisky and snuff, robbed him and then thrown his body from a window. They denied the charge but the principal witnesses against them were two brothers named Shillingshaw, both less than 12 years of age, who had been sleeping under a bed in the same house and watched the whole scene. The boys had been kept in prison since the murder because they had nowhere else to go. At the trial in Edinburgh, a third person, Ann Marshall, was also found guilty but her sentence was commuted to transportation. There was no such mercy for McFarlane and Blackwood, for they were to hang. 'We have not got justice,' remarked the woman. 'There is a higher judge for us. We are innocent.'

On being returned to Glasgow, McFarlane and Blackwood were lodged in Duke Street prison. There McFarlane asked the governor if he would be allowed to marry his co-accused. The request was turned down but McFarlane had his mind set on making an honest woman of her – figuratively speaking, at least. On the day of their death, 11 August, they were both moved to the South Prison before being led out to the scaffold. A crowd estimated to be 40,000 strong rippled far into the Green and before them McFarlane shouted, 'Helen Blackwood, before God and in the presence of these witnesses, I take you to be my wife. Do you consent?'

The stunned ocean of faces waited to hear the woman's response. 'I do,' she said.

'Then before these witnesses, I declare you to be what you have always been to me, a true and faithful wife, and you die an honest woman.'

The officiating clergyman intoned, 'Amen,' the bolt was drawn and the newly-weds plunged into the gaping maw beneath them. T.M. Tod remarked in his *Scots Black Kalendar*, 'This marriage, we understand, was not recorded in the Registrar General's book.'

McFarlane and Blackwood insisted on their innocence to the last, as did weaver Andrew Stewart, who was condemned for a street assault. Although he admitted he had struck the victim, he insisted that he had not participated in the subsequent robbery. Peter Mackenzie tended to believe him and considered the case a miscarriage of justice.

The victim was Italian Filippo Testi, who, Mackenzie wrote, was a 'mild, fine-looking young man, who scarcely understood the Scots language'. He earned a living as a street trader, selling ornaments and little works of art from a board that he carried about Glasgow on his head. Belfast-born Andrew Stewart was a weaver who lived in Bridgeton with his parents and had never been in trouble with the law.

One Saturday in August 1826 (Mackenzie says it was May but he was writing from memory long after the events), Stewart came to Glasgow to be paid by his employer. With money in his pocket, he tarried too long, visiting the Theatre Royal and lingering in the Boat Tavern in the Saltmarket with some friends. As he made his way home via the Gallowgate, he encountered Filippo Testi in East Nile Street. The Italian had lost his way and in his faltering English asked Stewart directions. The 25-year-old weaver, his mind befuddled with drink, did not understand him and began to believe that Testi was trying to make a fool of him. The Italian tried again but Stewart still did not understand him. Then he put his hand on Stewart's shoulder. Stewart shrugged him off. Testi became more excited in his questions, desperate to make himself understood. Finally, Stewart took offence and punched him. If he had been sober, perhaps he would have been more patient. But he was not and Testi fell to the ground. A policeman standing nearby saw the punch and 'sprang his rattles', panicking Stewart who ran off down Charlotte Street and onto the Green, leaping over an iron gate that police had earlier locked to prevent anyone from getting into the park at night. The officer followed, leaving Testi stunned on the ground, but lost Stewart in the dark.

Testi was being stalked by 'a gang of ruffians' who had been told by a woman that he had money on his person. These 'street blackguards' materialised from the darkness and pounced on the man while he lay prone in the street. They robbed him of his gold watch and chain, his gloves, his tobacco and 'five or six segars'. They also relieved him of two one-pound notes, a guinea note and ten to twelve shillings in silver. The gang was seen rifling his pockets but anyone who attempted to prevent them was threatened. They did not stop until other officers arrived, alerted by their colleague's rattle. The gang, like Stewart, bolted for the Green, where they argued over the division of the spoils.

Stewart, meanwhile, had made it home, where he told his mother what had happened. Two days later, they came for him while he was eating breakfast. The officer who had chased him identified him and charged him with assault and street robbery. Police also arrested George Buckley and James Dickson, on whom they found Testi's wallet. The Crown case was that Stewart had acted along with Buckley, Dickson and others to attack and rob Testi. The young weaver insisted he had never seen the men before. He told the police his story. Yes, he had struck the blow but it was in anger, not in the course of a robbery. He had not meant to hurt the man. He repeated it to lawyers. He told anyone who would listen. He was not believed.

The jury, by a majority, condemned Stewart for assault and robbery but acquitted Buckley on a not proven verdict. The young man had been identified by witnesses, while Buckley — a known crook — had not. One witness prevaricated so much that he was jailed for two months for contempt, to be fed nothing but bread and water. Dickson, however, was found guilty of robbery. He had, after all, been found in possession of part of the booty. He was to be transported for life but Stewart was to die. The judge said that street robbery was an atrocity and that it was 'necessary to make a terrible example, especially in the case of the poor foreigner'.

'So it is,' replied Stewart, 'but I am not guilty in the way imputed to me.'

The case excited sympathy in the liberal minds of Glasgow and it was hoped that a reprieve would be forthcoming. On the day set for the execution, 1 November, supporters turned up early at the post office in Nelson Street in order to catch the London mail coach. They hoped that a letter would reach them from the Home Secretary saving the young weaver's life. No letter was sent. Andrew Stewart walked up the scaffold steps followed by the tall frame of Tam Young. The young man's mother stood by the steps and cried out, 'My son! My son! My innocent son! May the God of Heaven receive you into his everlasting arms.'

Another Irishman died that day. Edward Kelly had been convicted with another man, whose sentence of death was respited, of robbery in the Bridgegate. The victim, James Fleming, had picked up a prostitute and while in her company she had learned that he had a sum of money about his person. When he left, she alerted some of her 'abandoned colleagues', who set about him in the street, dragged him into a close and robbed him of over £100. Kelly, a 21 year old 'never bred to any regular business', and his co-accused were arrested while they were splitting the loot. A third man got away with around £40 of the haul and was never caught.

CHAPTER FOUR

WORKERS UNITE

Universalist preacher Neil Douglas might have believed that everyone would ultimately be saved but he must surely have had his doubts about George III and his son, the Prince Regent, whose private life was an almost constant source of scandal. Douglas rented the Andersonian Institute in Glasgow for his tirades and in May of 1817 he was slated to discuss the Prophecies of Daniel, chapter 5, verses 7–23. Knowing his penchant for fiery invective, Glaswegians turned out that Sunday afternoon in their droves. The hall, it was said, could have been filled twice over. Among the crowd were two police officers sent by the town council to monitor his speech. The Reverend Douglas did not disappoint. George III, he said, was like Nebuchadnezzar, the Babylonian king who was known for his 'infidelity and corruption'. As for the Prince, he was 'a poor infatuated creature' too much in the thrall of Bacchus. The minister was arrested after the service and appeared before the High Court of Justiciary in Edinburgh charged with preaching sedition. Noted liberal lawyer Francis Jeffrey, later rector of the University of Glasgow, took on his defence and subjected the two officers to such a withering cross-examination that the charges against the old man fell. Douglas was warned by the court to be more careful of his language in future.

The scent of sedition was strong in the early nineteenth century as workers battled for their rights. The Industrial Revolution had helped create the fortunes of a few but there were many who suffered as increased mechanisation began to make manpower redundant. In 1810, angry weavers attacked the homes of Glasgow mill-owners. Six years later, there was a riot in the Calton during which a 'steam loom factory' was attacked. The subsequent unrest saw cavalry galloping through the streets.

That does not mean that there were no attempts to relieve the situation. A number of charitable projects were set up, including a scheme by Glasgow's council to employ more than 300 jobless locals to improve Glasgow Green and the Ramshorn Kirk. However, the authorities stamped down hard on the men who demanded liberty, equality and fraternity.

The reinvigorated Radicals demanded political reform. They wanted votes for all, not just the propertied classes. They wanted unfair laws repealed. They wanted cheaper food. They wanted the right to join trade unions, or 'combinations' as they were also called, which had been banned in 1799. In Scotland, they wanted more – they wanted independence. The orators spoke of Wallace and Bruce and the Covenanters. Scotland should be free, they preached, from the yoke of English oppression. Spurred on by their fiery words, the spinners and the weavers and the labourers and the artisans mobilised.

In 1812, hand-loom weavers in Glasgow and district withdrew their labour over pay cuts. They were very highly paid for the day but their income had fallen from around fifty shillings a week to ten. They had already had one dispute with employers over trade-union membership and found themselves locked out of the factories until they signed an anti-union agreement. Now, though, they were back and ready to fight for their rights. Under a 150-year-old piece of legislation, the town magistrates were empowered to grant a pay rise and did so, albeit grudgingly, but the employers ignored the instruction. The matter went to the Court of Session, which, perhaps surprisingly, sided with the workers. Still the mill-owners refused to part with their silver. The weavers went on strike for nine weeks, the stoppage spreading the length of the country and involving 40,000 workers in all. Even though the weavers were legally in the right, the magistrates joined with the employers in condemning the action. In the end, the strike was broken when lobbyists for the employers convinced the authorities that the leaders could well be guilty of sedition and they were arrested. Five of them were jailed and the strike fell apart. But in the following years, the tide of resentment simply gathered in strength.

In London, the political parties – the Whigs and the Tories – took fright at the vehemence of feeling across the nation but did nothing to meet any of the workers' or reformers' demands even halfway. Instead, they dug their heels in and passed legislation that cracked down on what would now be called civil liberties. They banned any gathering they deemed seditious and suspended habeas corpus. 'Nothing was viewed with such horror as any political congregation not friendly to existing powers,' wrote Lord Henry Cockburn. Weavers and other workers were brought to trial for daring to question the status quo. Cockburn himself was part of a dream triumvirate of lawyers to defend gratis Glasgow weaver Andrew McKinley on a charge of high treason in 1817 (the other two were Francis Jeffrey and James Moncreiff, later Lord Advocate). However, the case collapsed when it was revealed by John Campbell, one of the accused, that he had been offered a reward by Advocate Depute Drummond in return for giving evidence against McKinley.

In 1819, more than 50,000 men, women and children gathered in Manchester, at a place called St Peter's Field, to demand reforms. Presented with such a formidable body of protesters, the local magistrates lost their nerve. The Riot Act – which demanded that they disperse – was read and then cavalry armed with sabres were ordered to break up the meeting. Estimates vary, but between 11 and 18 people were killed and some 400 to 700 injured.

Four years earlier, Wellington had won the Battle of Waterloo and so this incident was swiftly dubbed the Massacre of Peterloo. The following year, a group of conspirators was caught in London's Cato Street plotting to murder the cabinet and seize control of the Bank of England. Five men were sentenced to die for their part in the plot.

Churchill said that 'compared with most Continental countries, Britain came lightly out of these years of disturbance'. He was, of course, more concerned with English history and so completely ignored events in Glasgow.

* * *

By 1820, the city of Glasgow was reaching out across the fields to envelop weaving villages such as Anderston, Bridgeton and Calton. The area was already seen as a hotbed of discontent thanks to the rapid growth of its industrial base. The cotton kings had been battling against striking factory workers since the latter part of the previous century. The workers lived in squalor, leading what Glasgow historian Charles Oakley termed 'an almost brutish existence'. When times were hard, work could be hard to find, even in the factories. For many, the mantle of breadwinner had passed from father to child, and some children worked a thirteen-hour day, six days a week.

As calls for reform grew, the authorities became increasingly jittery. On 11 September 1819, cavalry were used to control a rally in Paisley held to memorialise the dead of the Peterloo Massacre. It led to a week of rioting. The streets of Glasgow were filled with 'crowds of idle populace' so detachments of cavalry and a number of special constables were wielded like a club to clear them. By the end of the year, fears of a workers' uprising reached Edinburgh, where Tory and Whig came together to defend their property. Even that old defender of the Radicals Henry Cockburn took up arms in readiness to defend his city. The anticipated uprising, however, never took place.

Then, in the early part of 1820, came the Cato Street conspiracy and government paranoia rose dramatically. Across Britain, local magistrates and their law enforcers looked to their own patches for home-grown dissidents. The conspiracy had been uncovered – some said promoted – by government agents, and Glasgow's police chief

James Mitchell wished to do the same – to root out the leaders of the local Radicals.

They had been drilling some of their followers in public – Glasgow Green was one such parade ground – seemingly in preparation for some future military action. Among their ranks were former soldiers who were passing their fighting skills on to the army of disaffected workers. Metal was taken from iron foundries to be turned into pike points. Spears called 'wasps' and barbed devices called 'clegs', for injuring horses, were stockpiled. Lead was taken from roofs to be turned into pistol balls. Mitchell, though, had spies in their midst and he wrote in March that the organising committee of what he termed 'the rabble' was due to meet in Glasgow. By the end of the month, he was telling his masters that 'we apprehended their committee of organisation, due solely to the efforts of an informant who has served his government well'.

The arrests were made on 21 March 1820 in Marshall's Tavern on the Gallowgate. The raid was kept secret from the Radical rank and file, an easy enough task, for security precautions dictated that the identities of the committee members be shielded from their followers. According to Mitchell, the committee 'confessed their audacious plot to sever the Kingdom of Scotland from that of England and restore the ancient Scottish Parliament'. Mitchell, though, wanted more. He wanted to apprehend the rest of the rabble: 'If some plan were conceived by which the disaffected could be lured out of their lairs – being made to think that the day of "liberty" had come – we could catch them abroad and undefended.'

What he proposed was the use of agents provocateurs to agitate the Radicals into staging a rebellion that could then be effectively crushed by the military. The body did not know that the head had been severed, so Mitchell's army of spies was sent out again to whip up the already existing fever for rebellion. They burrowed their way into the confidences of the remaining Radicals and were active in promoting the idea of armed insurrection by claiming that a rising had already begun.

His agents may have been among the 20 Radicals who delivered to a printer's in the Saltmarket a manifesto calling on the people to take up arms 'agin the Government'. It went on: 'Liberty or Death is our motto, and we have sworn to return home in triumph – or return no more.' They called for a general strike until their demands for greater rights and fairer laws were met. The document was signed 'By order of the Committee of Organisation for forming a Provisional Government'.

The call to arms caused great alarm and the city's anxious magistrates imposed a curfew. All shops were to be closed by 6 p.m. and the inhabitants in their own homes by 7 p.m. Non-Glaswegians had to be out of the town by the same time. They also warned that 'the military would be employed in the most decisive manner against all those coming forward to aid in the rebellion'. Artillery batteries were deployed at all the bridges across the Clyde, while soldiers guarded the main buildings.

The strike call, meanwhile, was answered. Workers downed tools not only in Glasgow but across west and central Scotland. Sixty thousand men, women and children – weavers, spinners, colliers, wrights and labourers – walked away from factories and mills in the first general strike in history. Rumours spread, fanned by Mitchell's agents, that an uprising had begun in England, that mail coaches had been stopped on the road, that a force was gathering near the Campsie Hills to the north of the city under a Scottish-born French army officer, that another army was mustering at Cathkin, south of Glasgow. Emboldened by the stories, men gathered in Paisley, Kilbarchan and Stewarton.

At a place called Fir Park or Firhill, where the Necropolis now stands, around 60 men debated attacking the ironworks at Carron near Falkirk. Many of those present felt their force was too small and declined to go. The remainder, under the command of Auchinairn-born Andrew Hardie, a former member of the Berwick Militia and a veteran of Waterloo, marched off in the belief that they would pick up more recruits along the way. At Condorrat, a small village to the north now swallowed up by Cumbernauld, the 27-year-old Glasgow weaver and his 30 men met up with another small force led by local man John Baird. Also a former soldier, 31-year-old Baird had seen action in Spain under Sir John Moore, the Glasgow-born hero of Corunna. Unsurprisingly, the authorities knew in advance of the plan to sack the munitions factory at Carron and a detachment of the 11th Hussars under the command of Lieutenant Ellis Hodgson was dispatched to counter any attack.

On 5 April 1820, he was waiting for them at Bonnymuir, a drab stretch of moorland in the shadow of the Kilsyth Hills. What followed wasn't much of a battle. The Radicals – wet, tired and hungry after their long tramp from Glasgow – took shelter behind a wall and began firing. The cavalry spurred their mounts over the wall and routed the ragged bunch of men. Lieutenant Hodgson was wounded in the hand by a pike and had a horse shot out from under him, while a sergeant was shot in the side. The Radical 'army' suffered four wounded and had nineteen taken prisoner, including Hardie and Baird. The government forces also took possession of their meagre arsenal, which included five muskets, two pistols, eighteen pikes and about a hundred rounds of ball cartridges.

Glasgow was awash with military personnel. The bridges continued to be covered by artillery, while cavalry trotted through the streets and infantry were in place in St Enoch Square, the Gallowgate and Eglinton Street. Still, though, the Radicals rallied men to their banners. In the weaving centre of Bridgeton, an old man beat a drum to gather a force of 200 men armed with pikes, blunderbusses and pistols. In Tradeston, a bugle called around 60 pikemen together. Everywhere were banners and flags and speeches and calls for action. And everywhere there were arrests. But no action. Talk there was in abundance and posturing aplenty, but very little violence.

Mitchell's men, though, were still active. The village of Strathaven, to the south-east of Glasgow, was a strong weaving centre and on 6 April a message was delivered to the Radicals there that the hour had come. They were to make for Cathkin, where a stronger force was waiting to launch further attacks. Among them was 63-year-old weaver James Wilson, known as 'Purlie' because it was claimed he had invented the purl stitch. He was a veteran of the reform movement and, carrying a banner that read 'Scotland Free or a Desart [sic]', he and 25 like-minded Strathaven men set off for Cathkin. However, at East Kilbride they were warned that a party of soldiers waited for them ahead. Wilson had mistrusted the message from the off so he returned home. Some of the others went on, carefully avoiding the soldiers, to reach Cathkin. They found no larger force, so they split up and returned home too. However, many of them had already been identified and that night ten, including Wilson, were arrested in their homes.

There was one more flashpoint. On 8 April, five Radical prisoners were to be moved from Paisley jail to Greenock, escorted by the Port Glasgow Militia. The soldiers marched the prisoners through the streets with fifes whistling and drums rattling – a display of martial superiority that only served to enflame the passions of the mob. More men and women joined the crowds to jeer as they passed and the prisoners were bolstered with the sentiment, 'Cheer up, you will soon be relieved from your situation.'

Stones were thrown but there was no direct assault until the column reached the jail. Then the volley of stones increased and the crowd surged forward to attempt to free the men. The soldiers fired above their heads and this seemed to cow the mob sufficiently to allow the officers to lodge the prisoners in the jail. However, as the militia marched homeward they were attacked by the protesters once more. Shots were again fired, at first overheads and then into the crowd. This made a bad situation worse and the soldiers were rushed. Iron railings were hauled from their fixtures and used as weapons. During the resulting street fight, nine people were killed, including an eight-year-old child, while many others were wounded. The crowd launched another attack on the jail and this time managed to free the prisoners.

Twenty-two days later, in London, the five Cato Street conspirators were led to their deaths outside Newgate. They sucked oranges as they followed the dignitaries to the scaffold. After they were hanged, a man in a black hood surgically removed their heads with an amputation knife.

A yet more brutal fate awaited the Scottish insurgents, although first the authorities would have to trample over the spirit, if not the letter, of the Act of Union. The men had been accused of high treason and their cases were to be heard under English, not Scots, law. In return for a fee of 2,000 guineas, an English barrister, John Hullock, was sent north to advise his Scottish counterparts. On 23 and 24 June, a special commission court of oyer and terminer (from the French 'to hear' and 'to conclude') opened in Stirling. A grand jury of 22 people was empanelled and over the two days Andrew Hardie, John Baird and others were found to have been involved in treasonable acts and referred to trial. Hardie, Baird and 20 others were found guilty.

Turning to the sentence, the Lord President intoned, 'The sentence of law is that you and each of you be taken to the place of execution, there to be hanged by the neck until you are dead, and afterwards your head be severed from your body and your body be divided into four quarters, to be disposed of as His Majesty may direct. And may God in his infinite goodness have mercy on your souls.' The words must have caused a shiver among the condemned men. However, 20 of them were reprieved and transported. Twelve years later, they were all pardoned. For Hardie and Baird, though, there was nothing but doom ahead. 'I can hold out little or no hope of mercy,' said the Lord President, 'as you were selected as the leaders of that band in which you were associated. To the others, clemency might be extended, but I counsel you to prepare for the worst.'

In Glasgow, James Wilson was found guilty of 'compassing to levy war against the King to compel him to change his measures'. The jury recommended mercy because of his age but the Crown was not feeling compassionate. Lord President Hope said Wilson was 'a miserable and sinful creature, about perhaps shortly to appear at the mercy seat of Almighty God, where you must answer not only for this crime of which you have been convicted, but for all the sins and vices of your past life'.

Wilson was unimpressed and unsurprised by the sentence. 'You want a victim,' he retorted. 'I will not shrink from the sacrifice. I have neither expected justice nor mercy here. I have done my duty to my country. I have grappled with her oppressors for the last forty years and having no desire to live in slavery, I am ready to lay down my life in support of these principles which must ultimately triumph.'

On 30 August 1820, Wilson was brought from the condemned cell in the South Prison and taken to the scaffold on the Green. The council and government knew that the sentence was unpopular and were taking no risks. A crowd of over 20,000 was kept in order by members of the 3rd Dragoon Guards, the 38th Regiment and the Rifle Brigade – all soldiers who had patrolled the streets at the height of the troubles. There was some violence when the Dragoons charged a section of the crowd, sending some of the panicking spectators flying into the less than fragrant Molendinar Burn. Tam Young was to be the hangman and on the scaffold Wilson looked across the mass of faces below him and commented, 'Did ye ever see sic a crood?'

Tam glanced around him and observed, 'Oh, aye, I've seen as big a crood as that afore.'

After Wilson had been hanged, his body convulsing on the end of the hemp, blood streaming from his ears, his corpse was taken down and laid with his head on the block. The hangman was not to sully his hands with the beheading; there was a specially hired headsman for that, dressed in black, his face hooded, said to be a medical student from the university. However, this was to be no surgical procedure such as had been seen in Newgate. An axe was wielded with some measure of confidence and Wilson's head then held aloft, sawdust soaking up the gush of blood. 'Behold the head of a traitor,' cried the headsman. The crowd grew restive and cries of 'Shame!' and 'Murder!' had the soldiers fingering their weapons nervously.

The remains were placed in a black coffin that had been lying open on the platform throughout the proceedings and it was later interred in Glasgow Cathedral burying ground. Wilson had requested that he lie 'in the dust of his fathers' in Strathaven, so within a few nights his corpse was spirited away by his daughter, niece and friends and buried in his home town. A pamphlet issued on the day of his death condemned the execution as 'Murder! Murder! Murder!' saying, 'May the ghost of the murdered Wilson haunt the pillows of his relentless jurors.'

On 8 September, Hardie and Baird died on a scaffold erected outside the courthouse on Stirling's Broad Street. Young had been imported from Glasgow to conduct the hanging, at a fee of ten guineas for each man, while the 'decapitator' may have been either the same hooded man who had performed the duty on Wilson or an Edinburgh man who demanded a fee of 20 guineas a head. The turning-off went without a hitch but the headings were not as smoothly done as the previous execution. The men's bodies had hung for 25 minutes before they were taken down and laid on the block. The headsman wielded his axe twice on Hardie but, a broadsheet noted, 'a third slight touch was necessary to sever some of the adhering fibres and skin'. The head was then held up and the roar of 'This is the head of a traitor!' was met by cries of 'Murder!' Perhaps this unnerved the axeman, for when he turned to Baird's body his first blow missed the neck and smashed the jawbone. As the crowd screamed, another stroke was needed to finish the job. The quartering of the bodies was waived, and Hardie and Baird were buried together in an unmarked grave in Stirling. In 1857, they were found – the damaged jawbone confirming Baird's identity at least – and removed to Glasgow's Sighthill Cemetery.

In a final letter to relatives, Hardie – said to be an ancestor of Labour Party founder James Keir Hardie – wrote, 'No person could have induced me to take up arms in the same manner to rob and plunder. No, my dear friends, I took them for the good of my suffering country.'

The strike of 1820 flowed away with the blood in the sawdust, the dreams of nationalism with it. Four years later, the anti-combination laws were repealed and trade unions were once again made legal.

Master of Police James Mitchell resigned in 1821 and James Hardie, a Justice of the Peace and no relation to the 'martyred' weaver, was appointed superintendent. In addition to the existing ranks, the Glasgow Police now had as senior officers three lieutenants, a rank peculiar to the Glasgow force. One of these, Peter McKinlay, was in 1819 – while the Radical scare was gathering pace – appointed a 'criminal officer'. He was the city's first detective, although it would be more than 40 years before the Glasgow force would be allowed to investigate a major crime on its own.

Where McKinlay found the time to solve crimes is a mystery, for as well as keeping a note of all incidents and descriptions of everyone who was arrested, he inspected every prisoner in custody every day, ensured that those who could not pay for food were fed, inspected the various patrols before and after their tours of duty, recorded all fires, noted the names of all streets swept and reported on the condition of closes. He also had to note the names, ages and number of prostitutes arrested. After two years, McKinlay was allowed the services of an assistant to help with what was obviously a heavy workload.

In 1825, a purpose-built central police station was erected in South Albion Street. By this time, the police commissioners who supervised the force had become disenchanted with Master of Police Hardie and he was dismissed. Merchant John Graham took over until his death in 1832, when F.G. Denovan, the former Bow Street Runner and master of police at Leith who had investigated James MacKoull's links with the Begbie murder, became the city's top cop. He instituted a number of changes to the force, but railed against the political machinations involved in the job and when three new lieutenants were appointed without his approval, he resigned after a few months.

The city was going through yet another rough time. Unemployment was again on the rise and with it the growth of street crime. Gangs were beginning to come to the fore and street battles were common. In his 1973 book *The Thin Blue Line*, Glasgow police historian Douglas Grant wrote that many of these disturbances were the result of religious conflict and that 'as many as 100 persons armed with sticks and stones took part'. He also said that 'the moment the police intervened the antagonists forgot their differences and joined forces against the law'.

Meanwhile, from 1819, the Burgh of Calton had its own force. Although it was formed with the assistance of Glasgow Council, there was a certain rivalry between the Glasgow officers and their counterparts in outlying districts. Should a Glasgow officer pursue a felon across a boundary line, he could find himself locked up on charges of exceeding his authority. Calton must have been an exceedingly dangerous area, for its officers were issued with a cutlass for protection. In 1822, a bodysnatcher had an arm severed by one such weapon when disturbed by police in Abercrombie Street.

The city of Glasgow itself had what Charles Oakley called 'a doubtful reputation'. Cartoons from the period show the city as lawless. In one, from the *Northern Looking Glass*, a group of children is busy trying to haul down the statue of Sir John Moore from its plinth in a George Square where women still hung their washing. In another, religious differences are exemplified by the goading of an elderly Jewish man with a pig's trotter by an unpleasant-looking gang of men and women. In a third, from the same publication, a gang creates a disturbance as the London coach readies to set off. They are seen manhandling passengers to prevent them from getting on, grabbing gentlewomen for a kiss and leaning from windows with rum bottles in their hands. While all this was going on, although it is not seen in the cartoon, 'dippers' would have seized the chance to pick a pocket or two.

In 1822, George IV visited Scotland (the first visit by a ruling monarch to the country since 1650) but Glasgow was not on the itinerary. Five years earlier, a report to Parliament had dubbed the city 'one of the places where treasonable practices prevail to the greatest degree' and things had not changed. As the city moved from the 1820s into the 1830s, revolution was again in the air. Workers still demanded better wages, better conditions and better prospects. Social conditions had not improved. An 1839 report on housing recorded:

> I have seen human degradation in some of the worst places, both in England and abroad, but I did not believe until I visited the wynds of Glasgow that so large an amount of filth, crime, misery and disease existed in one spot in any civilized country.

Lord Shaftesbury said the city was 'amazing' but he had walked its 'dreadful parts' – the area around the Cross and down to the river. He continued, 'It is a small square plot intersected by small alleys, like gutters, crammed with houses, dunghills and human beings.' It was this small area that bred 'nine-tenths of the disease and nine-tenths of the crime in Glasgow; and well it may'. He concluded:

> Health would be impossible in such a climate; the air tainted by exhalation from the most stinking and stagnant sources, a pavement never dry, in lanes not broad enough to admit a wheelbarrow. And is moral propriety and moral cleanliness, so to speak, more probable? Quite the reverse.

Moral propriety concerned Superintendent Graham in 1831. In that year, the city was estimated to have 2,850 pubs and almost 1,500 brothels. These figures did not take into account the shebeens, illegal drinking dens, that proliferated around the old town and offered cut-price booze. Whisky could be brewed illegally anywhere that a makeshift still could be set up. The hooch the shebeens sold was made of varying quantities of real whisky, water, vinegar and meths (known as 'finish', and some drinkers really were finished off by it). Their product was cheap, it was effective as a means of blotting out the miseries of life and it was readily available. The law took a dim view because the trade denied the authorities their tax revenues. The 'shebeeners', like their counterparts in 1920s America, grew adept at hiding their goods. Special containers were made to fit under their clothing to allow them to transport it from still to point of sale.

Cheeky they may have been, but they would fight to safeguard their trade and they formed gangs to protect their territory and equipment. In 1815, customs officers raided a still between Union Street and Mitchell Street. They arrested two men and tipped about 50 gallons of spirits into the street. One of the men seized the chance to set light to the raw alcohol and escape in the confusion. He returned shortly afterwards with around a dozen friends and attacked the excisemen as they were dismantling the still. They liberated the equipment from official hands, injuring an officer during the ensuing battle.

Prostitution was also a problem. If social conditions led to poverty, homelessness and drunkenness, then they also led to more women taking up the oldest profession. Standing orders were issued to all police officers to arrest any woman found walking the streets after dark. In any one night, up to 70 women could be found enjoying the comforts of the central police station. In court, they were fined and released again to ply their trade or they were sent to the Bridewell in the hope that they would see the error of their ways.

The death rate was high: 32 people in every 1,000 per annum, compared with 15 in London. Glasgow became known as the unhealthiest city in the United Kingdom. Of course, the kind-hearted and well off among the city's merchant classes provided funds for social welfare. Trusts were set up, societies formed, committees organised. But it was never enough to stem the tide of misery. And there were new immigrants to the city every day.

And always there was crime, particularly in the new parts of the East End, where citizens were advised not to go abroad at night. Theft, violence, murder were commonplace among the dingy closes, poorly lit alleyways and dung-heaps of the city. Squalor, crime and degradation were never more than a stone's throw from the more affluent parts of the city. And the throwing of stones was seldom far off either, as labour relations never seemed to improve.

In 1837, the entire country was in the grip of a recession. Many workers found themselves without a job, while those who were lucky enough to stay in employment had their pay drastically sliced. It was in this year that the cotton spinners withdrew their labour, followed soon after by the colliers of Lanarkshire. Around 80,000 workers were involved in the strikes and again the city streets were filled with thousands of disaffected men and women, and heaven help any blackleg worker, known then as 'knobsticks' or simply 'knobs', who fell foul of them. Stones were thrown, beatings were dished out, faces were scarred with vitriol or acid, and, on 22 July, one knobstick was shot dead.

Striking was one thing but murder was another. The mill-owners and mine bosses offered a reward of £500 for the arrest of the men responsible. That was a lot of money – and times were hard. It was a matter of when rather than if someone decided to collect it. Three days after the killing, Sheriff Allison met two men in a dark vault under the Old College in the High Street. In the guttering light of a lantern, the men told the sheriff that the murder of the knobstick was only the start of a war of terror. Strikers planned to embark on a killing spree of workers and bosses until their demands were met.

Clearly, such a bloody plan could not be allowed to proceed and the informers told the sheriff that the committee responsible for the plan were to meet on Saturday, 29 July in the Black Boy Tavern on the Gallowgate. He reported the tip-off to the new superintendent of police, Henry Miller, and that Saturday night the two men stalked the dark and dangerous streets around the Gallowgate. Much has been made of the sheriff's bravery; he was armed only with a stick, but he did have 20 stout police officers to back him up. The tavern was situated in Black Boy Close, a 'vile den' near Glasgow Cross, and the 20 officers were stationed at various points around it with orders to arrest anyone who tried to leave. Sheriff Allison, along with Miller, Procurator Fiscal Salmond and Principal Sheriff Officer Nish, entered the dingy tavern. In an upstairs room, reached by a rickety ladder, they found 16 men with a quantity of cash spread out on a table. A single gaslight hung from the ceiling, casting a pale glow over the cramped little room. Sheriff Allison positioned himself under the light to ensure no one could put it out and try to escape, and then one by one Superintendent Miller called the members of the committee by name and told them to climb down the ladder into the waiting arms of his officers.

The following Monday, the three-month strike was broken. The cotton spinners met on Glasgow Green and decided to return to work, and before long the tall chimneys of the factories were belching their black smoke again. The 16 men were charged with conspiring to keep wages up, disturbances at factories, appointing a secret committee to do unlawful acts, attempting to set fire to houses and factories, and assaulting 'new hands' (strike-breakers). The trial was set for 10 November but then postponed at the last minute to 27 November. There were more than 150 witnesses and in the end the men were found guilty, by a margin of one juror, of conspiracy and causing of disturbances at factories. The other three charges were found not proven.

On 8 January 1838, they were sentenced to seven years' transportation. After three years of rotting in the unspeakable hell of the Woolwich prison hulks, they were pardoned. But the damage to their cause had been done. Their union had already collapsed, while the employers moved quickly to replace men with machines, until cotton spinners were as endangered as hand-loom weavers, who had been replaced by the power loom. On the other hand, some employers had gone out of business thanks to the effects of the three-month stoppage. Wages had remained static, or if they did rise, it was by very little. Between the years 1836 and 1846, the average weekly wage of a cotton spinner rose by just 1 shilling, from 25 shillings to 26. Meanwhile, a miner's wage dropped from 30 shillings to between 15 and 20 shillings. Hand-loom weavers, although the trade was dying out, were better off by one shilling in those ten years (from six shillings to seven), while bricklayers and joiners enjoyed rises of six shillings and two shillings respectively.

In a report to the Select Committee on Combinations of Workmen after the strike, Sheriff Allison told MPs that the unions merely wanted to 'establish a monopoly of skilled [workers] against the efforts of unskilled industry'. However, too many strikes occurred, he said:

> in consequence, not of a general contest about wages but of some quarrel with the individual. Such as about an unpopular manager, or their having admitted hands not members of the union, or their having admitted too many apprentices, or something of that kind. In consequence of that, the trades union is exercising a continual control over the masters and over the other workmen engaged in the business.

Workers in other trades, such as hand-loom weaving, were being prevented from getting into the cotton-spinning trade by combinations who wished to keep the work for themselves – or their own relatives. They were, the committee noted, 'preventing the free circulation of labour'.

Although many respectable citizens did what they could to ease the lot of the working classes, the poor were expected to live in rotting, infested homes and do back-breaking work for very little pay. The city was still growing and people were crammed into subdivided rooms in tenements that had been overcrowded to begin with. This was the advent of the 'single-end', a one-room apartment measuring as little as 7 ft by 16 ft into which as many as nine people could be squeezed.

By 1848, the old resentments, aggravated by high unemployment, boiled over again – and the Glasgow Police would find themselves at the centre of a storm of protest over their handling of a riot. By that time, the old Glasgow force had grown to incorporate men from the Gorbals, Calton and Anderston. This necessitated reorganisation, and so the old Glasgow force area became known as the Central Division, Anderston the Western, Calton the Eastern and the Gorbals, naturally, the Southern.

On Monday, 6 March, almost 5,000 people gathered on Glasgow Green. Compared with the numbers that turned up on an execution day, it was a small assembly, but they were not there to see a felon turned off to oblivion. They were there to protest over the lack of jobs and the treatment of workers. Fiery invective pierced the air, fists were raised in outrage and the common folk decided that food and a decent wage were their rights. What happened later became known as the 'Bread Riots'.

The reaction of the authorities was at first one of appeasement. They pledged to provide work for the jobless and food for the hungry. But the crowd was in no mood to be placated and thousands marched through the streets to the City Hall, where the council was in session. The protesters made their voices heard in Candleriggs and Ingram Street but there was no violence. Having made their point, they dispersed.

However, there were elements in the crowd who did not wish to leave it at that. A mob made up of young men and women – many of them street toughs out for a 'rammy' – pulled up the railings surrounding the Green and stormed into the town centre, looting gun stores in Stockwell Street and the Trongate. In one, they threw the female owner through the glass window and made off with her entire stock of firearms and ammunition. The shopkeeper next door, however, beat the raiders off with a stick. The rioters surged away, firing their stolen weapons in the air and attacking another gun shop in the Royal Exchange. More enterprising elements, seeing the chance to turn a profit, robbed a jeweller in Buchanan Street, making off with £2,000 worth of goods.

The mob rampaged unchecked by the police. Douglas Grant points out that there were only 130 serving officers on duty, armed only with batons and smaller coshes known as 'life preservers'. There would have been very little they could have done against a much larger force armed with stolen firearms. What was more, word had spread and more gangs had begun looting and pillaging on both sides of the river. A few daring officers did make arrests but it wasn't until a cavalry troop arrived that the majority of rioters decided enough was enough and melted into the warren of alleyways.

The ashes of unrest still glowed below the surface. The Riot Act had been read in various streets and in the Saltmarket the cavalry had drawn sabres and sliced their way through a group of rioters. Citizens were ordered to stay in their homes that night, while able-bodied men were urged to volunteer as special constables. Over the next two days, ten thousand public-spirited Glaswegians turned up at St George's Church to form this one-off militia. Rioters tried to erect barricades to fend off the troops but these were breached and more arrests made. As the Monday night wore on, the streets gradually quietened and the cavalry and special constables settled themselves into the Royal Exchange, ready to spring into action if the tinderbox city erupted again. Tuesday dawned with a feeling of suppressed menace in the air. The trouble had not passed, everyone knew that, so large groups of special constables patrolled the streets, backed up by the military.

Then word came from the Calton of a plan to launch an attack on Campbell's silk mill in John Street. A force of police, including 17 army pensioners known as 'foggies', were sent out to meet the troublemakers head-on. There was a pitched battle in the streets and the rioters were forced back towards Glasgow Green. There they regrouped and, their numbers swollen by reinforcements, stormed onto John Street again. The police wielded their batons and the pensioners battered the attackers with their muskets and hacked at them with their long bayonets. The mob threw stones and wielded sticks, iron bars and any kind of weapon they could lay their hands on. The police retreated up the street, bombarded by stones from all sides, but at Main Street in the Calton they made their stand. A man dropped a foggy with a stone and was taken into custody. His pals tried to free him, so the pensioner force was ordered to charge the mob and open fire. Miner David Carruth died, his body being borne away on a window shutter, while four others were wounded. Two later died, one being James Alexander, a special constable cut down by 'friendly fire'.

After that, there were sporadic outbreaks of further violence but the city gradually fell into an uneasy peace. The role of the police during the two days of mobbing and rioting came under scrutiny and on 24 March, Police Superintendent William Henry Pearce, who had been appointed almost exactly one year before to head up the new supersized force, resigned. At the beginning of the riot, he had been the only officer seen on the streets, dodging from one flashpoint to another. However, he was the man in charge and as such he felt he had to carry responsibility for the lack of confidence the public had in his force. Henry Miller, now a prison governor, returned to his old post but only briefly, for ill health forced him to resign in December 1848. Glasgow's new top cop was serving officer James Smart, who as assistant superintendent in the Eastern Division had been the man who had sent the special constables and foggies to the John Street battleground. A former travelling salesman in the tea trade, he had first become a police officer with the Metropolitan Police. In 1831, he'd returned to Glasgow to join the Gorbals force and four years later had become assistant superintendent with the Calton Burgh Force, absorbed by the Glasgow force in 1846.

In 1862, the title of his office was changed. No longer would the chief of the City of Glasgow Police be called superintendent. From then on, he would be known as the chief constable.

CHAPTER FIVE

POISON GIRLS TOGETHER

Poison, they say, is a woman's weapon, the perception being that there is something decidedly unmanly in slipping a victim a noxious substance rather than facing up to him with a weapon. Like all generalisations, it does not bear up under scrutiny.

In Glasgow in 1828, a husband and wife team used laudanum to dull the senses of their victims before they plundered their pockets. No one knows for certain how many men they robbed in this way, or how many they killed by dosing them with too strong a mixture. Although convicted of only one killing, they almost certainly murdered many more, making them two of Scotland's most prolific – if forgotten – serial killers.

They called it 'tipping the doctor' – lacing drinks with laudanum and then rifling the pockets of the insensible victim. Although it was fairly common in the nineteenth century, John Stuart and his wife Catherine seem to have taken the practice to new levels. The Glasgow girl married Stuart over the anvil at Gretna when she was only 16 and he was a thief, if not out of the top drawer: sheep-stealing, *The Scotsman* later observed, was his 'boldest adventure'. He picked pockets, he cheated at cards, he became a 'coiner' (a counterfeiter), he drank, he whored – and he raised his standing among the 'idle and unprincipled profligates' he called friends when he broke out of Stranraer jail.

Coining proved too much like hard work and the couple decided to try tipping the doctor. All they had to do was select their mark, load him up with booze laced with laudanum and then rip him off at their leisure. The beauty of it was that they could spend their time in taverns and inns and still make some cash. The pair set off from the south-west for Glasgow, where they believed there would be richer pickings.

Laudanum was a highly addictive mixture of opium and alcohol, viewed as a cure for all ills and used by the poorer classes as a soporific. It was easily obtainable and an ideal tool for ruthless crooks. It was also very dangerous and it was not long before the Stuarts killed their first victim, a little man in a Glasgow bar who was simply grateful for some convivial company. Another was left to die in a Bridgegate tavern, having been robbed of 30 shillings. During a sojourn in Ireland, they robbed and killed a drover, taking the 20 sovereigns he had hidden in the tail of his coat.

The man who proved to be their downfall was farmer and merchant Robert Lamont, who had left his home on the island of Ulva to make his annual pilgrimage to Glasgow to buy supplies. The 50-year-old father of four met the Stuarts on the *Toward Castle* packet steamer as it made its way from Lochgilphead. Below decks, they plied Lamont with drink, 'tipped the doctor' and took from him twelve pounds in banknotes, seven guineas and some silver coins. Lamont was found seriously ill before the boat berthed and died the following day. The Stuarts were arrested on board with the cash and Lamont's hand-stitched silk purse on their person. A small bottle of laudanum was also discovered.

They were sent to Edinburgh to languish in Calton Prison until their trial. Stuart, though, believed that no prison could hold him. He and eight other 'stout and desperate ruffians' planned to kill their way out using home-made weapons. The plot was uncovered and spikes sharpened into daggers found under Stuart's bed. 'It was no more than anyone else would have done,' he said when confronted. He was described at the time as 'ardent and fearless – resembling in these respects the lower animals, which rush forward with an impetuosity which nothing can impede'. His wife, though, was 'very penitent' and had been haunted with visions of their first victim, the little man in Glasgow who had been so cheered by their company.

Before they were hanged on 19 August 1829, Stuart admitted that they had killed eleven men. A contemporary broadsheet stated, 'With the exception of Burke [William, the notorious Edinburgh murderer] no criminals have excited so much detestation.' In the midst of a torrential downpour, over 10,000 people thronged Edinburgh's Lawnmarket to watch the deadly duo die. Just before the lever was pulled, Stuart reached out as best he could to grip his wife's hand and together they fell through the trap. He died instantly but she jerked and choked on the rope for a few minutes before she was finally still.

Nine years later, a woman who poisoned her neighbour and a lodger caused something of a fashion sensation – for the tartan she wore on the city gallows was subsequently shunned by the women of Glasgow for a number of years.

Elizabeth Jaffray, sometimes known as Nickleson, Shafto or Jeffrey, murdered her two victims in Carluke, Lanarkshire. Ailing Ann Newal, or Carl, died on 5 October 1837 after eating some meal and water with whisky prepared by her 'kindly' neighbour, who told her the mixture contained medicine. Jaffray's lodger, a Highland miner called Hugh Munro, met his death on 30 October after a meal of porridge and then some rhubarb. The poisoner's motive was that old faithful, money. The Crown stated that she owed Munro £5 but could not pay it back, so decided that murder would be the cheapest way out of the debt. However, villagers believed that she wanted him out of the way to allow her to take in a more profitable lodger. It was believed she had discussed the easiest way to poison someone with poor Mrs Newal, which had made her a liability.

After a trial that lasted 18 hours, Mrs Jaffray was found guilty and sentenced to hang. However, 'a few Quakers and other eccentric individuals' campaigned to have her sentence commuted. A broadsheet noted that 'these characters say it was a mighty piece of unheard-of cruelty to execute BURKE!' The writer continued:

> But we have no patience with them. Their mawkish ravings are an outrage on nature and common sense. How humane, and kind, and charitable they are to the cold-blooded murderer – while not a sigh is given for the innocent butchered victims!

Mrs Jaffray was hanged in sight of the monument in Glasgow, and a large crowd clustered on the Green to see her go. She had refused to confess to her crimes and feeling against her ran high. She stepped onto the platform wearing a shawl in the distinctive red-and-black check of the Rob Roy tartan and such was the general revulsion felt for her crimes that the fabric immediately went out of favour.

The poison she had used was arsenic, which she had purchased under the pretext of poisoning rats. That very substance was alleged to have been used by two other women in the west of Scotland, one of whom is the most famous suspected murderer in Glasgow's criminal history.

* * *

Everyone knew that Christina Gilmour was unhappy in her marriage to Renfrewshire farmer John Gilmour. And when he died after a violent illness in 1843, tongues wagged about the rat poison she had purchased not long before. What made matters worse was that she had fled the country. After she disappeared, the heavy mort-safe that protected the man's corpse from bodysnatchers was hauled off and the remains examined by experts. The rumours proved correct: his body was riddled with arsenic traces.

A dogged Renfrewshire Police detective traced Christina's movements to Liverpool, where she had taken ship for New York in the company of a man. Superintendent George McKay took a faster vessel and was on the quayside to meet her. Her companion, who had proved to be far from a gentleman during the voyage by making unseemly advances, vanished into the crowds.

The 24-year-old suspected murderess gamely battled extradition by feigning insanity but the Scottish cop was determined she was going to return home with him to face the music. And in January 1843, she was in the High Court at Edinburgh charged with murder.

During the two-day trial, black-clad Christina Gilmour, a simple gold wedding band on her left hand, listened dispassionately to the evidence. She listened as her purchases of arsenic were raised and her late husband's extended, agonising death outlined. She watched as medical witnesses produced a grisly succession of the dead man's internal organs to prove that he had been poisoned.

The law prohibited accused persons from giving evidence but their declarations could be read into the record. Gilmour denied murdering her husband. The arsenic was not to kill rats, as she had claimed at the time, but to kill herself, such was her unhappiness. Her husband was not a bad man but he was not the man for her. Her defence counsel raised the possibility that John Gilmour had killed himself. He already kept arsenic around the house for the control of vermin and he had shown a somewhat dramatic nature during the couple's courtship, when he had threatened to kill himself if Christina, holding out for her true love, did not agree to marry him. He knew his wife was unhappy – it was even said that the marriage was unconsummated – and it was possible his earlier thoughts of suicide had resurfaced.

The jury was out for only an hour. Christina, a cup of water in her hands, sat immobile as the 15 men delivered their verdict on whether she would live or die. The case had been a major talking point in the dining rooms and drawing rooms of Glasgow's middle classes; Renfrew was not so very far away, after all, and Christina was very much of their stratum. They were fascinated by the case and the courtroom was crammed with west-coast sensation-seekers who had made the trip to the capital. The packed courtroom was hushed, as if everyone present was holding their breath, and the solemn voice of the clerk floated towards the high ceiling: 'The jury, after a careful and mature consideration of the evidence brought before them in this case, are unanimously of the opinion that John Gilmour died from the effects of arsenic poisoning . . .'

That much was expected; the medical evidence had been compelling. The question now was, had the defence created even a shadow of doubt that she had laced his food and drink with the poison? Journalists' eyes watched for a sign of emotion from the woman in black sitting in the dock but there was none. Then the clerk spoke again: '. . . but find it not proved against the prisoner at the bar, as libelled.'

The courtroom erupted and the judge demanded order, finally quietening the public gallery with strong threats of contempt. Still Christina's blank expression did not change. There was not so much as a flicker of emotion as she left the court. She later returned to her father's home in Ayrshire. She died in Stewarton, aged 87, having never married again.

But in 1857 she must have been aware of a similar case being heard in the High Court of Justiciary in Edinburgh. The accused was a young, beautiful woman from a good family. The circumstances included the use of arsenic and the removal of a man who was, quite simply, in the way. The case scandalised Victorian society with its heady mix of passion, sex and murder. It has inspired articles and books and plays, and at least one film, directed by none other than David Lean. The question remains, though: did Madeleine Smith kill her lover?

She was only 19 when she first met Jersey-born Pierre Emile L'Angelier. He was a lowly clerk in a seed merchant's warehouse and as such was not a fitting match for the eldest daughter of wealthy Glasgow architect James Smith. Educated at a London boarding school, she was a fine beauty, with fair skin, dark eyes that could entice any man and long hair 'of polished ebony'. She liked to flirt and she liked to enjoy herself, and her beauty, combined with a powerful personality, meant she could have had her pick of the eligible men in Glasgow. But she was also feisty, single-minded and adventurous, and each of these qualities would come to the fore over the next two years.

L'Angelier had engineered a meeting through a mutual acquaintance in April 1855 and Madeleine had been captivated by his Gallic charm. Ten years older than the girl he would come to know as 'Mimi', he had spent some time with the National Guard in Paris during the revolution of 1848. This appealed to the 19-year-old girl's repressed Victorian romantic spirit. It is to his credit that, although experienced in the intrigues of *l'amour*, he did not see the redoubtable Miss Smith as just another conquest. He wanted to make her Mrs L'Angelier in a proper manner and that meant with the permission of her parents. His station in life, however, precluded the stern Mr Smith from even countenancing such a match and Madeleine was forbidden from seeing the handsome pen-pusher again.

Madeleine, though, was not the girl to meekly accede to such an order. She continued to see Pierre. She smuggled him into the family home, first in India Street and then, from 1856, in Blythswood Square. When the Smith family went to Rowaleyn, their summer home in Row (present-day Rhu, on the Clyde near Helensburgh), he followed and the couple kept up their midnight liaisons. At some point, probably in the house's wooded gardens, the relationship became physical. 'My own, my beloved husband,' Madeleine wrote afterwards, 'if we did wrong last night it was in the excitement of our love . . . I did not bleed in the least last night but I had a good deal of pain during the night. Tell me, pet, were you angry at me for allowing you to do what you did?'

L'Angelier may not have been angry but he was certainly disappointed. He seemed to find fault in many things she did and she was forced to grovel at his feet for forgiveness. The letters she wrote to him in the early stages of their relationship are peppered with phrases like, 'I ought never in any way to vex or annoy you', 'If I do anything wrong and you check me, I shall never, never do it again . . . you shall love me and I shall obey you', 'It is my duty as a wife to do so. I shall do all you want of me.' She talked of her faults and how he would correct them. She talked of being his 'wife in every sense of the word', another clear indication that their relationship was sexual. Even that was thrown back in her face, for he blamed her completely for their having succumbed to their passions. 'I am sad at what you did,' he wrote to her, 'I regret it very much. Why, Mimi, did you give way after your promises?' He even obliquely suggested that she was not a virgin. 'I do not understand, my pet, your not bleeding, for every woman having her virginity must bleed,' he wrote. 'You must have done so some other time. Try to remember if you ever hurt yourself in washing, etc.'

Madeleine's ardour, though, was cooling. She was young, she was flirtatious and the constant belittling finally got to her. Apart from that, someone else had been paying her attention. Merchant William Minnoch lived next door to her family in Blythswood Square and was a much more desirable candidate for son-in-law. Madeleine thought so too and tried to break off the relationship with Pierre but he would hear nothing of it. She was his Mimi and if she tried to end things, then he would take her letters – her passionate, revealing, indelicate letters – to her father and her new beau. L'Angelier stalked her, watching her whenever she was out with Minnoch or her family. Madeleine felt forced to continue her correspondence and the illicit meetings. When he could not creep into the house, he stood outside her basement bedroom window and accepted hot chocolate through the bars.

Then L'Angelier began to take ill. In February 1857, he was stricken with sharp, piercing abdominal pains and vomiting. The symptoms continued until finally he was found dead in his room. His friends and his employers were suspicious of this sudden and lethal decline in his health and demanded a post-mortem. His body was exhumed from the Ramshorn kirkyard and his stomach revealed 82 grains of arsenic. Madeleine's letters were found, leading the procurator fiscal to believe that he had his culprit. But like Christina

Gilmour before her, Madeleine, perhaps seeing the writing on the wall, had taken flight.

She did not get far, for her brother and William Minnoch found her on the steamer heading for Rowaleyn. As Glasgow's courts were still not considered good enough for such high-profile proceedings, the trial took place in Edinburgh. It lasted nine days, during which the Crown tried to paint a picture of a cold-hearted young woman who had purchased arsenic ostensibly for the poisoning of rats but who had served it to her erstwhile lover in cups of cocoa.

Since the Arsenic Act of 1851, all purchases of the substance had to be made by persons over the age of 21 and known to the chemist. The substance itself, white in colour, had to be stained with either soot or indigo and the purchaser's details recorded in a poisons book. None of these regulations had prevented Miss Smith from obtaining the poison, which she later claimed she used in diluted form as a cosmetic to wash her face, arms and neck. It was certainly common for women to tone up their complexions with arsenic-based lotions. Both sexes also used arsenious acid as a tonic and it was prescribed for the treatment of fevers. L'Angelier had on more than one occasion claimed he was 'an arsenic eater', taking it to improve his health and his appearance. The defence used this to suggest that perhaps he had poisoned himself. He also suffered habitually from stomach trouble. (A later theory suggested that L'Angelier had visited a spa where the medicinal waters might have been thick with the poison).

The main problem facing the Crown was that although they had motive – the victim had become something of a liability to Miss Smith's future happiness and had threatened to betray their liaison to her father and her new suitor – they could not prove Madeleine had even seen L'Angelier on the three occasions specified in the indictment, let alone given him a drink laced with poison. Also, the medical evidence was ambiguous. The defence experts thought that given the amount of arsenic found in the stomach, there should also have been traces of soot. It was further suggested that L'Angelier would have tasted the mixer, or at least felt it scratching his throat. In their minds, it

81

followed that, before he died, he would have mentioned something to his landlady or the doctor who attended him.

The Crown's experts refuted this, saying the soot would have evaporated and the strong cocoa would have masked the taste. There was also a diary kept by L'Angelier in which he had written:

Thursday 19th February. Saw Mimi a few moments. Was very ill during the night.

Friday 20th February. Passed two pleasant hours with Mimi in the drawing-room.

Saturday 21st February. Did not feel well.

Sunday, 22nd February. Saw Mimi in the drawing-room. Promised me French Bible. Taken very ill.

The defence, naturally, battled hard to have the diary excluded from evidence – and won. It was felt that had L'Angelier been alive to give evidence, it would have been admissible because he would have been open to cross-examination. Of course, had he been alive, the point would not have been debated in the first place. Madeleine did not deny having given L'Angelier cocoa on a few occasions but added, 'I never administered, or caused to be administered, to Mr L'Angelier arsenic or anything injurious, and this I declare to be the truth.'

Public sympathy was with Madeleine. The case consumed prodigious amounts of newsprint and Smith's cause was further strengthened by the fact that L'Angelier was a 'foreigner'. Even writing some years after the event, crime writer F. Tennyson Jesse called him 'that little, scheming, sensual, iron-willed lady-killer'. Madeleine, though, captivated all who saw her. One contemporary report said she entered the court 'with the air of a belle entering a ballroom or a box at the opera. Her steps were buoyant, and she carried a silver-topped bottle of smelling salts. She was stylishly dressed, and wore a pair of lavender gloves.'

The defence was careful to remind the jury that murder was a capital crime. Madeleine's counsel opened his remarks with, 'Gentlemen, the charge against the prisoner is murder, and the punishment for murder is death.' Who can say how much the thought of sending the calm, self-possessed young beauty in the dock to the gallows helped convince 13 of the men on the jury that the case against her was not proven? Only two believed beyond the famed shadow of a doubt that she was guilty. The courtroom was filled with cheering spectators and the judges called for order.

Madeleine Smith, still calm, still dignified, was taken from the court by her brother, through a side door, and spirited away to Rowaleyn. Her parents, who had 'taken to their beds' during the trial, were waiting for her, having sought refuge from the scandal in the country. The lack of support from her mother and father in court must have hurt her deeply but she could take some solace in the warmth of feeling from other quarters. In a letter to the matron of Edinburgh Prison, Madeleine stated, 'I think I must have had several hundred letters, all from gentlemen, some offering me consolation, and some their hearths and homes.' She also noted that, 'the feeling in the west is not so good towards me as you kind Edinburgh people showed me. I think it shall be necessary for me to leave Scotland for a few months.' She was, though, 'not at all pleased with the verdict'. William Minnoch was out of the picture. The letter says, 'My *friend* I know nothing of. I have not seen him. I hear he has been ill, which I don't much care.'

So if Madeleine Smith did not kill L'Angelier, what happened? He could have taken the arsenic himself, either in a suicide attempt or, more dramatically but perhaps more unlikely, as a way of punishing the woman he loved by framing her for his murder. The suicide angle is strengthened by his reaction to an earlier failed romance, when he threatened to take his own life (a parallel with the reaction of John Gilmour to being rejected by Christina in the decade before). He could have taken the poison by accident; as a known arsenic eater, perhaps he just ate too much. He was also painted as a womaniser and even a blackmailer, so perhaps someone else took it into their head to remove him from the earth.

Madeleine later married London artist George Wardle and became part of the smart set, being noted, it is said, for having the daring to uncover the legs of her dining table. It would be interesting to see the faces of her dinner guests if she ever offered them cocoa. She subsequently moved to New York, married for a second time, raised a family and died, aged 93, on 12 April 1928. Her gravestone in Mount Hope Cemetery, New Jersey, bears the name Lena Wardle Sheehy.

Her case had been plastered across newspapers the length and breadth of the country, and in the weaving village of Eaglesham, to the south-west of the city, an itinerant tailor named John Thomson had often spoken of it to friends. The 26-year-old lodged with tailor James Watson from June 1857 and had many conversations with his landlord about the redoubtable Miss Smith. Thomson believed Madeleine should have been hanged. He had become fascinated by a mention of prussic acid in a report on the case and had asked Watson's photographer brother John what it was. 'I said it was the kind of stuff that, if she had got it and had given sixpence-worth of it to L'Angelier, she could not have got out of his company till he was dead.' In other words, had L'Angelier been given prussic acid, he would have died instantly. Thomson wondered where such a substance could be found and was told that photographers regularly use it.

The tailor had developed a fixation on Agnes Montgomery, who worked in the village cotton mill. The 27-year-old woman lived in the rooms directly above her sister, Janet, who was married to James Watson. Agnes often denied that there was anything of a romantic nature between her and Thomson but they had been seen together by other workers. She refused to come away with him to Glasgow and continued to ignore him in public, even making a fool of him in front of her friends.

At around 5.20 p.m. on Sunday, 13 September, Janet found her sister dying in her room. The door had been locked from the outside and had to be forced. She was retching, half paralysed and her fingers were cramped and claw-like. Thomson ran for the doctor but the woman died within the hour. A glass lay on a table with some sediment caking the bottom. A bottle of beer was also seen when she was discovered but this disappeared.

Thomson had been the last person to see her alive. He had been with her that afternoon and was spotted leaving her rooms. However, there seemed at this stage to be no evidence of foul play and she was buried in the local churchyard, where her grave can still be seen. However, James Watson was deeply suspicious of his lodger – and recalled the conversations about prussic acid. He became convinced that the man was responsible for Agnes's death. However, before Watson could convince anyone of this, Thomson decided things were too hot for him in Eaglesham, so he surreptitiously relieved his landlord of one pound and headed for Glasgow.

James Watson reported the theft to the Renfrewshire county police. He also opined that Thomson might be guilty of murder. The matter had to be reported to the procurator fiscal of Paisley, who was at that time attending circuit court in Glasgow. And here fate – or coincidence – steps in. While the police were talking to the procurator fiscal, it was discovered that Thomson was at that very moment in court on a charge of theft.

When he had reached Glasgow, he had returned to his previous lodgings in John Street, which he had left under a cloud, having been suspected of stealing another guest's clothing. At 11 p.m. on 25 September, the landlord, Archibald Mason, woke to find Thomson in his room, a bottle of 'good Paisley whisky' in his hand. 'Father,' said Thomson, 'will you have a dram?' The 65-year-old agreed but after one sip handed it back, saying it had a strange taste. His wife was made of sterner stuff, for she downed half a glass before concluding it was a bit off. Thomson did not attempt to take a drink. They agreed that Thomson could stay the night, planning to alert the police in the morning. When his wife began throwing up in the night, Mr Mason grew suspicious of the whisky and took some to a doctor, who declared it was heavily laced with methylated spirits.

The following morning, Thomson was arrested for the theft of the clothing and taken to court. It was while he was there that he was also arrested for stealing James Watson's cash – and the murder of Agnes Montgomery.

Investigations revealed that Thomson had sent a boy to buy some prussic acid from a Glasgow chemist. Another witness had seen him walking across the green and stopping beside a tree on the day of the murder. A search of the spot uncovered the missing key to Agnes's door. More damningly, John and Janet Watson's three-year-old daughter said she had been in Agnes's house when 'Jack', as she knew him, had offered the murdered woman 'some ginger' (in fact beer). Agnes had taken some of the beer, then vomited violently. The girl had also seen Thomson smash a small glass bottle under his heel in the back garden. He had given her sweets to keep her silent but she finally told all under pressure, wailing, 'I'm no to tell, for Jack is to give me a bawbee [a halfpenny].'

Thomson was hanged in Paisley on 11 January 1858. A crowd of 20,000 crammed into the space before the county buildings where the gallows had been erected. By that time, the Watsons and the others who had befriended him in Eaglesham had learned his true nature. His real name was Peter Walker and he had killed once before. At the age of nine, near Tarbert where he had grown up, he had thrown a young boy into a quarry and watched him drown. In 1853, he had been jailed for theft at Inveraray Court. He had been apprenticed to a Lochgilphead tailor and had fallen for the boss's daughter. In a bid to impress her, he had overspent, found himself in debt and so had broken into the shop to find cash. When he turned up at Eaglesham after his sojourn in Glasgow, he was a ticket-of-leave prisoner (released on licence).

Perhaps, when Madeleine Smith read of his case in the papers, she permitted herself a small smile . . .

CHAPTER SIX

POLICE McCALL

He was an imposing man, even by the standards of the Victorian era. Tall, balding but with a thick bush of mutton-chop whiskers to compensate, he walked down the platform of the city's Queen Street Station with a purposeful stride. He was smartly if inexpensively dressed and the two constables who flanked him looked strangely shabby in their blue uniforms. Passengers filed off the Edinburgh train and Superintendent Alexander McCall of Glasgow Police's detective division allowed them to surge around him as he scanned their faces, looking for one man amongst many. Then he spotted him, also a tall man but sporting a long, carefully groomed and ever freshly pomaded beard. His balding pate, however, was disguised without much success by a comb-over. He was a distinguished man, a professional man, but to McCall he was nothing more than a man who had quite ruthlessly killed two women, one his wife.

Dr Edward Pritchard might have got away with it, too, if someone's pricked conscience had not brought the eyes of the Glasgow Police upon him. It led Superintendent McCall to this platform to meet the murdering medic as he returned from his wife's funeral. For McCall, it was all in a day's work. For Pritchard, it was the beginning of the end.

Hampshire-born Edward William Pritchard was the son of a sea captain and seemed destined, like many of his family, to enjoy a professional life on the ocean wave. However, it was to the medical profession that he seemed drawn, so, like one of his brothers, he mixed the two by becoming a naval surgeon. Despite being a lacklustre student, he was admitted to the College of Surgeons and passed the Navy Board examinations before taking up the post of assistant surgeon.

In 1850, he met pretty Mary Jane Taylor, the daughter of Edinburgh merchant Michael Taylor. She was visiting her uncle in Portsmouth when she was introduced to the handsome young doctor at a ball. Romance followed and by the autumn they were married. The following year, he resigned his commission and set up in practice, with his in-laws' financial help, in Hunmanby and Filey in Yorkshire. He fancied himself as a man of letters – writing books on local matters and on his travels abroad and submitting articles to medical journals – but he was an indifferent doctor. He spent six years in Yorkshire and the best that could later be said of him was that he was 'fluent, plausible, amorous, politely impudent, and singularly untruthful. One who knew him well at Filey describes him as the "prettiest liar" he ever met.'

Pritchard's hands were made not to heal but to wander and his affection for the ladies did not endear him to his patients. He was also a man 'whose imagination overran the limits of probability, as much as his expenditure overran his means'. He left Yorkshire with a cloud over his character and a deep hole in his finances. He purchased a diploma stating that he had qualified as a Doctor of Medicine at the University of Erlangen in Germany and travelled abroad as personal physician to a wealthy gentleman. In June 1860, he set up practice again, this time in Glasgow. Almost from the start, he tried to insinuate himself into the city's medical establishment but was constantly rebuffed. He used Masonic connections to attempt to further himself but even that failed. The art of photography was by then popular and he had himself photographed in his Masonic robes and these pictures made into calling cards. Still he could not break into the solid circle of the Glasgow glitterati.

Given the cold shoulder by his professional contemporaries, he sought fame by other means. He turned to the arts, obtaining a seat on the board of the Glasgow Athenaeum. He also delivered a series of lectures on his travels, but in these fact was intermingled with fantasy. He had a walking stick that he claimed was a gift from the Italian hero Garibaldi but it was later proved that Pritchard had had the cane inscribed 'To William Edward Pritchard from his friend General Garibaldi' himself.

It has been suggested that the doctor was intimate with Elizabeth McGirn, who worked in the Pritchard household in Berkeley Terrace. However, this cannot be confirmed as poor Elizabeth died in most mysterious circumstances in 1863 when her room caught fire. No one else was injured in the blaze. Elizabeth died in her sleep as the flames raged through the room, perhaps caused by a gas jet being left on at the head of the bed. Despite her right arm being burned almost away and the flesh on her chest eaten by the flames, her corpse looked almost at peace. Whispers suggested Dr Pritchard had got her pregnant and murdered her to avoid scandal. However, the post-mortem failed to substantiate the rumours and no action was taken against Pritchard. After an insurance settlement was reached, he and his growing family – he had five children by this time – moved first to Royal Crescent then to a house in Clarence Place, Sauchiehall Street.

It was here, in October 1864, that Mary Jane first began to show symptoms of the illness that would kill her. Severe headaches led to vomiting and deep depression. It was felt prudent that she spend some time away from the travails of family life and recuperate under her mother's care in Edinburgh. Jane Taylor nursed her daughter well, for by Christmas she was back at her own hearth. But by January 1865, her illness had returned, more violently than before. She could not keep food down and during severe attacks of cramp the fingers of her hands stiffened and froze. Her ever solicitous husband treated her for irritation of the stomach. He also told a visiting physician that his wife suffered from catalepsy but the doctor later dismissed this diagnosis by saying that Pritchard's skills were 'a little at random' and that he was not 'a model of accuracy, wisdom and caution in applying names to things'.

Then Jane Taylor arrived to take charge of her daughter's care. The 70-year-old woman was all Victorian hustle and bustle, and she soon had matters under control, supervising meals, supervising visits, supervising everything. It must have come as a blow to the still ailing daughter when her mother seemed to contract the same sickness. It was a greater shock when she died on Saturday, 25 February – just two weeks after her arrival.

Dr James Paterson had been called and attended the woman while she was ill. Pritchard tried to suggest that the old woman had perhaps taken too much laudanum, which she used as a headache medicine. Dr Paterson disagreed. 'If a person is in the habit of taking opium to a great extent,' he said later, 'you generally find they are not good in colour. They are generally thin in features and hollow around the eyes – in fact, not of a healthy appearance generally.' Pritchard then suggested that the woman might be suffering from an apoplectic fit but Dr Paterson suspected something else. He suspected poison.

His suspicions were made all the keener when he saw Mary Jane Pritchard. He thought then that someone in the house was administering poison. Further, he was an experienced enough physician to suspect that the poison in question was antimony. Used as an emetic, in larger or continual doses it brought about cramps, vomiting, diarrhoea and depression. Towards the end, the victim can turn cyanotic, or blue. He recognised all these symptoms in the two women and knew in his heart that they were being systematically poisoned.

However, he kept his own counsel.

Why this good doctor remained silent is a mystery. He claimed later that it was not his place, that he had no right, that he was 'under no obligation'. That was the position he took then and that was the position he took at Pritchard's trial – a position that went unchallenged in court. He made one other visit to the Pritchard house, to see Mary Jane, and what he saw only confirmed his fears. But officially he did nothing – apart from refusing to certify the cause of death in Mrs Taylor's case. He noted that the death 'was certainly sudden, unexpected and to me mysterious' and referred the registrar to Dr Pritchard, who stated his mother-in-law's death was due to paralysis followed by apoplexy. For that to be the case, it would have to have been the other way around but no one commented on that.

On 18 March, Mary Jane died. Pritchard put on a great display of emotion for the servants, one of whom knew that much of what she saw was play-acting. Mary McLeod had been intimate with her master for some time; he had even been caught kissing and groping her by Mrs Pritchard on one occasion. The wife had called the husband 'a nasty, dirty man' and consoled the then 15-year-old girl. The affair continued until McLeod fell pregnant but that inconvenience was surmounted when Pritchard gave the girl 'some medicine' that induced a miscarriage. He bought her gifts and he promised her marriage – if his wife were to die.

While he was in Edinburgh burying his wife beside her mother in Grange Cemetery – having earlier demanded that the coffin be unscrewed so that he could kiss his wife's dead lips for the last time – events in Glasgow were turning against Dr Pritchard. The procurator fiscal received a letter signed 'Amor Justiciae', or 'lover of justice'. The anonymous writer stated:

Dr Pritchard's mother-in-law died suddenly and unexpectedly about three weeks ago in his house in Sauchiehall Street, Glasgow, under circumstances at least very suspicious. His wife died today, also suddenly and unexpectedly and under circumstances equally suspicious. We think it right to draw your attention to the above, as the proper person to take action in the matter and see justice done.

91

The writer of this note has never been revealed but it is strongly believed that it was Dr Paterson belatedly taking action. He denied this was the case both verbally and in the press.

Dr Pritchard was arrested by Superintendent McCall as he stepped off the train. He was escorted first to the North Prison on Duke Street and later to Calton Prison in the capital to await trial. Even when the bodies were exhumed and traces of the poison found, he denied murdering his wife and mother-in-law by administering antimony in various drinks and foods. McCall himself transported the various samples to Frederick Penny, professor of chemistry at Glasgow's Andersonian University (later to form part of the University of Strathclyde). Professor Penny confirmed the results of the post-mortems.

Pritchard's trial in Edinburgh was a sensation. As the Madeleine Smith trial had already proved, the public liked nothing better than to see the middle classes in the dock, and demand for space in the courtroom was high – so high that special arrangements had to be made for the admittance of the public. Pritchard denied everything, of course, but it did him no good whatsoever. The final nail in his coffin was the evidence of Mary McLeod. He had tried to implicate her in the murders and she had, in fact, been arrested on the same day as he. Despite even this, she appeared unwilling to testify against the man who had first got her pregnant, then given her something that had caused her to miscarry. When the judge lost patience and threatened her with jail if she did not speak out, she finally told the court that Pritchard had promised to marry her if his wife died.

Whether his passion for the serving girl was what moved him to murder is unclear. McCall's investigations had revealed that Pritchard's finances were in disarray and there was an insurance policy on his wife, although it was not worth enough to merit such drastic action. In the end, the motive for Mary Jane's murder was a mystery, although it was clear that her mother had had to go when she managed to place herself in the way. But the prosecution did not need to prove motive; they just needed to prove that murder had been done by the accused. At the end of the five-day trial, the jury took only fifty-five minutes to decide that Pritchard was a double killer. For the judge, there was only one sentence. The black cap was placed over his wig and Pritchard was sentenced to hang – and may God have mercy on his soul.

On Friday, 28 July 1865, an estimated 100,000 people made their way to the Green to see Pritchard die. A light drizzle had been falling all night but they endured the damp for a glimpse of the most hated man in Glasgow. Few of them would even have suspected that they were to witness the final public execution in the city. Superintendent McCall would have been there, just one of the 750 police officers on duty to maintain order. Pritchard had spent the few weeks between his trial and execution in the North Prison but had, on the Thursday night, been brought to the now almost empty South Prison for ease of accessibility to the gallows on the Green.

The finisher was William Calcraft, imported from London for the job and the longest-serving executioner England ever knew. A murmur grew among the crowd when his distinctive white hair and thick bushy beard were spotted as he climbed the steps of the gallows to begin his checks. Then, 45 minutes later, at 8 a.m., Pritchard himself appeared. In a final touch of hypocrisy, he was impeccably turned out in mourning clothes. Calcraft adjusted Pritchard's long beard as he put the noose around his neck, and then he pulled the lever. According to one observer, the doctor 'shrugged his shoulders more than half a dozen times, his head shook and his whole body trembled'. The hangman knew his job, though, and Pritchard's lifeless body was soon swaying on the rope, the kid gloves he had been holding slipping from his fingers. The air of professionalism was marred, however, by the way the body was allowed to tumble into the coffin below the platform. It landed with such impact that it smashed some of the wood and joiners had to be called to repair the damage before it was interred in the prison yard, with only the letter 'P' scratched on a stone wall to mark it out from the others. Years later, the body was exhumed during work on the site. Someone stole Pritchard's skull and, of more practical use, the elastic-sided boots he had worn at the execution.

For Superintendent McCall, the Pritchard case was over. It was another feather in his cap and no doubt helped him reach the pinnacle of the force's hierarchy. Three years earlier, he had supervised the first murder investigation handled solely by the city's officers. Until then, crimes had been probed by the procurator fiscal's office with the help of detectives. But when in 1862 the hideously mutilated body of a woman was discovered in a room in a well-to-do house, it was decided that the Glasgow Police were now of age to go it alone.

They did not cover themselves with glory.

* * *

McCall had been made a detective inspector in 1850, rising over the following 12 years to superintendent of the Central District. By 1862, the force had embraced, albeit belatedly, both the telegraph system and photography as aids in the fight against crime. The city continued to face the usual problems and the police still handled everyday crimes on the rapidly proliferating streets. The Victorian era was supposedly one of family values but there was yet a market for all forms of vices and perversions. A man would still seek out a 'doxy' (a prostitute) and a drink. In the decade beginning 1860, the beat officers wheeled between 45,000 and 64,000 drunks every year to stations on special 'drunk barrows', which were still in use 60 years later. Shebeens were still hawking rotgut whisky at knock-down prices. One of the most notorious was Mother McGuire's in the Saltmarket, where customers needed a password to gain access and a series of hoists and pulleys were in place to swiftly haul the illicit beverages away should the joint be raided. Sunday drinking was outlawed in the city in 1853 but the popular Clyde steamers – like the one on which the Stuarts claimed their last victim – were exempt from such restrictions. The first 'booze cruises' were born, giving rise to the expression 'steaming drunk'. Criminal gangs continued to roam the streets, robbing the unwary and fighting among themselves. In

1868, one Peter McGuire was fined three guineas for 'having fought a pitched battle with Michael Rody in the presence of fifty Glasgow roughs'.

Glasgow was growing, gradually spreading further in all directions to eat up villages and burghs. The gardens of the tobacco lords had long since vanished under a teeming, seething pile of wood and brick tenements that were a breeding ground for disease, unrest and crime. The wealthy families moved to more fragrant areas in the west and their old homes were subdivided for multiple occupancy. In some parts of the city, there were as many as 1,000 people per acre.

The town council applied for permission to remove some of the ghastlier parts of the old city and the City of Glasgow Improvement Act was passed in 1866. Six acres of buildings, in the High Street, the Gallowgate, the Saltmarket and the Gorbals, were swept away. Thatched cottages, medieval buildings, rickety tenements were hauled down. Gone were the narrow lanes and dark passages where the shadow people of the city's underworld watched and waited for victims. These were the 'rookeries' and 'thieves' kitchens' where criminals thrived, and they exist now only in the photographs taken by Thomas Annan at the behest of the council. In their place were erected 'model tenements'.

Its remit and expertise had grown with the city but in 1862 the Glasgow Police force had still not been trusted to investigate a murder on its own. That changed with the brutal slaying of Jessie McPherson.

The attractive serving girl was found in her room by her employer, wealthy accountant John Fleming, at 17 Sandyford Place. Mr Fleming and his family had been away for the weekend at their holiday home on the Clyde, leaving Jess with her employer's 87-year-old father, James. When Mr Fleming returned on the Monday, the old man told him he had not seen Jess since Friday. He mentioned at this point that 'she's cut'. This could be taken to mean that she had left or, as subsequent events indicated, something more sinister. The door to her basement room was locked but the key was not in the hole, so Mr Fleming was able to use a spare. The room was dim and when the blinds were raised he found Jess on the floor. Her face had been hacked to pieces and the lower half of her body was naked. Someone had tried to clean up the blood that had splashed on the walls, but the stains were still visible.

Mr Fleming contacted the authorities and the police arrived accompanied by a surgeon, who, on examining the body, declared that the woman had been dead for three days and that the hideous wounds to the head and neck had been caused by a meat cleaver or something similar. Deadly they may have been but the blows were comparatively weak and could have been made by a woman or a somewhat frail old man. Two cleavers were found in the house, one of which had been recently scrubbed clean. Traces of blood led from the kitchen to the maid's room and it was thought that the woman had been dragged there face downward. A trio of bloody naked footprints – a woman's – were also found on the passage floor and a quantity of Jess's clothing, as well as some household silver, had been stolen. Enquiries were made in city pawnbrokers to see if anyone had tried to offload the stolen goods. The floorboards carrying the footprints were removed for later comparison against any suspects.

Superintendent McCall was in charge of the case and he realised there were few suspects. It looked like the murder was the result of a robbery gone wrong, but why was the body hidden in the locked room? And why had the robbers interfered with the dead woman's clothing? And who had left the footprints? John Fleming, his wife and their children had all been away from the city at the time of the murder and the only person left in the house was the elder Fleming. The old man said he'd heard a few squeals in the early hours of Saturday morning but had dismissed them as the noise of 'loose characters' who often gathered on a stretch of empty land nearby. He had thought it strange that Jess had not brought him his porridge as usual and had checked her room but found it locked. He did not raise the alarm when she did not appear during the remainder of the weekend but prepared his own meals and attended church as normal. He thought she had gone away to visit friends, he said, but despite attending services three times that weekend, the respectable Highland gentleman had not mentioned her disappearance to anyone.

McCall was unconvinced by the man's story and three weeks later had him arrested for the murder. However, while the old Highlander was being examined by a magistrate, who committed him to prison pending trial, another clue turned up, one that took McCall and his men in a new direction. A pawnbroker told police that a woman had brought in items of clothing and cutlery on the Saturday. These were identified as having come from the Fleming house and had been pledged by a Mary McDonald for six pounds and fifteen shillings. Enquiries revealed that Mary McDonald was actually Jessie McLachlan, a friend of the dead woman and a former maid in the Fleming household.

Her home at 182 Broomielaw was searched and other stolen items were found, including articles of Jess's clothing. She and her merchant seaman husband were arrested but he was later freed when he was able to prove that he had sailed on the steamer *Pladda* on the Thursday before the murder. McLachlan had been short of cash but following the murder had the means to redeem items she had previously pawned and pay off some rent arrears. When questioned, she claimed that the silver had been pledged on behalf of old Mr Fleming, who had wished to raise money for a holiday in the Highlands. Mr Fleming, though, had money in his bank accounts, so this seemed unlikely. She also claimed that the items of clothing found in her possession had been brought to her for cleaning and alteration on Jess's behalf. When she'd heard that her friend had been murdered, she'd decided to keep them.

McCall listened to her stories and did not believe a word. Old Fleming had been released, denying that he knew McLachlan, although this later proved to be false. Her foot was smeared with bull's blood and a print taken, which appeared to match the one left at the murder scene, although this was far from conclusive. She denied having been anywhere near Sandyford Place that night but witnesses had seen her in the area. Although there was nothing to prove beyond a shadow of doubt that she was in the house at the time of the murder, the evidence against her was deemed compelling enough to have her committed for trial.

From the start, it was clear that trial judge Lord Deas was prejudiced against her, a not uncommon position for this particular judge. He prevented her defence from exploring old Fleming's past, which could well have put a different complexion on the matter. Although an avid churchgoer, he was an 'auld devil' who had subjected the curvy Jessie McPherson to unwanted advances. And she was not the first, for ten years prior to the murder he had been called before his kirk session to answer charges over 'the sin of fornication with a servant'. He was also prone to pulling a cork with those below stairs. However, Lord Deas did not allow counsel to explore this thread. His four-hour charge to the jury was one-sided enough to draw criticism from the press.

Fifteen minutes after retiring, the jury returned with their guilty verdict and his lordship lived up to his nickname of 'Lord Death' by placing the black cap on his head. Before he did so, Jessie McLachlan stood up in the dock and defiantly threw back her veil to declare, 'I am as innocent as my child, who is only three years old this day.' Her lawyer then read a prepared statement – accused persons were not allowed to give evidence on their own behalf until 1898 – in which she alleged that Fleming senior had murdered Jess. The three of them had been drinking together, she said, and she had been sent out for some more whisky. When she returned, she found Jess lying semi-conscious in her room, her face cut and bruised and her clothes in disarray. Although Fleming said that the woman had fallen down and somehow lost her clothing, Jessie knew he had been making sexual advances again. Fleming feared that the truth would come out and asked Jessie to swear on the family Bible that she would not tell anyone what had happened. He promised to reward her and she agreed. She then went to fetch a doctor but before she left the house she heard a commotion in Jess's room and returned to find the drunken old man hacking at the injured woman's head and face with the meat cleaver. The already weakened victim could do nothing to halt the murderous attack and by the time Jessie arrived on the scene she was lying motionless as each succeeding stroke beat down on her flesh, sending blood flying to the ceiling and the walls.

Jessie McLachlan's silence was bought with her own freedom, for the old man threatened to implicate her in the horror unless she kept her mouth shut. He gave her the clothing and silver to make it look like a robbery.

Lord Deas dismissed the whole story as 'a tissue of wicked falsehoods'. He then sentenced her to die on 11 October. 'May the Lord have mercy on your soul,' he said.

'Mercy!' retorted the still defiant McLachlan. 'Aye, he'll have mercy, for I am innocent.'

She did not hang. The handling of the trial, the strong suspicion that the real killer was old man Fleming and the lack of clear evidence linking McLachlan to the actual murder led to outcry in some sections of the press. A petition was raised in which 100,000 signatures called for clemency. The Government heeded the call and set up an inquiry, which decided: 'She can never be hanged but as she concealed and adopted it she must be severely punished.' No further light could be shed on what actually happened in Sandyford Place that night in July. The sentence of death was commuted to life in jail. When told, McLachlan responded, 'Then am I tae be kept in jail all my days?'

Meanwhile, the public turned its attention to the Fleming family. It was generally believed that the 'auld devil' had murdered Jess and a piece of street doggerel recorded the public opinion: 'I wish I was in the land of Canaan, spinning ropes to hang old Fleming.' When he left the courtroom after giving evidence, he found himself jeered in the streets. To escape attention, he moved to Dunoon but angry locals pelted him with stones in the street. The old man died on 16 September 1864, exactly two years after the opening of the trial, and was buried in Anderston Old Church. He never admitted any involvement in Jess's murder.

In October 1877, Jessie McLachlan was released from prison. She lived with her husband in Glasgow until 1880 and, on his death, moved to America with her son. There she married a second time. She died on 1 January 1899 in Port Huron, Michigan. She continued to deny her guilt, saying it would all come right at Judgement Day.

Seven years before Jessie McLachlan died, a woman named Isabella McLennan or McGregor confessed on her own deathbed in Dundee that she had murdered Jess McPherson. She claimed that the contents of a box to be opened only on her death would reveal all but it merely contained reports on the case.

Glasgow Police were criticised for their handling of the case but that was largely unfair. McCall and his men had focused on old man Fleming from the start but there was little, or no, evidence directly linking him to the killing, apart from his presence in the house. The evidence against McLachlan was circumstantial, to be sure, but it did link her to the crime. By her own admission, she knew Fleming had killed her friend but kept her mouth shut. As Sheriff Archibald Alison commented to the inquiry, it was likely that she was 'an accidental and constrained accessory of the crime, but not an actor in it, except accessory to the murder after the fact'.

McCall's supervision of the Pritchard case three years later went some way to restoring the force's good name but its successful outcome owed more to the doctor's own failings than the investigative skills of the detective bureau. Even so, McCall was a highly respected officer – and the execution of Pritchard left him free to embark on the case that would set him apart from his contemporaries. He had no way of knowing that the man he would soon be hunting was among the crowd on the Green that day, or that his chase would take him across the Atlantic to the toughest streets of a tough city. Nor did he know that he would one day attain the position of chief constable, a goal cherished by, in the words of satirical magazine

The Bailie, 'many a Hielan' Tonalt and Lowland Sandie . . . when first they don the uniform blue, the martial helmet and the useful cape, the white gloves of purity and become entitled to "move on" the lieges with the voice of authority'.

* * *

In 1866, Superintendent McCall was told by officials of the Union Bank of Scotland that someone was forging their banknotes and passing them in Glasgow, Edinburgh, Greenock, Dalkeith and Stirling. The process used was lithography and when the detective heard that a Glasgow photographer had recently sold a printing press of the type required, three rollers and seven lithographic 'stones', or engravings, he began to believe he had his man. He had the equipment taken from its new owner to the central police office, where he had a lithographer examine it. The printer found impressions of a one-pound Union Bank note in one of the stones, while a subsequent search of the photographer's Sauchiehall Street studio revealed engravings and banknote paper. Superintendent McCall put two and two together to come up with a very sizeable sum indeed. The problem was, his forger had left the city.

English-born John Henry Greatrex was a photographer who specialised in making the kind of pictorial *cartes de visite* of which Dr Pritchard was so proud. Like Pritchard, he was a tall, striking man with a full beard and a way with women. A lay preacher, the 38-year-old had been issuing religious tracts on Glasgow Green when Pritchard met his maker. But business was failing and he decided that although there was a commandment against stealing, there was no stricture specifically about forgery. He first tried taking pictures of banknotes but the results were singularly unconvincing. His mind then turned to lithographic printing and he recruited copper engraver Sewell Grimshaw to help perfect his scheme. If they were to make money, they must first spend it and neither man had the capital required. Enter Sewell's brother Tom, who had some disposable income and was not afraid to risk it on their venture. The equipment duly purchased and tests made, the men began to churn out the notes in Greatrex's premises in Hope Street, and later on the corner of Sauchiehall Street and West Campbell Street. They produced around £1,300 (approximately £89,000 in today's terms) in dodgy notes and then set about passing – or 'uttering' – them around central Scotland.

McCall's investigations further revealed that family man Greatrex had been conducting an affair with Jane Weir, one of his employees. She had been working for him for around four years and it was during the execution of the counterfeiting scheme that they had become intimate. Her romance with the photographer had developed to such a point that he had felt confident enough to confess to her how he was making a living. He even showed her the results of his labours – banknotes, she said, 'bundles of them in the room where they were wrought'. She never at any time thought to 'peach' on him and soon found herself deeply involved in her lover's criminal enterprise. Deciding that Aberdeen would be a fine place to pass their product, Greatrex sent Jane to the Granite City, planning to follow her after he and the brothers Grimshaw had completed their tour of the central towns and cities. He joined her there and, using the name Rivers, they shared a bed in Forsyth's Hotel.

It was during this illicit sojourn in the north-east that Greatrex learned that the jig was up. McCall and his men were following the trail. The real break, however, came when the Grimshaws were arrested in Edinburgh while passing a note in exchange for an umbrella. When their luggage was searched, it was found to contain a quantity of counterfeit cash. Greatrex read about the arrests on 3 October and knew that sooner or later they would track him to Aberdeen, so he hotfooted it to London, taking a room under the name of Gray in Brown's Private Hotel in the Strand. Jane followed him a few days later and they stayed at Brown's for around a week before moving to lodgings in Waterloo Road. But Greatrex was growing increasingly nervous about the progress being made by McCall and his team and concluded, like Christina Gilmour, that they should flee to New York. He decided it would be safer for them to travel separately, so he booked himself a first-class passage on the steamer *Hermann* out of Southampton. One week later, Jane followed – second class for her – on the SS *Deutschland*.

McCall tracked their movements to Aberdeen, then to London and finally to Southampton. He was not about to let something as insignificant as the Atlantic Ocean prevent him from nabbing his man, so on 19 November 1866 he arrived in the USA in the company of a witness who knew Greatrex by sight. The problem was that New York was teeming with people. Boats arrived every day from Europe with new immigrants, and the Glasgow copper, a fish out of water, had a daunting prospect ahead of him. How was he to find two Scots in a sea of nationalities in an alien city?

Then he hit on a daring notion. Despite Greatrex's money-making skills, he would be short of cash in New York, so he and Jane would be looking for work. The Glasgow detective ran an advertisement in a number of newspapers posing as a photographer looking for a female assistant to work in his studio. The clincher was the phrase 'a Scotch girl preferred'. He received a variety of applications and one, amazingly from a Jenny Weir, took him to a lodging house in Renwick Street, on the lower west side of Manhattan in what is now known as SoHo. Weir and her 'husband' were out when he called, so he chatted to the landlady, asking her about her lodgers, who were using the name Mr and Mrs Parker. He described the people he was searching for and the woman said it sounded like Mrs Parker but her husband did not have a beard. He was, however, in the habit of quoting from the Bible.

McCall knew he had tracked them down so he and his companion waited in the street for them to return. They were soon rewarded by the sight of a man of similar build to Greatrex but clean-shaven. When the man approached the steps to the boarding house, McCall took a chance and intercepted him. Up close, he was certain he had his man and Greatrex was escorted to a nearby police office, where the extradition process was begun. Jane Weir was found later in their rented room. McCall did not arrest her but strongly advised her to return to Scotland and give evidence against her lover. It was 27 November; McCall had been in the land of the free only eight days.

Greatrex and the Grimshaw brothers stood trial in May 1867. The 72-page indictment ran to a total of 21 charges, with 164 witnesses listed against them. Greatrex, a newspaper noted, was 'more than usually pallid' perhaps because the long flowing beard and moustache for which he was known were gone. Among the witnesses was Jane Weir, who took the stand hesitantly, which did not endear her to the judge. She had kept the court waiting, which was not a wise thing to do then or now. She was a figure of scandal. She had not only conducted an affair with a married man, a man she knew to be a felon, she had fled the country with him, posing as man and wife.

In court, Weir tried to hide her face from onlookers and her voice rarely rose above a whisper. When asked, as is courtroom tradition, to identify the accused, she had to be forced to look around the room. At the end of Weir's testimony, as the court adjourned for the day, Mrs Greatrex stepped to the dock and embraced her husband through the rails. 'She was evidently much affected,' wrote a reporter.

Jane Weir was attacked by Greatrex's counsel, who said that she had testified against a man 'on whose bosom she had lain' and had feigned illness to elicit sympathy from the jury. He felt nauseated by her, said Greatrex's lawyer. His client had been painted as the destroyer and she the victim. 'As if they were not equally guilty,' he railed, 'both wilfully and knowingly plunging themselves into guilt.'

The charges could have brought transportation or even death but in the end Greatrex and his accomplices were lucky. The jury took 40 minutes to find them guilty and the photographer was sentenced to 20 years in jail while the brothers were each given 15 years. Greatrex had shown tremendous interest throughout the three-day hearing, using his copy of the indictment as a notebook, but on hearing the sentence he slumped in the dock and covered his face with his hands.

The case was a triumph for McCall and he became one of the best-known detectives on the force. Three years later he rose further, being appointed chief constable on the death of James Smart. Speaking of his predecessor, McCall said that 'at his death, he left the police force of the city in a state of organisation and efficiency inferior to none in the Kingdom'. However, the boys in blue were still viewed with a mixture of distaste and suspicion by many sections of society, and McCall, it is said, did more than any other to improve relations between the force and the public. An article in the Wednesday, 26 February 1873 edition of *The Bailie*, a publication dubbed by Glasgow writer Maurice Lindsay 'the *Private Eye* of the 1870s and '80s', was particularly damning in its assessment of the force prior to McCall's tenure. It noted that until McCall took charge the city was 'police-ridden to a disgraceful extent'. It continued:

> Ignorant Highlanders, scarcely capable of uttering or understanding the Queen's English, and as boorish and insolent as they were ignorant, moved us on and off at their will. The slightest remonstrance at unjust treatment either of ourselves or of others produced . . . a whistle for the neighbouring Celt, ending in a walk to the nearest station and a charge for disorderly conduct.

McCall, it seems, changed all that, and the police became more professional, courteous and effective. Under his leadership, there were a number of advances in the Glasgow force. The rattles and clappers used by officers for decades to alert colleagues (the latter device giving birth to the term 'run like the clappers') were abolished in 1880 and the whistle brought in. In 1858, the Clyde Port Authority had created its own police force to patrol the city's burgeoning dockland. In 1866, it had become the Glasgow force's Marine Division – and for decades afterwards Partick police station would still be known as 'the Marine'. In 1881, the city bought its first river patrol vessel, a rowing boat that remained in service for many years. More dramatically, the newfangled telephone apparatus was introduced in a limited fashion in 1880, although political indecision prevented it from being fully used until 1886, when every police station was linked with the general exchange.

McCall remained in office until 1887, when illness struck. In the winter of that year, he was pensioned off and moved to the south of France in a bid to regain his strength. On 29 March 1888, he died. He was buried in the Necropolis, Glasgow's great city of the dead, near the Cathedral. Charles Rennie Mackintosh, whose father had been a police officer who had served with McCall, received a commission, perhaps his first, to design the headstone, a Celtic cross.

However, before McCall's death, the city had a brand-new threat to deal with.

CHAPTER SEVEN

THE IRISH QUESTION

In the 'Hungry '40s' the Irish fled their homes in unprecedented numbers, forced to emigrate by the grinding poverty and the famine caused by potato crop failure in their homeland. Those with means made the perilous crossing to America, the land of milk and money. Those with less disposable income made the shorter crossing to London, Liverpool or Glasgow. In the first quarter of 1848 alone, close to 43,000 Irish people, eager for a fresh start, were delivered to Scotland by boats that berthed on the Broomielaw.

The newcomers were not welcomed with open arms. Scottish crops had also failed and unemployment was rising. With the Industrial Revolution came industrial disputes and the Irish workers, willing to work for low wages, were viewed with contempt. Then there was religious division, for the bulk of the Irish were Roman Catholic and the city was predominantly Protestant. The Roman Catholic hierarchy was not reinstated in Glasgow until 1878, when the Pope appointed an archbishop for the city, and dear green place Glasgow might have been, but it was resolutely Orange.

Nonetheless, employment was found, for many on the public works, canals and railways, and the Irish became very much a part of the fabric of the city. However, there remained an underlying tension, often exacerbated by the political situation in Ireland, that occasionally seethed to the surface right up to the latter half of the twentieth century.

Of course, there had been Irish people in the city prior to the great rush of the 1840s, and, being human, some had found themselves involved in crime. In 1828, Alexander McKinnon – who was either from Tralee or the Highlands depending on which broadsheet you favour – arrived in the city to sell eggs and did well, for he eventually had around £10 in notes and coin. The notes he shoved into one stocking and the coins into the other for safe keeping. However, the cash was not safe for long. He chanced to meet 25-year-old beauty Bell McMenemy, who invited him to a house for some whisky and the promise of other delights. The flame-haired colleen from County Tyrone introduced McKinnon to a man who she claimed was her brother. As the three walked in the streets, the brother suddenly grabbed their mark by the neckcloth and felled him with a blow from a brick. As McKinnon lay insensate, blood streaming from the wound on his head, the pair rifled his clothing until they found his cash and made off.

Although seriously injured, McKinnon found two policemen and reported the crime. Their enquiries led them to Bell and her consort Thomas Connor, who, aged 21 or 23, was described as 'a bad boy ever since he was able to crawl'. His mother was no help, for she encouraged him from an early age in 'evil practices'. A broadsheet commented that 'whenever he committed an act more characterized by dexterity and skilful depravity than another, he was sure to be rewarded by the caresses and applause of this most abandoned and most unnatural woman'.

He had first come to the attention of the authorities when he stole an anvil from a Renfrewshire smithy. No one ever worked out how he did it alone, as the anvil would have needed three men to lift it. For that, he was banished from the county. His mother introduced him to Bell, who worked legitimately as a steam-loom weaver in Paisley. The young woman had never been in trouble but thanks to the influence of Mrs Connor she was 'hurried on from one crime to another with a rapidity which gave her no time for reflection'.

Connor and McMenemy were sentenced to death for the assault and robbery of McKinnon. Calls were made for commutation of their sentence due to their age but Connor's past spoke against him, while McMenemy was deemed to have gone too far down the road to sin. They were hanged before the courthouse on 22 October, McMenemy being the first woman to die on the gallows in the city since 1793.

On 10 December 1840, John Green, a ganger on the Edinburgh and Glasgow Railway, was murdered at Crosshill, about three miles north of the city in Bishopbriggs. 'National feeling' was given as the motive for the murder. Three Irish labourers, Dennis Doolan, Patrick Redding and James Hickie, were convicted of the crime and sentenced to death. Hickie, though, was reprieved, despite being described at the time as 'one of the most perfectly ignorant men in the world, as he can neither read nor write' – a condition, in spite of the tone of the remark, in which he was far from alone in Glasgow at the time. The curious thing about this case is that the judge, sitting at the Justiciary Circuit Court in Glasgow, decreed that the two men facing death be executed not on the Green but at the site of the murder.

The authorities received word that friends of the two men planned to stage a rescue attempt, so there was strict security all along the route. The Crown resolved on such a show of force, such an exhibition of the law's might and majesty, that any would-be attacker would think twice. The gallows were erected and a detachment of infantry placed on guard, with two pieces of artillery present to deter any rescue party. Then, at 8 a.m. on Friday, 14 May 1841, the city saw one of the strangest processions ever to grace its streets. The gates of the South Prison opened and out trotted a troop of cavalry, followed by the City Marshall and then Doolan and Redding in an open carriage, their arms pinioned. Their seats were elevated so that the large crowds along the route – said to be 75,000 strong – could get a clear view. One reporter recorded:

Thousands of men, and women too, turned out on this occasion without compunction, delicacy, or shame. None who saw the great multitude could doubt the popularity of the show. A royal triumph could not have excited a stronger desire on the part of the public to witness it. Windows were taken and paid for, and the housetops were crowded.

More cavalry followed, along with the executioner John Murdoch, the sheriff, the Lord Provost, magistrates and finally another detachment of cavalry. The entire parade was flanked on either side by cavalry, infantry and police. In all, there were about 200 horsemen and 600 to 700 foot soldiers, all bristling with weapons. Any brave soul who dared to try to break the two men free would have a fierce fight on his hands. The grim procession made its way up the Saltmarket onto the High Street and then north to the Kirkintilloch Road, often having to force its way through the crowds jostling for position on the streets, before finally reaching the place of execution at Bishopbriggs.

Poet Alexander Smith was a boy of ten when he witnessed the execution. In his essay 'A Lark's Flight' in his 1863 collection *Dreamthorp*, he recalled the dark events of that day:

> I got a glimpse of the doomed, blanched faces which had haunted me for so long, at the turn of the road, where, for the first time, the black cross-beam with its empty halters first became visible to them. Both turned and regarded it with a long, steady look; that done, they again bent their heads attentively to the words of the clergyman.

As they stood at the nooses, a silence fell on the crowd, wrote Smith:

> Everyone was gazing too intently to whisper to his neighbour even. Just then, out of the grassy space at the foot of the scaffold, in the dead silence audible to all, a lark rose from the side of its nest, and went singing upwards in its happy flight.

There was to be no such happy escape for the two Irishmen. Perhaps they scanned the crowds staring expectantly back at the platform; perhaps they saw the faces of workmates who had downed tools for the day in protest at the executions. Doolan was stout and heavy, so his drop was set by Murdoch at 18 inches shorter than that of his slender friend. Doolan craned his neck for one last look at Redding just as the drop opened, and the knot was seen to shift slightly from under his left ear to the back of his neck. It meant that as he plunged through the trap he did not die instantly, his neck snapping, like Redding, but struggled for several seconds. Murdoch was unmoved by the spectacle, saying that the man should have stood still. 'But see, sir,' he said to a magistrate, 'hoo kindly Redding's slippin' awa'.' After the prescribed time, the bodies were cut down and returned to Glasgow to be interred that evening behind the prison walls.

It was 'national feeling' that prompted what the newspapers dubbed the 'dynamite outrages' of 1883. The political situation in Ireland was always volatile, with landowner and peasant forever at loggerheads. The gentry were mostly English or Scottish 'colonists', absentee landlords who believed they deserved their inheritance since James I and VI had sent their ancestors to 'civilise' the Irish. The locals were afforded little or no protection under law from the greed of the more ruthless owners and could be evicted at will. Sir Winston Churchill, who became a hated figure for his ruthless attempts to stamp out the IRA as Secretary of State for War in the 1920s, wrote that this was part of a deliberate attempt to turn the Irish worker into a 'day labourer after the English pattern. But Ireland was not England; the Irish peasant clung to his land; he used every means in his power to defeat the alien landlords.'

Fierce nationalism led to calls for Home Rule and the abolition of unfair land laws. With the British government seemingly uncaring about the lot of the Irish common people, acts of violence grew. In March 1881, the Irish authorities were given the power to detain anyone they thought fit for as long as they thought fit. However, at the same time as these 'acts of coercion' were imposed, new land laws considerably lessened the injustices that had prevailed. This, though, was not enough for nationalist leader Charles Stewart Parnell and his Irish-American backers. They wanted complete freedom for the Emerald Isle and sensed that Prime Minister Gladstone was somewhat sympathetic to their cause. Parnell fought for reform through Parliament and popular agitation in Ireland and was arrested for his passionate speeches. That was the signal for more terrorism. In 1882, Parnell was released on the understanding that he would attempt to quell the wave of violence in return for more sympathetic laws. A new Chief Secretary for Ireland was appointed but was stabbed to death while walking in a Dublin park within hours of landing.

The Fenian Brotherhood was formed in the United States in 1858 as a way of uniting all Irishmen across the globe against British rule in their homeland. The group was named after the mythological warriors the Fianna, and the term 'Fenian' gained currency in America and Australia as well as in British cities like Glasgow, Liverpool and London. In 1866 and 1870, members staged two unsuccessful raids into Canada, while in 1881 they launched a submarine, the *Fenian Ram*, in New York harbour with the intention of attacking British shipping.

With cash aid from expatriate Irishmen and Americans sympathetic to their cause, the Brotherhood was also behind a series of attacks on the British mainland, including the so-called Fenian Rising of 1867. In that year, a band attacked a prison van carrying some of their colleagues through Manchester. A police sergeant was killed in the fighting. (A similar event would erupt in Glasgow in 1921.) In London, an explosion targeting a wall of Clerkenwell Prison was designed as a means of freeing Richard Burke, one of the ringleaders of the Manchester attack. It killed 12 people, including children, and maimed others. The act turned those who looked favourably on the Irish cause against it and the authorities resolved to bring the bomber to justice.

In Glasgow, 27-year-old Michael Barrett was arrested, ostensibly on a firearms charge, and implicated in the Clerkenwell bombing.

An informer, Dublin man Patrick Mullany, claimed that Barrett had told him he had carried out the attack along with another man. A young witness identified him as being the man who had placed the wheelbarrow filled with explosives at the wall. Despite a string of people testifying that Barrett was actually in Glasgow at the time, the jury found him guilty and he was sentenced to death. There was discomfort with the verdict at the time, and to this day Republicans continue to insist that Barrett was innocent. But the prison bombing had turned public opinion totally against the Irish and a scapegoat was required.

Back in his County Fermanagh home, Barrett's mother appealed to her local MP but her words fell on deaf ears. On 26 May 1868, outside the walls of Newgate Prison, the young man died on the rope, watched by a 2,000-strong crowd singing 'Rule Britannia'. He was the last man to be hanged in public in Britain, as a law had already been passed ensuring that future executions would be performed behind prison walls. William Calcraft, the finisher of Dr Pritchard, performed his duties with his usual efficiency. The Irishman is said to have met his end calmly but still protesting his innocence. His body was interred beneath the uneven flagstones of Newgate's Birdcage Walk, the narrow corridor where condemned prisoners took their exercise and where their predecessors were buried.

The events of 1867 focused Prime Minister Gladstone's mind on alleviating the Irish problem. However, the Fenian Brotherhood continued to take the fight to the hated English. There were bomb attacks on London but they had little effect. They bombed Liverpool and in January 1883 they came to Glasgow, where they had a lot of support from expatriate Irish. That no one died was something of a miracle, as the principal target of the attacks, in a bid to disrupt the city's power supply, was a gasometer in the South Side. It was the first time that Irish radicalism had raised its head in the form of organised violence on the city's streets.

The initial explosion rocked the south of the city at just after 10 p.m. on Saturday, 20 January. Residents from Pollokshields to

Langside felt a 'profound shock' followed by a deep rumbling that lasted for a second or two. Then the gas lamps in the streets and houses dimmed and seemed in danger of going out. To the north, the sky was alive with a fierce red glow and many believed that there was a blaze at the riverside. The 'profound shock', the rumble and the glowing sky had all been caused by an explosion at the Tradeston Gasworks.

The plate-iron gas cylinder had been constructed on the south side of Lilybank Road in 1870. Standing 160 ft tall and with a 60-ft diameter it had become something of a landmark on the south side of the river. The main gasworks was across the road but the only people on duty were the nightwatchman and the gas 'tester', John Gibson. The latter had just completed his duties at the gas holder when he felt the force of a loud explosion and the huge metal cylinder trembled to its foundations. He looked up to see fire leaping into the air through a hole in the roof and there was a sound like 'the simultaneous discharge of artillery'. Holes were punched through the side of the structure and there was a loud hissing noise, then a second explosion. The metal plates ground together as the massive holder threatened to collapse.

The blasts shattered windows in nearby houses and could be heard as far away as Maryhill to the north-west. Nearby residents screamed as doors were blown open and scorching hot air roared into their homes, singeing faces, hands, necks. One woman leaped out of her window with her baby in her arms. She was slightly burned but the baby, thankfully, was unhurt. Eleven people suffered burns and contusions. In the houses, plaster cracked and roofs caved in. The worst hit were single-storey structures in nearby Muirhouse Lane, where a carpet-beating firm and a ropery caught light and firefighters battled to prevent them from being totally consumed.

A valve was swiftly turned to prevent any more gas entering the stricken holder, while supplies were diverted from another source. Meanwhile, crowds had turned out to see the spectacle and had to be controlled by police officers under the supervision of Superintendent

Donald. Chief Constable McCall, referred to, like many a chief constable after him, as 'Captain', also visited the site. The flames licked out of the hole in the roof and another in the side of the cylinder.

At first, it was thought that the fire had started in the carpet-beating factory but that was soon discounted. This had been a deliberate attempt at sabotage and a guard was placed on the gas holders at Dawsholm, while sentries at Maryhill Barracks were doubled.

As firemen battled the flames at Tradeston into the early hours of Sunday morning, reports came in of another blast, at Buchanan Street railway station. And this one, it was firmly believed, was the result of dynamite. The explosion centred on a disused coal shed very near the platform. Thankfully, no one was on the platform, although men working nearby were showered with bricks hurtling in all directions. Apart from shattered windows and damage to a chimney at a bottle works in Canal Street, there was very little disruption. A spokesperson for the railway company played the matter down, saying that the 'authors of the outrage' had merely saved them the cost of demolishing the shed, as it had been superseded a few months before by a new facility at St Rollox. Captain McCall, though, took the matter very seriously. He had already received threatening letters from members of the local Fenian organisation and was determined to bring the men who had brought chaos to his city to justice.

But the bombers were not finished.

On the Sunday, a group of young men and women were making their way from Springburn over the stone bridge that carried the Forth and Clyde Canal over Possil Road. On the parapet of the bridge, they found a small tin box, described as the kind 'commonly used by ladies for carrying bonnets'. Curious, they opened the box, which contained something resembling sand. One of the men was a gunner in the Royal Artillery who really should have known better. He stuck his hand in the 'sand' and set off a small explosion, which severely burned him and slightly injured five of his friends. A quick-thinking individual kicked the box to the ground, where it continued to burn for a further 15 minutes. The size of the explosion suggested that the bombers had been disturbed. Had they managed to complete their preparations the bridge might have been breached and the area flooded.

Tension rose as guards were mounted at railway stations and bridges. The city spent a few anxious hours awaiting the next attack but none came. Now the search for the bombers really began.

Captain McCall was in constant touch with the Home Office, for the bombings were seen not as simply a local problem but part of a national situation. At first, it was thought that a Fenian activist named Timothy Featherstone was behind the attacks. He was known to have been in Glasgow that day and had purchased nitric and sulphuric acids, used in the manufacture of explosives. He and others had been arrested in Liverpool following attacks similar to the Glasgow incidents. Enquiries spread to London and even Antwerp, from where consignments of nitroglycerine had been dispatched to Britain.

However, the real breakthrough came from a Glasgow beat officer who covered the Saltmarket, including Jail Square and the Green. It was in the shadow of Nelson's Monument that Constable William Porter's copper's nose began to twitch. He had become aware of a large body of Irishmen congregating regularly in the square or near to the monument. He knew some of them but could not discover what they were up to – or the nature of the documents they frequently consulted. Whenever he moved within earshot, they clammed up and the papers disappeared. He even tried observing them through a telescope but could learn nothing. When the explosions took place in January, he began to detect the cordite-tinged odour of nationalism. However, it was not until three months later that he was able to piece it all together, when a fruit hawker named George Hughes alleged that he had been assaulted by some of the men in Jail Square. As if to strengthen his accusation, Hughes went on to tell the police constable that the men had been behind the bombing outrages. However, a reward of £500 offered for information leading to arrests may have enticed him to break ranks and inform on the others, although he firmly denied seeking or being offered any cash.

Hughes had been a member of an Irish nationalist group called the Ribbon Society, having been introduced to it by Peter Callaghan, a labourer who lived in Rose Street. Hughes told PC Porter all about their meetings on the first Monday of every month in Lennox's public house in the Saltmarket, during which he had taken an oath to support the brotherhood and pay half a crown entry money, a shilling of which went towards drink. He confirmed the policeman's own suspicions about the men gathering in the square and on the Green. More tellingly, Hughes spoke of a meeting 'Grand Master' Callaghan and street vendor Patrick Drum had had with two men from America. One of these American visitors was none other than Timothy Featherstone, who went on to show the society members how to use dynamite.

The police did not jump in with both feet, which was unusual for those days. Instead, they set up surveillance on the men Hughes had named. Then, on 31 August, Captain McCall decided that it was time to swoop and ordered a series of arrests. The police were dispatched in force to bring in the men but there was no trouble. Callaghan and Drum were among the first lifted, along with Terence McDermott, a chemical worker from Dobbie's Loan, Thomas Devaney, a quarry labourer from Portugal Lane in the South Side, Patrick McCabe, a general dealer from Rose Street, and Henry McCann, a shoemaker from Stirling Street. Two days later, another three men were arrested: labourer James Donnelly from Villiers Street, hammerman James Kelly from Kirk Street in the Calton, and Dennis Casey, described as a 'scavenger' with no address. Another man, chemical worker James McCullagh or McCulloch, was arrested in Cuthbert Street, Hebburn on Tyne.

The trial took place in Edinburgh and rumours were rife that fellow Ribbon Society members were to stage a rescue. The ten men, described as 'a miserable and dejected looking lot', were transported under heavily armed guard from Glasgow and kept in the cells below the courthouse for the duration of the five-day hearing. Meanwhile, a detachment of Gordon Highlanders patrolled Parliament Square and police officers on court duty were issued with revolvers. Thoughts of the 60-plus roster of prosecution witnesses led to the railway lines between Glasgow and Edinburgh being heavily protected. In addition to the armed guards on the trains, the lines were watched overnight and a considerable police presence maintained at stations in the two cities and on every platform in between. Even the bridges across the line were watched. The authorities were taking no chances.

The accused, to a man, pleaded not guilty. During Hughes' testimony, McCullagh rose to his feet and shouted, 'You are an infamous liar!' The officer sitting behind the accused had to force him back to his seat. Hughes claimed he had been prompted to speak to PC Porter when an argument with McCann led to him being punched. He also stated that Devaney had threatened the lives of officers making enquiries after the bomb blasts, saying:

> Last night I had a very narrow escape. I laid myself down on the top of the bed after I came home to have a sleep when I heard someone speaking to my wife at the door. I looked out and saw two detectives talking to her. If they had attempted to take me, I would have blown them to eternity. I would have blown them to atoms before they would have taken me.

This prompted an outburst from Devaney in the dock, who also declared Hughes was a liar.

Defence counsel insisted that the men were innocent and that the outrages had in fact been carried out by Featherstone and four other men who had been sentenced for similar attacks in London. The jury were unconvinced and every one of the men was found guilty. Five were sentenced to life for treason while the rest were given seven years each for conspiracy. They were detained for a few days in Calton Prison, then removed, under conditions of great secrecy, to Chatham jail. A decoy van left the prison and travelled along Princes Street to draw away any unwanted attention, while a second carried the prisoners to a nearby railway station, where they were placed in a special carriage, which was then taken to Waverley Station and linked up with the morning train to London.

Their releases from prison years later continued to make news even beyond these shores. On 25 December 1898, the *New York Times* reported that Terence McDermott had been freed on the orders of the Home Secretary. 'McDermott does not appear to be any the worse for his punishment,' the newspaper stated, 'and says he has done with dynamiting, and will start in life afresh, with the few pounds which he earned in prison.' By 1901, the last of the men was released and four years later the obligation of the lifers to report to the police was removed.

Irish terrorists had another stab at Glasgow's gas supplies in 1890, when devices went off at the cylinders at Dawsholm in the north-west of the city. A number of people were injured in the blasts. In this instance, the police drew a blank and no one was arrested. The bombers and the gunmen would be back, while for almost 100 years Glasgow would act as a fundraising centre and an armoury for both sides during the Troubles across the Irish Sea.

The world was changing, looking forward to a new century. The city continued to expand, as did its police force. Its beat now included Possilpark, Springburn, Pollokshields, Crosshill, Govanhill and Maryhill. In 1891, the first police boxes were erected in Glasgow. Designed by Fire Engineer Eggar of the city's fire brigade, the 14 cast-iron signal boxes consisted of a telephone in a shelter with a gas lamp on top. The public could contact the central police station from the box, while headquarters was able to light the lamp by phoning the box, its red filter casting such a glow that a passing policeman could not help but notice it and call in for instruction. At first, the boxes were sited only in outlying areas, but slowly they spread across the city, and they remained in use until 1932.

Developing means of identifying criminals had occupied the authorities for centuries. The old ways of brandings and mutilations were as much a means of warning others about the criminal leanings of the recipients as they were punishments, but these had, thankfully, been phased out. In 1879, Alphonse Bertillon, a clerk in the records office of the Paris police, began to develop a system based on the existing theory that no two individuals shared the same physical measurements. After a few years of tweaking, his system – known as anthropometry – was accepted as a valid means of identifying criminals. The Glasgow Police began to keep detailed records of arrested felons' personal measurements, such as the length of arms, legs, fingers and feet and facial shape. Photography had been in use in Glasgow since the early 1860s and the faces of crooks were recorded – the famous 'mug shots'. In such pictures from those days, the accused person was required to hold up their hands to show any distinguishing characteristics like deformities, wounds or scars, while a carefully placed mirror to show the profile gave the cops two views for the price of one.

However, while the Bertillon system was being introduced, the Glasgow Police were also looking at a new means of identification, one that would reverberate through the criminal justice system long after the French clerk's process was dismissed as unworkable and unreliable. The basic truth behind fingerprinting – that no two people have identical prints – had been known in China for centuries. In the seventeenth century, Italian anatomist Marcello Malpighi was the first to describe the whorls, ellipses and triangles that differentiate one person's hands and fingers from another's. The first crime was solved using fingerprinting in Tokyo in 1879, when a handprint left at the scene of a theft was examined and compared with that of a suspect by Scottish doctor Henry Faulds, who then made a study of the use of fingerprints as a form of signature. The subsequent paper written by Dr Faulds was attacked by a man named William Herschel, who had been pursuing a similar line of thought for a number of years. It was, however, scientist Sir Francis Galton who in 1892 pulled everything together, creating a classification system for fingerprints that allowed a workable process to be developed.

This was perfected by Sir Edward Henry, an inspector general of the Bengal police who set up Scotland Yard's fingerprint bureau. The first murder to be solved with fingerprints took place in Argentina in 1892, the first European one in Paris in 1902, while the first British killing to be cleared up using the system happened in London in 1905. In 1952, Glasgow Police took it a step further by convicting a man for blowing a safe on the evidence of an imprint from his big toe. William Gourlay had sought to confound the fingerprint squad by using his feet in the process but became the first man in Britain to be sent down for putting his foot in it.

The dawn of the new century marked the centenary of the Glasgow force. It had come a long way since it first mustered in the Tron Kirk's Session House on 15 November 1800. It had started off with 77 men, most little more than watchmen, but by 1900 had 1,355 men on the roster. They faced the same problems as their predecessors – along with general crime there was still social unrest, poverty and drunkenness. In 1899, Glasgow Corporation bought an Ayrshire mansion with the idea that they could house some of the city's 'degraded and drunken women' there. It was hoped that by removing them from 'bibulous temptation' and force-feeding them a diet of 'pure air and horticultural work of a light nature' the authorities might entice them away from the delights of the demon drink and degrading behaviour. The project was not a success but that did not prevent the city fathers from hatching a later scheme to send drinkers to the Isle of Shuna in Argyll and, as late as the 1930s, to the deserted island St Kilda.

Murder, larceny and violence would remain the three staples of the city's criminal life. The police might have increased their ranks, but they were still hopelessly outnumbered.

CHAPTER EIGHT

THE WRONG MAN

A new century, but old ways still persisted. In Glasgow at least, however, capital punishment seemed to be going out of favour. There had not been a sentence of death pronounced in a Glasgow court for ten years – and thirty-year-old Patrick Leggett was banking on the court's leniency.

He had been separated from his wife for seven years and had taken it into his head to kill her. He had told people that he planned to do her in but felt 'as there was no hanging nowadays he would probably get 15 years for it'. In September 1902, he beat Sarah Jane to death in her Whiteinch lodgings. He then tried to escape from the gathering crowd by jumping into the Clyde but was fished out by a ferryman. On being taken to Partick Police Office, he said that he hoped his wife was dead. He got his wish – and also the chance to put his theory about sentencing to the test. In October, he appeared in front of the Glasgow circuit of the High Court of Justiciary. His defence gamely insisted that he was insane and that an upbringing filled with 'bad influences' had wrecked any sense of right or wrong. However, his escape attempt proved that he knew he had done wrong and the jury was having none of the lawyer's pleas. The fifteen men took only five minutes to return a unanimous guilty verdict. A petition of 10,000 signatures pleaded for the man's life but the sentence of death was carried out on 10 November in Duke Street Prison.

In 1904, two pronouncements of doom were handed out within minutes of each other. On 5 July, Joseph Calabrese, an ice-cream merchant from Kilbirnie who spoke only Italian, faced the jury for murdering his wife and family with a hatchet in April. His lawyer told the court that Mrs Calabrese had 'given way to drink' and the long-suffering husband had succumbed to an 'irresistible homicidal impulse'. The jury, after half an hour of deliberations, decided he was guilty but recommended mercy on the grounds that he had suffered extreme provocation. Nevertheless, the judge, Lord Adam, his voice so hushed it could barely be heard, donned the black cap and sentenced him to die in Ayr Prison on 26 July.

Destined to die on the same day, but in Glasgow's Duke Street Prison, was Thomas Gunning, who had reduced the body of his girlfriend Agnes Allen to a bloody pulp and then made the mistake of boasting about it to friends. Found guilty by a 9–6 majority, Gunning was hanged on the due date, although Calabrese was luckier: in his Ayr cell, he was told through an interpreter that his sentence had been commuted to penal servitude for life.

Even after those two sentences, the July 1904 sitting of the Glasgow circuit was not finished with the death penalty. The day after Calabrese and Gunning faced the judge, Pole Adonias Ujavichis, who used the anglified name Adam Black, was found guilty of stabbing his son to death in Hamilton. As was usual, the jury recommended mercy, but the judge was obliged to pass the death sentence, although this was, in the words of Secretary for Scotland Andrew Graham Murray in a letter to Lord Provost Sir John Ure Primrose, 'respited until further signification of His Majesty's pleasure'. Despite the fact that only one man reached the gallows, this sitting subsequently became known as the 'Black Assize' as it had been more than sixty years since three men had been sentenced to die at the one circuit.

The next year, a judge felt obliged to comment on the number of garrotting cases that came before him in Glasgow. He was prompted by three cases in which men were 'seized by the throat' and robbed. In one, the victim, 'somewhat the worse for liquor', was knocked down in College Street and robbed. Two men were charged but one claimed he had only been walking past the scene of the crime as the police arrived. Nevertheless, both men were sentenced to three years. The other two cases were of a similar nature and newspapers reported that one judge, Lord McLaren, said that 'robbery by garrotting was one of the worst crimes with which he had to deal, and unfortunately there was always a large number of them in that Court'. The practice, along with the city's enduring love of blades, was one of the reasons why officers had worn leather neck protectors under the high collars of their uniforms since 1812.

On 18 October 1910, a murder case was heard in the county buildings because the judiciary buildings were being renovated. The accused was Sulleyman Adam, a 23-year-old 'lascar', an East Indian sailor, charged with the murder on 27 August of the 'serang', the bo'sun on board ship who supervised the native workers. The crime had been committed while the steamer *Newby Hall*, out of Liverpool, had been berthed in Queen's Dock on the Clyde.

The accused made for an unusual figure in a Glasgow courtroom, dressed as he was in a white linen jacket and trousers, his feet bare. He spoke no English and an officer of the Lanarkshire constabulary was appointed as interpreter. The evidence suggested that an argument had broken out among the 'coolies' and when the bo'sun tried to stop it he was stabbed. The judge stated that the evidence against Adam ruled out culpable homicide, and the young man was found guilty by a majority of the capital crime. The jury recommended mercy but the judge was obliged to don the black cap and sentence the man to death. The sentence was later commuted to life.

In 1913, the newly refurbished court buildings were reopened amid much fanfare. The trumpets blew and the drums rattled and the great and the good of the legal establishment turned out in their finery to herald a new era of crime and punishment. On 7 July, the Lord

Justice General unlocked the huge main doors with a ceremonial golden key and commented, 'The less we have to do in these rooms the better it is for us and the better it is for the people of Glasgow.' Unfortunately, the refurbished court would be as busy as ever.

Four years before, the city had witnessed another of its celebrated murder cases, although the trial was heard in Edinburgh. Popular legend has it that it brought about the creation of a court of appeal in Scotland. In fact, it had already been established before the details were heard. It did, however, prove the need for one.

* * *

In July 1928, Sir Arthur Conan Doyle sat in a courtroom in Edinburgh's High Court of Justiciary for four days listening to lawyers argue a case that had caught his attention almost twenty years before. As he listened to the legal points being won or lost, he scanned the faces of those present. Suddenly, he wrote, his eyes were arrested:

> One terrible face stands out among all those others. It is not an ill-favoured face, nor is it a wicked one, but it is terrible none the less for the brooding sadness that is in it. It is firm and immobile and might be cut from that Peterhead granite which has helped to make it what it is. A sculptor would choose it as the very type of tragedy. You feel that this is no ordinary man, but one who has been fashioned for some strange end. It is indeed the man whose misfortunes have echoed round the world. It is Slater.

The injustice done to Oscar Slater by the Scottish legal establishment remains an outrage a century after the events with which it began. The case, sparked by a murder in 1908, stands alongside that of Madeleine Smith as perhaps the city's most famous historical mystery. It was obvious to many even at the original trial that Slater was innocent and some commentators have alleged that the authorities conspired to ignore facts and manipulate evidence to win the day. However, for evil to triumph, it is only necessary for good men to do nothing – and there were a number of good men in Glasgow, London and Edinburgh who refused to sit back and do nothing. For one honourable police officer, it meant the end of his career.

The violent act that caused the scandal took place in a respectable street in Glasgow's West End. Spinster Marion Gilchrist could be called eccentric, perhaps even reclusive. The 81-year-old woman was of independent means and kept jewellery to the value of £3,000 hidden away in her wardrobe. She protected her privacy with an iron will, had the door of her first-floor flat at 15 Queen's Terrace on West Princes Street strengthened by double locks and had until recently kept a dog, but it had been poisoned. No one was allowed access unless she knew them. She had an arrangement with her downstairs neighbour that she would bang on the floor should she ever need assistance. But on 21 December 1908, someone breached those defences. It was her custom to send her maidservant, Helen Lambie, down the street for a newspaper of an evening, and that night was no exception. The young woman was gone for about ten minutes.

At about 7 p.m. on that Monday night, musician Arthur Adams, who lived in the flat below, heard a noise from above as if something had fallen. The arrangement with his elderly neighbour in mind, he climbed the stairs to see if he could help and through the locked door heard another noise, 'as if it was someone chopping sticks'. Receiving no answer at the door, he returned to his sisters below and for the next few minutes the noises from Miss Gilchrist's flat continued, gaining in volume until it sounded as if 'the ceiling was like to crack'. Adams went back upstairs, meeting Helen Lambie on the way. She unlocked the double locks and they both walked in. It is at this point that the mystery takes an unusual turn.

As Mr Adams and Helen entered the hallway, a man emerged from the bedroom. Lambie did not acknowledge him nor show any surprise or fear. One might even say she expected him to be there. Mr Adams noted that the 'most gentlemanly-looking man', who he took to be a relative, walked past them 'quite pleasantly' before darting out the door and rushing down the stairs like 'greased lightning'. He felt that Lambie knew him, although she did not speak to him. The descriptions they gave to police later were combined to form a picture of a 25- to 30-year-old man, 5 ft 8 to 9 in. tall, of slim build, clean-shaven with dark hair. They said he was wearing a light-grey overcoat and a dark cloth cap.

They found Miss Gilchrist in the dining room, her head mashed to a pulp, blood spatter on the fireplace. In the bedroom, her personal papers had been rifled – she had kept them locked in a wooden box – and jewellery lay scattered on the floor. All that appeared to be missing was a heart-shaped diamond brooch.

Mr Adams and the maid rushed back downstairs to intercept the man but the rainswept, gaslit street was empty. Arthur Adams called his own doctor – coincidentally also named Adams – while Lambie hurried to Miss Gilchrist's cousin to tell her what had happened. It was not until Dr John Adams arrived that police were called. While he waited, the GP surveyed the scene of the crime and surmised that the leg of a smashed chair had been used to inflict the bloody wounds. Also evident was a bloody palm print beside the fireplace. A coal box, which had been moved slightly from its customary position beside the fire, was damaged and carried traces of blood.

Police very swiftly found a third witness, 14-year-old message girl Mary Barrowman. She said that she had been passing the house when a man burst out of the door and almost knocked her down before running towards West Cumberland Street and Woodlands Road. Despite having seen him only for an instant in the dimly lit street, she was able to provide a much fuller description. She narrowed his age to between 28 and 30. He was tall, thin and clean-shaven. His nose was slightly turned to one side, she thought to the right. He wore a round hat known as a Donegal and a fawn-coloured overcoat, which might have been a waterproof. He had on dark trousers and brown boots.

At first, police were convinced that the murderer was known to Miss Gilchrist and thought, given the disparity in descriptions, that perhaps there were two men involved. However, all other lines of enquiry were abandoned on Christmas Day, when information came in that a man named Oscar Slater had been trying to offload a pawn ticket for a diamond brooch. Slater was something of a ne'er-do-well, a gambler living with his mistress at St George's Road under the name Anderson. His real name, though, was Oscar Joseph Leschziner; he was a 39-year-old German Jew who often claimed to be a dentist or a diamond trader. However, he did not fit the various descriptions given by the three witnesses. He was of medium height and heavy build. More importantly, he had a short black moustache. His nose, however, which appeared to be broken, could have been said to turn to one side.

Here was a suspect the police could really get behind – and when they discovered that he had fled the city, they set off in pursuit. On 27 December, Chief Superintendent John Ord wrote to chief constables across the country to ask that their forces be on the alert for Slater. It was believed he might have fled to Nottingham, so on 27 December that city's top policeman received a letter saying that 'a man named Oscar Slater alias Anderson, describing himself as a dentist . . . left this city hurriedly and may have gone to your City as two single railway tickets were issued for passengers by the 9.30 p.m. train'.

A telegram sent that night by Glasgow's chief constable, James Verdier Stevenson, to 'Handcuffs, London' (presumably shorthand for Scotland Yard) said in customary unpunctuated form: 'Slater supposed left Glasgow with train due Euston 6-30 am Saturday His nose has been fractured and slightly twisted to one side Supposed accompanied by a woman about 30 tall stout good looking dark hair dressed dark costume set sable furs large blue or black hat.'

Meanwhile, the following day's press carried an advertisement placed by the chief constable asking for any hotel proprietor, landlady or lodging-house keeper to communicate without delay 'any information to the Subscriber regarding the sudden or unexpected disappearance of any Lodger or Boarder on the night of the murder or after; of any person of a suspicious nature sought for or obtained lodgings about the time stated'.

The public became enthusiastically involved in the hunt, which had received widespread newspaper attention. Anyone with a theory or a suspicion wrote to the police; at least one urged them to 'look for a relative' while a man signing himself 'The Prince of Darkness' wrote from Edinburgh on 18 January claiming responsibility and gloating that he was 'still at large'. He also admitted stabbing a woman in Dublin on 9 November.

Although some officers continued to believe that two men had been involved, the focus rather quickly narrowed on Slater. He had left his homeland to avoid conscription and had drifted around Britain and abroad as far as New York. He frequented and ran gambling clubs. He was a rogue, of that there is no doubt, but no killer. Neither is there any real evidence that he was a pimp, as was claimed in court but never substantiated, although he was living with French prostitute Andrée Junio Antoine, better known as Madame Junio, at the time of the murder. In court, emphasis would be placed on his flight from justice and it would be claimed – again falsely – that he had run from Glasgow as soon as his name appeared in the newspapers as a person of interest and that he had tried to cover his steps as he made his way to Liverpool and on to New York. However, he and his partner had planned to quit the city some weeks before the murder and actually left before the police made his name public. Furthermore, he travelled to Liverpool and lodged there quite openly under the name Oscar Slater. It is true that he had a habit of using other names – Anderson and George being two – but for a man who lived on the fringes of the law, such a pose was commonplace. Although it is also true that he had booked passage under the name Otto Sando, this was no flight from justice. His move to the States had been planned and in fact it was his intention to move on to San Francisco, where he was to run a gaming club with an old friend. What was more, the brooch he had pawned was not the one taken from Miss Gilchrist's house and had in fact been pledged prior to the murder. That did not seem to matter to Glasgow's finest. The varying descriptions of their suspect didn't matter either; all they needed was a little bit of 'tweaking'. Oscar Slater was a seedy character, a liar, a cheat and a foreigner to boot. If ever there was a usual suspect, he was it.

While attempts were made to track him down and bring him back from New York, the two different descriptions furnished by Lambie and Barrowman – the short-sighted Arthur Adams having stressed that he could not identify the man again – were duly finessed. Lambie had insisted that she would not be able to identify the man she saw that night but police worked on her. They showed her a picture of Slater. They badgered her and Barrowman until the two differing descriptions merged into one, 'which made it much simpler for all concerned', said crime chronicler William Roughead. During the extradition proceedings, Lambie and Barrowman were taken to New York and just happened to be in the corridor when a handcuffed Slater was brought by. A Glasgow detective pointed him out and said, 'That's the man.' Later, in front of a New York judge, they had no difficulty in picking him out.

Slater could have fought the extradition proceedings. The brooch 'clue' had already been proved false and all that was left was the evidence of Lambie and Barrowman, which was far from conclusive. However, Slater elected to accede to the Crown's request and return to Scotland. He was innocent of the crime and believed that the truth would out. His belief in the legal system, though touching, was to cost him 19 years of his life.

The motive, the Crown insisted, was robbery. But if that were the case, why was there only one item of any value stolen and others left discarded? And how would a man like Slater – a stranger and obviously foreign – get in the securely locked door? Reports suggested that Miss Gilchrist would have been extremely unlikely to let him in and there was no sign of forced entry. No murder weapon had been found. Dr Adams' theory that the chair leg had been used was ignored or discounted, for he was listed as a witness but never called, which was unusual given that he was the first medical man on the scene and had actually pronounced life extinct. However, in Slater's bags the police found a small hammer, which they insisted had been used to inflict the killer blows. No traces of blood were found on this weapon and there was no explanation as to why he would hold on to it during his supposed flight from justice.

A series of witnesses were produced who identified Slater as a man seen watching Miss Gilchrist's apartment. However, in what was becoming a motif for this investigation, each of these witnesses had previously been shown, or had seen in the press, a photograph of the suspect. In an ID parade, he had appeared with eleven other men – nine plain-clothes cops and two railway officials – who looked nothing like him. During the trial, a police officer was asked if it would be fairer to exhibit a suspect in a parade of similar-looking men. 'It might be the fairest way,' the officer conceded, 'but it is not the practice in Glasgow.' Only one of the witnesses had spoken to the mysterious watcher and she had not noted anything foreign about his speech. Slater spoke with a pronounced accent. One of Arthur Adams' sisters said she had seen a man in the street at 6.55 p.m., five minutes before the murder, and identified Slater by his profile. Unfortunately, she said that the man she saw was wearing a heavy tweed overcoat and 'had the appearance of a delicate man'. Naturally, this did not gel with the now accepted description of what the suspect was wearing or the fact that Slater was powerfully built and deep-chested.

Slater produced witnesses who placed him in another part of the city at the time of the murder. At 6.12 p.m., he was in Central Station sending a telegram; at 6.30 p.m., he was in Renfield Street dressed in a waterproof and a bowler hat. Madame Junio and their maid insisted he was home at 7 p.m. But most of the witnesses were dismissed as low life whose acquaintance with the truth was, at best, a passing one.

A ticket girl at Kelvinbridge railway station had identified Slater as a man who had burst through the barrier sometime between

7.30 p.m. and 8 p.m. The prosecution picture was that Slater had 'taken a train to some remote part of the city and then come strolling back to his house'. The Crown contended that nothing more was known of his movements until 9.45 p.m.

But there was one witness who was neither a low life nor a friend of the accused. Grocer's assistant Duncan MacBrayne knew Slater as a customer and had told police that he had seen him at the door of his flat in St George's Road at 8.15 p.m. Slater was neither anguished nor flustered. MacBrayne was shown Slater in the police station and the suspect said, 'Oh, you are the man in the big shop in Sauchiehall Street.' Of course, it is not inconceivable that Slater could have reached his home from Queen's Terrace in that time, but his demeanour did not fit the picture the Crown was trying to paint. MacBrayne's name did not appear on the list of witnesses and he was not interviewed by the defence at the time of the trial.

Another witness, a female schoolteacher who saw two men running in the street in the opposite direction to the man Barrowman claimed to have seen, was cited to appear but was never called. She did identify one of the men she'd seen as the accused but said he was wearing a completely different style of coat and colour. The coat worn by the killer was, as William Roughead wryly noted, 'already in respect of hues [resembling] that of Joseph'.

The Crown had decided that the descriptions furnished by Lambie and Barrowman, now in accord, were the main plank in their case. The rest was mud-slinging. Lies were told at the trial, of that we can be sure, and not just by the witnesses. The Lord Advocate made his final speech without-the aid of notes. 'Possibly that accounts for its many inaccuracies,' observed noted English barrister Sir Edward Marshall-Hall, who took an interest in the case. Lord Guthrie's charge to the jury was one-sided and questioned the accused's character, which had not been properly explored in evidence. The judge had said, 'A man of that kind has not the presumption of innocence in his favour.' In other words, Slater was not a good man, therefore he did not deserve to be judged as one. What he ignored was the fact that every man is innocent until proven guilty of the particular charge he faces, irrespective of his background, nationality or religion. And it is strongly believed that all three of these facets coloured the establishment view of Slater.

Nine of the jurors thought Slater guilty, one found him not guilty and five thought the case not proven. Still protesting his innocence, and having been advised by counsel not to give evidence on his own behalf, he was sentenced to die, the date set at 27 May 1909. Two days before the due date, the sentence was commuted to life in prison.

Many rejoiced that a brutal murderer was no longer at large but there was disquiet over the case from the start. While Oscar Slater laboured away in the grim fortress that was Peterhead Prison, men of influence tried to have the case re-examined. Sir Arthur Conan Doyle, the creator of Sherlock Holmes, took an interest and was a stalwart campaigner over the next 19 years, despite Slater's personal life being a source of distaste to him. He believed that Miss Gilchrist was murdered because of a will and not her jewels – and that pointed to someone in the family. The august pages of *The Times* and *The Spectator* carried letters and articles attacking the verdict and finally, in 1914, with no court of appeal yet formed in Scotland, a 'Secret Inquiry' was held in Glasgow. It was limited in remit and no one represented Slater, although both the chief constable and procurator fiscal had input. Naturally, it was nothing but a whitewash.

That year saw the sacking of Detective Lieutenant John Thomson Trench. He had been with the Glasgow force for 21 years and was, as force historian Douglas Grant has written, 'a brilliant officer' who held the King's Police Medal for Meritorious Service. He had been on the squad investigating the case and believed that the old woman had been murdered by someone close to her. He also believed that Helen Lambie was intimately acquainted with the killer. He had discovered that on the night of the murder, when the maidservant ran to the home of the deceased's cousin, Miss Birrell, she had blurted out, 'I saw the man who did it. I think it was —' and here the only reference in the documents are the initials 'A.B'. Trench reported his findings to his superiors but was told that 'A.B.' had been fully investigated and cleared, even though no one had, as far as is known, mentioned him during the initial investigation.

Trench, though, was a man of conscience. He had already averted one Scottish miscarriage of justice based on suspect identification – the so-called Broughty Ferry case of 1912, which was very similar to the 1908 murder of Miss Gilchrist. An elderly spinster had been murdered in her own home, her house ransacked but little taken. A stranger had been seen around the house; he was identified by English police and a photograph shown to potential witnesses, who were later prepared to swear to their identification in court. Trench, whose expertise had ensured that he was called in on the case, was unconvinced and managed to prove that the man had been in Antwerp at the time of the murder. The Broughty Ferry case remains unsolved.

With no notice being taken of his pleas over the Slater case, Trench, with what he thought was an assurance from the Secretary for Scotland that there would be no backlash against him, took his information to lawyer David Cook. He in turn passed it on to the Scottish Secretary, who ordered the Secret Inquiry but tied its hands so much that there was no hope of the truth being found. When its predictable findings were returned, Trench learned he should not have put his faith in a politician. He had communicated official information to a third party and Glasgow Police took a dim view of him stepping outside the ranks. On 14 September 1914, John Trench, one of the best officers on the force, was ignominiously dismissed.

The war with Germany had begun and Trench enlisted in the Royal Scots Fusiliers but his vindictive superiors had not finished with him. It seems they would not be happy until his reputation was completely destroyed. Before he could be sent to fight, Trench and David Cook were accused of receiving stolen goods in relation to the recovery of items taken in a burglary. Everything he had done in the case concerned was done with the full knowledge of his superiors

– and he had received a glowing commendation from an insurance company. But that made no difference and the two men were brought to trial. Luckily, though, the system worked in the way it should and the judge ordered the jury to dismiss the charges. This low treachery in high places haunted the force for decades and it never apologised for its actions. Trench survived the war but did not live to see Oscar Slater – or himself – vindicated. He died on 13 May 1919. David Cook never fully recovered from his treatment at the hands of the system in which he had believed, and he died in 1916.

The breakthrough came in 1927 when Glasgow journalist William Park published his book *The Truth About Oscar Slater*, which was founded heavily on the information provided to him years before by his old friend John Trench. The book left many under no illusions that the original investigation had been anything but a shambles, with high-ranking officers conspiring to protect the real culprit, a man whom Helen Lambie had recognised. The man might have been related to Miss Gilchrist in some way but the two might not have been getting along well. He might even have been in the flat before Lambie left. During those ten minutes, perhaps he and the old woman quarrelled over a document, a will, and he lashed out in anger. He did not mean to kill but his passions were high. The old woman fell, losing consciousness when her head struck the corner of the coal box. Then he panicked. The wound was severe – there was blood – but she might survive long enough to name him. He was a respectable man and such a scandal would destroy him. So he finished the job off. He beat her with a chair until it broke into pieces, then he continued with a heavy chair leg. He beat her and he battered her until he knew she was dead. Then he threw a rug over her body and moved into the bedroom to look for the document he needed. He lit the gas, leaving behind a book of matches, and opened the wooden box. He hauled the papers out and rifled through them until he found the one he wanted. He was under pressure, not only because he knew Lambie would soon return, but also because someone had rung the bell. Then he heard the door opening and

Lambie talking to a man. There was nothing left for him to do but brazen it out, so he slipped the document into his pocket and walked into the hallway . . .

The book led to more questions and the questions led to pressure and the pressure led, finally, to Slater being released on licence on 14 November 1927. His case was to be examined by the newly formed Scottish Court of Criminal Appeal (a special act of Parliament had to be passed to allow his case to be heard) and the hearing began on 9 July. His counsel disputed the identification process, the decision not to introduce the evidence of Dr Adams, the Crown's claim that Slater had tried to evade justice and the unwarranted and uncorroborated attacks on his past and character. The appeal stood or fell on whether the jury's verdict was unreasonable or unsupported by evidence, whether any new evidence had been introduced and deemed viable, whether the non-disclosure of evidence by the Crown had caused prejudice and whether the judge had misdirected the jury. In the end, the appeal failed on all points but the misdirection – but that technicality was enough to have the conviction quashed and Slater exonerated.

He was granted £6,000 compensation, out of which he was expected to pay the costs of his appeal. He moved to Ayr, buying a bungalow at 25 St Phillans Avenue, and in 1937 married a woman named Lina. He made a modest living buying and selling jewellery but, being a German Jew, he was interned during the Second World War. He died, aged 76, on 31 January 1948.

Helen Lambie married a miner and moved to Illinois. Despite several attempts to discover more from her, she refused to discuss the case any further, although she claimed to continue to believe that Slater was the killer. As pressure grew, Mary Barrowman began to backtrack on her evidence.

The question of who 'A.B.' was has continued to plague writers. Trench meant well when he revealed the initials but he gave conspiracy theorists an ideal launch pad. Red herrings like the death of the dog and Miss Gilchrist's illegitimate daughter have been thrown in to muddy the waters. Even Helen Lambie and her boyfriend have been implicated. The name Austin Birrell, said to be a nephew of Miss Gilchrist's, was raised but it now appears this man did not exist. Another suspect was Wingate Birrell, a black sheep of the respectable family, who supposedly committed suicide after the murder, but there is evidence that he was in London on the night his aunt died. Another long-time suspect was Dr Francis Charteris, who later went on to become a professor at St Andrews University. He was very well connected and, through his lawyer brother, friendly with Lord Advocate Ure, who prosecuted Slater. One theory even has both men involved in the crime, Birrell committing the murder and escaping through the window while Charteris looked for the mysterious document and walked calmly out of the door. The will itself, however, may have been another red herring.

If another suspect had been named, why would police suppress any evidence linking him to the crime? Writers have suggested a grand conspiracy in which a class-ridden constabulary, perhaps under Masonic influence, ignored evidence linking a member of a well-to-do family with a brutal murder and actively framed a sleazy foreigner. And to keep their secret safe, they even sacrificed one of their own along the way. Thomas Toughill, who more than any other recent chronicler of the case has kept the scandal alive and who first suggested the possibility of collusion between Birrell and Charteris, revealed in *Oscar Slater: The Mystery Solved* that Prime Minister Ramsay MacDonald had in fact passed letters to the Scottish Secretary naming the real culprit. The city's criminal history is littered with the names of good men gone bad, but in this case any conspiracy may have been as simple as police officers seizing too eagerly on the person they deemed the likeliest suspect. Evidence was not followed but adapted to fit their preconceived scenario. This is 'prime suspect syndrome' and some officers, poor officers, continue to suffer from it.

However, the truth may be more mundane. In *Life Begins at Midnight*, former detective superintendent Robert Colquhoun put forward another scenario, based on information received from an old Glasgow criminal he named as 'Andy'. Crime writer and historian Richard Whittington-Egan picked up the clue and ran with it in *The Oscar Slater Murder Story*. This theory holds that the murder was an accident during a jewel robbery. A gang of thieves then active in the city had heard of Miss Gilchrist's hoard of jewellery and had watched her flat for some time. Two of them did the job, which went badly wrong and ended in the murder. Only that single item of swag was grabbed as one went out the window and the other daringly walked past Lambie and Adams into the hall. Whittington-Egan revealed the mysterious 'Andy' to be Richard Craig, a safe-blower active in the early part of the twentieth century. Craig, it seemed, had shared a cell with one Jimmy Inglis, who had formed part of the team casing Miss Gilchrist's flat, although he had been arrested prior to the robbery. Inglis said two men named Wilson and Jamieson were the killers.

The case of Oscar Slater remains a potent mystery in the panoply of Glasgow crime. Like the Madeleine Smith case it has prompted books, articles and a TV drama. Like the case of Madeleine Smith, we will probably never know the truth of it.

CHAPTER NINE

SQUARE GO

Women in Glasgow had been demanding the vote since 1870, although the Chartists had called for the right earlier in the nineteenth century. In the early days, apart from one large open-air meeting on Glasgow Green, the campaigners for women's suffrage contented themselves with discreet meetings and petitions to Parliament. In the early part of the twentieth century, a more militant strain strode purposefully to the front. In Glasgow, this was epitomised by the Women's Social and Political Union (WSPU), which was formed in Manchester in 1903 and reached the city in 1906. They met opposition from some men simply because they did not want women to have the right to vote, but other Edwardian decision-makers, including Chancellor of the Exchequor David Lloyd George, felt that, with 40 per cent of the male population still denied the franchise, a more universal suffrage was needed.

Between 1912 and 1914, many middle-class women showed that they were willing to throw aside the genteel manners of their upbringing and take the struggle for parity onto the streets. Windows were smashed in cities across the country. Acid was wielded against Royal Mail pillar boxes. Taking a page from the IRA's book, they bombed and cut telegraph lines. Empty buildings were firebombed.

Politicians were abused both verbally and physically, including Prime Minister Herbert Asquith. Women travelled to London to take part in protests and attacks. In February 1909, the *New York Times* reported that 'several big Scotchwomen were observed actively using their fists on the police' during a disturbance in London. Not all protests turned ugly. In August of the same year, three 'rain-soaked and benumbed but still valiant suffragettes' were brought down from the roof of Glasgow's St Andrew's Halls, on the site where the Mitchell Theatre now stands. The Earl of Crewe, Secretary of State for the Colonies, was due to speak to an all-male audience that night and the three women had planned to break through the roof, but the cold and wet Glasgow summer left them soaked and 'nearly perished'.

In March 1913, suffragette leader Mrs Emmeline Pankhurst addressed followers at the same venue. Knowing that many men would try to disrupt the proceedings, the organisers arranged for 300 stewards, including a group of beefy dock workers, to police the hall. Many of these men harboured little sympathy for the cause, but a few extra pennies were always welcome. Trouble began when a band of students from the University of Glasgow decided to heckle Mrs Pankhurst. The stewards took great delight in dishing out summary justice to the upper-class troublemakers.

While an organist provided musical accompaniment, the dock men dragged many of them from the hall and threw them out into the street. The remainder, a contemporary report stated, 'finding themselves outnumbered, did not renew the fighting, but were discreetly well-behaved'.

In March the following year, Mrs Pankhurst was arrested in Glasgow. As women tried to prevent the police from taking her away, she fell and was thrown bodily into the back of the van, where, it was claimed, she was forced to lie on the floor while officers fired insults at her. She was then taken by train to the capital. Police knew that the main London stations were swarming with her supporters so the 'Scotch Express' was halted at a small suburban station and she was taken by motor car to Holloway.

She was confident that she would, as on other occasions, be released under the 'Cat and Mouse Act', introduced the previous year to allow the Home Secretary to free hunger-striking suffragettes temporarily for health reasons. The practice until then had been to force-feed the women, in some cases through the rectum, but this was not popular, particularly with King George V, who found it distasteful. Nonetheless, one woman's heroine is another man's terrorist and many sections of the public had lost sympathy with the suffragettes (an originally derogatory term first coined by Lord Northcliffe's *Daily Mail*).

Sure enough, four days later, both Mrs Pankhurst and her daughter Sylvia were released again. Mrs Pankhurst was said to be in a very weak condition and on 15 March a band of followers tried to disrupt the Sunday service in Glasgow Cathedral by chanting, 'Oh Lord, we beseech thee to save Emmeline Pankhurst, Helen Crawford and all the brave women who are suffering for their faith.' However, a newspaper noted, 'the congregation took no notice of the demonstration'.

In October, at the High Court of Glasgow, two women – well-known artist Ethel Moorhead and Glasgow doctor's wife Dorothea Chalmers Smith – were sentenced to eight months each for breaking into an unoccupied house at 6 Park Gardens and trying to set it on fire. Women in the public galleries cried out 'Shame!' and began to sing 'The Marseillaise'. Three were arrested after they threw apples at the judge. They missed but a man on the jury was hit in the face.

On 24 January 1914, the glass walls and ceiling of the Kibble Palace at the Botanic Gardens in the West End erupted, sending a shower of glass shards flying into the night. A caretaker had just snipped the fuse on one bomb and narrowly escaped being ripped to pieces by the deadly debris created by a second. A police search uncovered footprints, by their size and style of footwear believed to be women's, and discarded food in bushes, suggesting that the bombers had waited for some time before setting the fuses. A black silk veil was also found and a box, used as a platform to help the women over the wall, was recovered. On 3 April 1914, three bombs went off in Belmont Church. On the same day, a band of suffragettes was found hiding in the cellar of an empty mansion near Rutherglen. Most escaped, leaving their cloaks behind, but one was caught. Also found were bottles of oil, cotton wool, matches and other inflammable material. In May, an attempt to disrupt the city's water supplies was foiled when the suspicions of a watchman patrolling an aqueduct were raised by the sight of some freshly turned earth. He then found two bombs and a half-burned fuse. Nearby lay a woman's handbag, two trowels, a recent issue of *The Suffragette* and a placard condemning the treatment of Mrs Pankhurst. Had the bombs gone off, the damage would have been disastrous, for the aqueduct carried half the city's water supply from Loch Katrine. In July, at Dalmuir just outside Glasgow, protesters unfurled a banner reading 'Your Majesty, stop the forcible feeding and torturing of women'. King George V and Queen Mary, then touring Scotland, paid no attention to the banner, or to one woman screaming denunciations of force-feeding through a megaphone. The crowd, however, took exception to the protest and turned on her, forcing her to beat a swift retreat.

When the war came, the cry lessened but did not die. Some suffragettes got behind the war effort; others joined the peace movement. Women across the country helped bolster the manpower shortfall in industry and services. They worked in factories, they worked the land, they worked near the front line. In 1918, the vote was extended to women over the age of 30 and then, finally, in 1928 they were allowed to vote on the same terms as men.

* * *

War with Germany was declared in August 1914 and patriotic Glaswegians, on both sides of the law, knew their country needed them. Thousands queued at recruitment offices, many believing that it would all be over by Christmas. No regulations prevented serving police officers from volunteering to fight and in the early weeks of the war 300 Glasgow men swapped the blue for the khaki. The less patriotic, or less able-bodied, among the city's criminals remained at home and continued in their old ways, so the city force found itself seriously undermanned. Four hundred temporary constables, paid five shillings for each shift, were taken on, while a further three thousand special constables helped guard important areas such as gasworks, power stations, waterworks and bridges. Germany's Zeppelins never reached the city on the Clyde but they did on one occasion bomb Edinburgh's High Street. The fear of sabotage by fifth columnists remained, though.

Christmas came and went with no sign of an end to the bloodletting, and in May 1915 Chief Constable James Verdier Stevenson ordered that no police officer could leave to join the forces. Despite this, by the close of the year, 692 men had left to fight on land and sea. The decision had already been taken to create the city's first policewomen and in September Miss Emily Miller became the first female to join the ranks.

When the war ended in 1918, a total of 748 men had left the force to fight; 145 of them did not return. Among the 26 medals handed out to them was a Victoria Cross to former Constable John 'Jock' McAulay who had braved heavy enemy fire to carry a wounded officer from the battlefield. He later returned to the city force and retired an inspector in 1946.

Shipbuilding and armaments manufacture on the Clyde had prospered even before the war boom. But workers believed they were being paid starvation wages and expected to live in substandard houses while their employers thrived on the profits they created. It was during the war that the banners of Red Clydeside began to wave, although the term was not yet used. In February 1915, armaments workers went on strike for higher pay. In March 1916, six union leaders of the Clyde Workers' Committee were arrested during a strike of three thousand munitions workers. Some union leaders, mainly miners, had opposed the notion of conscription, and in addition they wanted any wartime restrictions on disputes and pay lifted. The strikers and their leaders were seen as unpatriotic and actually aiding the enemy. 'Whatever might have been the rights and wrongs of those disputes of 1915–17, they undoubtedly prejudiced many people against Glasgow,' wrote historian Charles Oakley. 'The whimsical Wee Macgregor ceased to be the popular conception of what a Glasgow lad was like. Something less pleasant took his place and has persisted ever since.'

These new 'Glasgow lads' were men like John Maclean, a teacher turned anti-war protester and Communist, another former teacher, James Maxton, former sailor Willie Gallacher and Emanuel Shinwell. 'Manny' Shinwell was the bantam cock of trade unionists, as quick with his fists as he was with his tongue and, along with Gallacher and David Kirkwood, he guided the famous – or notorious – strike of 1919. He was not a native Scot, having been born in Spitalfields in London, but that was not what stuck in the throats of the more reactionary elements of the press, who noted with undisguised disdain that he was a Polish Jew. Some of his colleagues were loftily dismissed for being Irish. Shinwell had experienced casual racism as he grew up in Glasgow, educating himself in the public library and learning to box in a local gym. His working life began in a clothing factory as a machinist but it was in workers' rights that he excelled. His brand of fiery oratory struck a chord with his fellow workers and he rose in the ranks of the unions. In 1911, he was working with the National Sailors' and Firemen's Union (NSFU) and helped organise a six-week strike that began in the Glasgow docks and spread across the country. The strike won a national wage rate for British, European and black British subjects, although company owners still trawled the docks of foreign ports for cheaper labour. The following year, Shinwell formed part of a splinter group from the NSFU to join the British Seafarers' Union, becoming its Glasgow secretary. He also became president of the Glasgow Trades Council.

With the return of the soldiers from foreign fields in 1918, unemployment was expected to rise, as had happened a century earlier after the Napoleonic Wars. There were also fears of a depression, although it did not materialise until 1921. In a pre-emptive bid to stave off mass unemployment, trade unionists called for a shorter working week, from 54 hours to as low as 30, forcing bosses to hire more men to keep up production. Wiser heads, including Manny Shinwell, prevailed and a claim was made for a 40-hour working week. Other issues were raised, including high rents and housing conditions, but the resulting stoppage in late January 1919 became known as 'the 40-Hour Strike'. It would end with blood spilled in the heart of Glasgow and union leaders facing jail.

However, Shinwell's association with the sailors' unions was to help spark trouble before then. The 'race riot' of 1919 is a seldom discussed part of the disputes of that year and has been overshadowed by the violence in George Square a few days later. But it was part of the overall industrial unrest and also a telling indictment of the same casual racism that Shinwell himself experienced from the right-wing press – and perhaps of his own prejudices.

The merchant navy was hit as hard as any industry by the influx of men from the forces and the decline in world markets. The cry 'British jobs for British workers' was as loud then as it was in early 2009 when wildcat strikes hit the country over the granting of contracts to foreign workers while local men were idle. However, many men targeted in 1919 were British subjects – Africans and Afro-Caribbeans, skilled and unskilled workers, who had come to the 'motherland' before or during the war to help plug the manpower gap. Many had settled in Glasgow, married – some to white women, much to the outrage of certain newspapers, which used language to describe the men that would not be acceptable today – and raised families. The city was their home. They had their own private men's club, the Order of the Star of Bethlehem's Shepherds, formed at the end of the war by Cornelius Johnstone, a one-time sailor who was later convicted with two white men of running an unlicensed dance hall. The black community also formed its own political group, the African Races Association of Glasgow (ARAG).

During the war, they had run the gauntlet of enemy U-boats and warships, just like the white sailors. They had fought and they had died, just like the white sailors. But the war was over and the job pool in the merchant navy was draining. Union leaders, including Gallacher and Shinwell, imposed a 'colour bar' on the employment of black and Chinese seamen – and then banned them from membership. It was not a case of jobs going to British whites, for they were going to any white worker – Dutch, Norwegian, French – leaving some 'men of colour' without work. Debts increased, rents could not be paid, men – of all hues – starved. The white sailors were told that the 'foreigners' were stealing their livelihood. Many of the 'foreigners' believed that, even though they had not been born on this small island, they were British subjects and were entitled to work. Shinwell told sailors that overseas workers were undercutting their wages and urged them to take action. He was, to be fair, trying to gather support for a greater struggle, but a spark had been ignited that day and, fanned by Shinwell's fiery words, it was about to blaze.

Thursday, 23 January 1919 saw what the *Glasgow Herald* described as 'a riot unprecedented in the history of Clydeside'. Seamen had gathered at the mercantile marine yard on James Watt Street off the Broomielaw to sign on as crew members on the variety of merchant vessels crowding the port. Only a few hours before, Shinwell had addressed 600 of them and told them that the Government had refused to exclude Chinese labour from British ships, calling on the men to take action at once. To the average white man in those days of Empire, no colour but his own mattered. Feeling ran high and two factions, white and black, spat insults at each other. Words turned to action and there was pushing and shoving and punching. Then knives and even guns were drawn. Inevitably, a trigger was pulled and the first shots drew more men from the streets into the yard. A British sailor, 23-year-old Thomas Carlin, was slashed on the head and the battle burst out of the yard and onto the street. Around 30 black sailors backed away and holed up in a sailors' home on the corner of James Watt Street but the whites chased them and ripped through the building. The black sailors ran down the Broomielaw to their own lodging house, from where they took potshots at anyone who moved. Another seaman, 57-year-old Duncan Cowan, took a bullet in the neck just below the throat. Both he and Carlin were carted off to the Western Infirmary in an 'ambulance wagon'.

A handful of police tried to keep order, but reinforcements were needed and before long around 50 officers had waded into the battle. They stormed the lodging house and arrested around 30 of the besieged seamen, who went along quietly. Among them was Tom Johnston, a 23-year-old West African, suffering from gaping wounds on his back and leg. However, he was not taken to hospital like the two white wounded but was first dragged into a police van to be taken to appear before a magistrate. The court ordered that he be taken to hospital for treatment, where he remained for 22 days. It is believed the charge against him was subsequently dropped due to lack of evidence. The police, later accused of bias, did not arrest any white man for involvement in the riot. The Glasgow *Evening Times* noted that the arrested men 'although obviously of negro blood, bore familiar sounding names, such as Johnston, David Parkinson, Alfred, Pratt, with Tom Friday at the end of the list'. The only white subsequently arrested was 19-year-old Patrick Cox, and that was for police assault. He had been among a gang who had pounced on a Chinese sailor and struck a police officer from behind when he intervened.

Glasgow lawyer David Cook, the son of the man accused alongside Detective Lieutenant Trench, took the unenviable task of defending the 30 black men, all from the British colony of Sierra Leone, charged with rioting and recklessly discharging firearms. On 29 January, they appeared in court and Cook lodged not guilty pleas for 27 of the men, which were accepted by the Crown. The lawyer reminded the court of the men's war service and said that they were 'entitled to the protection of the British government'. Some, he said, had formerly sailed from Glasgow, but others had arrived from Cardiff to man ships in Glasgow harbour. Mr Cook observed, 'This gave offence to the Seafarers' Union, a body over which Mr Shinwell had some control. Being coloured, they could not become members of that union, though it was difficult to understand why, as this was a democratic body.' He also pointed out that some Chinese sailors had arrived in Glasgow and the 'coloured men got the benefit of the white men's umbrage'.

Three of the accused – Julius Parkinson, Daniel Pratt and Thomas Cole – pleaded guilty to a reduced charge of breach of the peace. They were given a choice of paying a fine of three pounds and fifteen shillings or spending twenty-one days in jail. Patrick Cox was found guilty of a more serious offence, police assault, but was also sentenced to pay the same amount or spend 20 days in jail.

In a passage headed 'Amusing Incidents', the *Evening Times* reported that:

> in the case of two who bore the same name the magistrate had some difficulty in distinguishing between them. Both said they belonged to Sierra Leone and when asked what part of Sierra Leone both replied Freetown. In an endeavour to find some distinguishing mark, Dr Neilson [the sheriff] asked them their occupation and found that both were firemen.

In the end, the court told the two men apart by their differing ages. Clearly, this was the kind of amusing incident that had the Glasgow newspaper-reading public chortling heavily over their suppers. It became even more thigh-slapping when another two men turned out to be from Freetown and both firemen.

The Glasgow race riot was just the first in a series of disturbances over the following months in ports all over Britain. Men died in these riots and in some cases troops were called in. There was further trouble in Glasgow in April, when two black seamen, Josie Kamarra and William Paul, were given a fine of thirty shillings each or seven days in jail for a breach of the peace. The police stated that around 50 black sailors had caused an obstruction on the Broomielaw on 2 April at around 7.30 p.m. When asked to move, Kamarra threatened to 'stab and shoot' any man who tried to interfere with him. He drew a knife to underline his point and the officer moved in for an arrest. Paul then shrugged off his jacket and waded in to rescue his friend, calling on the other men to join in. They did not and Paul was duly huckled off to the police station too. In June, police broke up a further fight between white and black sailors on the Broomielaw. One of the black men dropped a revolver and was fined five pounds.

Finally, the Government instituted a repatriation scheme, and by 1921, 2,000 black people had been returned to their former homes in Africa and the Caribbean. By that time, Manny Shinwell, Willie Gallacher and others had become working-class heroes thanks to 'Bloody Friday'.

On 27 January 1919, less than a week after the race riot, more than 3,000 men crammed into St Andrew's Halls for a meeting over the 40-hour-week demand. More jammed the streets outside. A call went out for other workers to join the strike and by the end of the month over 60,000 men had hit the cobbles. Shipworkers, steelworkers, factory workers, power workers all rallied round the flag. Only some of the tram workers resisted the call and kept a service running on the city's streets. Flying pickets – teams of men from one industry who targeted workers from another – were employed to urge, or intimidate, doubters into joining the ranks, and a daily newspaper, *The Strike Bulletin*, was produced.

The Government refused to intercede, privately siding with the bosses while officially stating that it was a matter for the two sides to work out between themselves. The employers were at first unconcerned, feeling that the dispute would peter out. However, as support grew, the men in power viewed the events with some alarm, many seeing the hand of Bolshevism in it. The Russian Revolution had taken place in 1917 and the threat of similar events occurring in Western Europe was taken very seriously. Germany had already seen blood flowing in its streets during an uprising by the Spartacists, socialists who took the name of the famed slave who had rebelled against Rome. Events in Glasgow were not designed to overthrow the Government, despite the hopes of Communist John Maclean, but what happened on Bloody Friday did strengthen feeling amongst the working classes against the bosses, the Government and the police.

After the meeting in the St Andrew's Halls, the strikers staged a march to George Square. A band played and the men sang, cheered and shouted slogans as they made their way to the Square via Argyle Street and Buchanan Street, a slightly circuitous route taken to enable them to attract more support along the way. The feeling against tram workers who failed to come out led to one man being arrested for pulling the trolley pole from the overhead power wires. Another man was later fined eight pounds and eight shillings for punching a woman driver in the face in St Enoch Square.

At George Square, Willie Gallacher, Manny Shinwell and other strike leaders climbed onto the bases of the pillars in front of the City Chambers and delivered more speeches. Gallacher urged those present to convince any doubters to join the struggle. 'Take them gently by the hand,' he yelled, 'and lead them from the evil preserve of their masters.' A red flag was passed over the heads of the men and handed up to him, and he waved it in the air, much to the delight of the strikers. It was then run up a flagpole nearby and the centre of Glasgow was filled with the sound of thousands of men and women singing the Communist anthem, 'The Red Flag'. Then Gallacher seemed to notice the eyes of the Glasgow Police upon them and addressed the boys in blue, urging them to join the National Union of Policemen, then also in dispute over pay. He said he understood that there were more Bolsheviks on the Glasgow force than anywhere else.

Strike leaders asked the Lord Provost to appeal to the Government to intercede in the dispute. They gave him until Friday, 31 October to come back with a reply.

On the Friday, strikers attended a mass rally in George Square. The square, seen now as the city's heart, had changed from the days when women used to hang their washing out there. In the late nineteenth century, it had become Glasgow's hotel centre and smart-looking buildings had grown up around it. At either side stood the impressive Merchants' House, erected on the site of a hotel in 1877, and the imposing City Chambers, built in the Italian Renaissance style, the very image of Victorian magnificence both inside and out. The City Chambers was designed to tell the world that here the full power of Empire was exercised. Queen Victoria was never a big fan of her nation's second city, despite having made the first royal visit to Glasgow (in 1847) since Bonnie Prince Charlie more than 100 years before, but she was delighted with the building when she opened it in 1888. By 1919, the large, open Square was mostly paved over and dotted with statues of great men. Former prime minister William Gladstone was there, Sir John Moore, the hero of Corunna, was there first, poet Thomas Campbell was there. But in pride of place, on a huge column, stood Sir Walter Scott, not a Glasgow man, but taking centre stage nonetheless.

It was proximity to the City Chambers and, perhaps more importantly, to the main post office on the periphery of the square that prompted the events of Bloody Friday. Memories of the 1916 Easter Rebellion in Ireland, during which rebel forces took possession of the Dublin post office building, remained fresh, and the authorities were fearful that the strike was merely the precursor to an uprising.

There had been a cold rain the night before, and the 60,000 men, women and children crowded together on the paving stones and flower beds, thousands of feet churning the earth into mud. They already knew that the Government had refused to intervene, for it had been printed in the morning papers, but the leaders duly met with the Lord Provost. The Government would not interfere, it said, because the strike was 'unofficial'. It was while Shinwell and Kirkwood were in the City Chambers that the strikers saw files of police officers lining up around them. In the enclosed square behind the imposing council building, another force of officers, some on horseback, waited. The Mounted Branch would not be formed until August 1924 but former Chief Constable James Smart had bought a number of saddles, and horses were hired. Chief Constable Stevenson was in charge on the day. He had already attracted controversy as the first non-Scot to be appointed to the position. A tough Irishman, he had proved his hard-nosed credentials on his home soil by wielding an iron fist in sectarian disputes. Events this day would not change his reputation. As Gallacher addressed the crowd, thousands more converged on the square – men brought their wives and children and the police grew restless in the electric atmosphere.

There are conflicting stories as to what sparked the riot. Police sources claimed that strikers prevented trams from moving around the square. When politely asked to stop, they turned ugly. Labour leaders said that police had allowed the trolleys to turn into the crowd, resulting in two men being knocked down. When organisers asked them to stop traffic, the attack began. Another version claims that the sight of a scarlet flag flying above the crowd made the police see red. Whatever the cause, the officers around the square led the onslaught, clubbing civilians down. When strike leader David Kirkwood emerged from the City Chambers, he was battered to the ground and subsequently arrested. Manny Shinwell was luckier – he was surrounded by a phalanx of strikers and moved clear of the carnage.

After the initial shock, the strikers regrouped and fought back. The now traditional weapons of rioters in the city – iron railings – were hauled from the ground, and men who were used to battle in the muddy ditches of the Western Front showed their mettle. Bottles were liberated from a truck and used as missiles. Willie Gallacher pushed his way through the sea of blue, grey and red to launch a personal attack on the chief constable. Still the police moved forward like a well-ordered machine, the piston-like rise and fall of their batons leaving the square dotted with the prone figures of men, women and children. Lists of the injured later showed that most of the wounds were to the head and scalp. The police were outnumbered, though, and their ranks withered and broke.

However, they were simply the shock – the awe was yet to come. Chief Constable Stevenson called in the reserve forces waiting behind the Chambers. The mounted officers surged from their hiding place and charged into the throng. Strike literature claimed that 'in a display of trick riding, two of them allowed their horses to fall'. This seems unlikely and the 'trick riding' claim merely a means of excusing the attack on the fallen officers and animals.

Sheriff Principal MacKenzie tried to bring order by reading the Riot Act, which prohibited gatherings of 12 or more people if they were behaving 'riotously and tumultously', which certainly covered the behaviour that day, on both sides. The act, first passed in 1714, told offenders that force would be used if they did not disperse within an hour, although this delay could be ignored if the authorities deemed it necessary. Force had already been used and the paper was snatched out of MacKenzie's hands, while a well-aimed bottle hit him on the arm. It was the last time the act was read in Scotland.

The police began to gain the upper hand, and Gallacher and Kirkwood, although in custody, were allowed to address the crowd, urging calm and telling the strikers to leave George Square and regroup on Glasgow Green. 'We are asking you to go on the march, for God's sake,' cried Gallacher. 'Are you going to do that for us?' The people gave a throaty answer in the assent and began to drift away, only to regroup in North Frederick Street. They marched to Glasgow Green via Glassford Street, the Trongate and the Saltmarket, gathering numbers as they went. Trams were halted, boarded and wrecked, windows were smashed, particularly in the court buildings and the central police station, which had moved to the Low Green (now Turnbull Street) in 1906. Anything that could be used as a weapon – railing, bottle, stick – was pressed into service when police charged again in Clyde Street. Further running battles took place on the Green and feelings continued to run high. When darkness fell, gangs of looters came out to pillage shops and stores. The cold January night was filled with the guttural roar of angry voices and the shrill shriek of police whistles.

The Government, now certain that a workers' revolution was taking place in Glasgow, dispatched 10,000 troops to patrol the city. They may even have been in transit prior to the riot beginning. Scottish soldiers of the Highland Light Infantry were locked into Maryhill Barracks for fear that they might revolt and join forces with the workers. Six tanks rumbled through the streets from their garage in the Saltmarket and machine-gun posts were set up on rooftops, while nervous and inexperienced young soldiers with bayonets fixed marched past surly Glaswegians.

There had been trouble in another part of Lanarkshire that day. A crowd of up to 6,000 men had tried to picket the coalfields, coming up against a small army of police officers at Bellshill Cross. The policemen staged a baton charge and eight strikers were subsequently arrested.

The Strike Bulletin called the events of Bloody Friday 'a brutal attack on defenceless strikers'. The police, it said, had 'once more been used as hirelings to bludgeon the workers' and the events looked like 'a prearranged affair by the master class' to satisfy their 'lust for broken skulls'. The Manifesto of the Joint Strike Committee, sent afterwards to trade-union offices across the country, called the events a 'dastardly attempt to smash trade unionism'. It read:

> Three years ago we were told by spokesmen of the employers that, after the war, the workers would have to be content with longer hours. Here then is the secret of the determination to crush by any and every means attempts to secure shorter hours.
>
> The organised workers of Scotland put forward an orderly and legitimate demand for the Forty Hours. The government's reply is bludgeons, machine-guns, bayonets and tanks. In one word, the institution of a Reign of Terror!

David Kirkwood, Manny Shinwell, William Gallacher and other strike leaders were charged with incitement to riot. After a trial that lasted eleven days, with a total of twelve men in the dock, only Shinwell and Gallacher were jailed, the former for five months, the latter for three. Kirkwood was able to prove, by using photographs, that he had not been involved in the riot, having been halted forcibly by a police baton as soon as he rushed out of the City Chambers. Despite a well-supported public petition against the sentences, the Scottish Secretary, Robert Munro, had deemed the strike and its aftermath a 'Bolshevist uprising' and refused to budge.

On 10 February, the strike was abandoned, having failed to gain the national support for which its leaders had hoped. They did not win their 40-hour week but there was a concession for engineers and shipbuilders of a 47-hour week. Years later, William Gallacher wrote that, in hindsight, perhaps they should have pressed for revolution:

> Revolt was seething everywhere, especially in the army. We had within our hands the possibility of giving actual expression and leadership to it, but it never entered our heads to do so. We were carrying on a strike when we ought to have been making a revolution.

The events of 31 January 1919 damaged the always delicate relationship between the police and the ordinary working man. The mutual distrust would continue, despite the fact that, apart from an incident during the general strike of 1926, police were not again used to suppress a dispute until the bitter miners' strike of 1984. It has often been argued by critics that governments look after the police to allow them to be used in such a way. What is not widely known is that in 1919 the police were themselves unhappy with their lot. However, in July, a report recommended that a constable's pay should start at three pounds and ten shillings a week, rising over ten years to four pounds and ten shillings, to be followed by further long-service rises. Glasgow officers accepted the offer, although their colleagues in other parts of the UK were less inclined to do so. In London and Liverpool, police officers went on strike and many were subsequently sacked.

Manny Shinwell and David Kirkwood enjoyed long careers in politics, both being elevated to the House of Lords. Gallacher, an ardent Communist, although elected as MP for West Fife in 1935, received no such honour. In October 1925, Special Branch officers travelled from London to arrest him in his Paisley home. The authorities were cracking down on the Communist Party of Great Britain, of which he was a founding member, and had staged various raids in London. He and fellow executive member Tom Bell, arrested in Glasgow, appeared in court and were then whisked down to London to face trial. The police took the view that the Party was financed by Russia with the principal aim of overthrowing the British government. They, and MI5, wanted membership made illegal. Gallacher and 11 other committee members were charged under the 1797 Incitement to Mutiny Act in that they had 'unlawfully conspired together to utter and publish seditious libels and to incite divers persons' to commit breaches of the act 'against the peace of our lord the King, his Crown and Dignity'. All 12 were later found guilty at the Old Bailey and Gallacher, thanks to his previous record, was sentenced to 12 months in prison.

On 1 June 1919, a young man who should have enjoyed a long career died. Constable William McGregor, aged twenty-six, succumbed to injuries he had received during riots six months earlier, which can only refer to the George Square incident.

He was not the first serving officer to die in the line of duty; he would not be the last.

CHAPTER TEN

IN THE LINE OF DUTY

A sk any police officer and he will tell you that the job is rather like the famous description of war: long hours of tedium punctuated by short bursts of action. Much of it is routine, too much of it paperwork. It can, however, by the very nature of the people with whom the average copper has to deal, be dangerous. The first name on the Scottish Police Memorial Trust's roll of honour is Aberdeen City watchman John Buchan, who was stabbed by a thief in February 1770 at Stonehaven market. The first Glasgow officer named is watchman John Colquhoun, who died on 4 April 1847 of a fractured skull received, it is believed, when he was assaulted while on night duty. The next named is Special Constable James Alexander who was killed when the military opened fire during the riots of 8 March 1848. The roll continues: John McArthur, like John Colquhoun, found dead on his beat with head injuries on 2 May 1861; Robert Campbell, killed by a drunk on 5 November 1863; Andrew Urquhart, felled by a poker during a domestic disturbance on 24 October 1897.

Not all officers were killed by 'customers'. Accidents and natural causes also claimed them. Constables Duncan Cameron and John McDonald both drowned in the Clyde while patrolling the docks, on 24 October 1860 and 21 February 1890 respectively. Police lore suggests that both men had partaken too heavily of the water of life during their tours of duty and succumbed to the water of death. Other officers have collapsed while on duty, been struck by trains or, in the case of Robert Murray in December 1895, been trampled by a runaway horse he was trying to stop. Runaway horses were a frequent menace on city streets and officers who managed to stop them were awarded the Corporation Medal. Legend tells of one tall officer on points duty at New City Road and Cambridge Street who halted one with a well-timed and well-aimed blow between the eyes.

However, it is the deaths of officers in the line that attract the most attention – and Glasgow has seen too many of them.

The end of the First World War brought many of the city's tough customers back from the front. They already knew how to fight; now they knew how to kill. The Armistice also saw a rise in the number of guns on the streets as soldiers returned home with souvenirs. Before 1870, no one needed a licence to own or carry a gun and any attempt to legislate gun control was blocked by MPs who believed that every man had a right to own a weapon. However, in 1870, the first licensing scheme was forced through and in 1903 a new Pistols Act was passed, which required that anyone purchasing a gun be registered and produce the ten-shilling licence fee prior to purchase. The gun laws were not tightened further until a police officer was gunned down in the street. Even then, certain 'war trophies' were still not covered.

On 18 January 1919, Constable James Campbell was walking his beat on what is now Tollcross Road but was then known as Great Eastern Road, near Parkhead Cross. The thirty-nine-year-old father of three had been on the force for eighteen years and was well regarded by his superiors, with a number of commendations from Chief Constable Stevenson on his record for his conduct. At around 11 p.m. on that Saturday night, he walked into the close mouth at 637 Great Eastern Road to check windows looking out onto the common back court. This 'superior class of tenement dwelling' was what was known as a 'high back', in that the back court was level with

The Tron Kirk, where the city police force based itself in the early days.

The plaque marking the site of the Session House, where the City of Glasgow Police mustered in 1800 after two false starts.

IN COMMEMORATION OF
THE MEN AND WOMEN
OF THE
CITY OF GLASGOW POLICE
FIRST FORMED 1779 - 1781
RE-FORMED 1789 - 1790
SUCCESSFULLY ESTABLISHED UNDER
THE GLASGOW POLICE ACT OF
30 JUNE 1800
&
MUSTERED WITHIN THIS BUILDING
(THEN KNOWN AS THE LAIGH KIRK)
ON
15th. NOVEMBER 1800
STOOD DOWN ON
15th. MAY 1975
ON THE FORMATION OF
STRATHCLYDE POLICE
ERECTED BY
THE GLASGOW POLICE & STRATHCLYDE JOINT
HERITAGE SOCIETY POLICE BOARD

The Tolbooth tower, all that is left of the complex that merged civic amenities with jailhouse and courthouse.

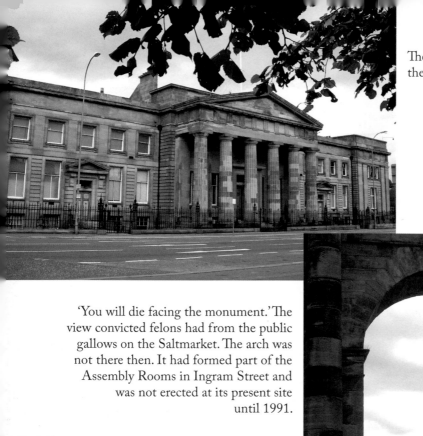

The old High Court on the Saltmarket.

'You will die facing the monument.' The view convicted felons had from the public gallows on the Saltmarket. The arch was not there then. It had formed part of the Assembly Rooms in Ingram Street and was not erected at its present site until 1991.

James MacKoull, as sketched by John Kay.

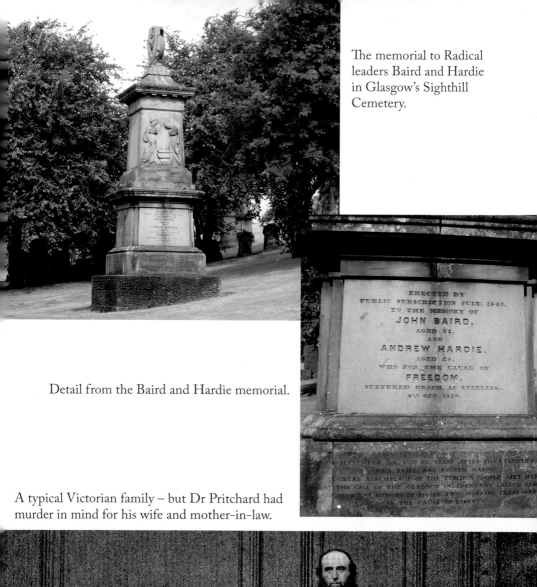

The memorial to Radical leaders Baird and Hardie in Glasgow's Sighthill Cemetery.

Detail from the Baird and Hardie memorial.

ERECTED BY
PUBLIC SUBSCRIPTION JULY. 1847.
TO THE MEMORY OF
JOHN BAIRD.
AGED 32.
AND
ANDREW HARDIE.
AGED 28.
WHO FOR THE CAUSE OF
FREEDOM.
SUFFERED DEATH AT STIRLING.
8TH SEP. 1820.

ON SEPTEMBER 5TH 1920 100 YEARS AFTER THE EXECUTION
JOHN BAIRD AND ANDREW HARDIE
GREAT ASSEMBLAGE OF THE COMMON PEOPLE MET HERE
AT THE CALL OF THE GLASGOW INDEPENDANT LABOUR PARTY
HONOUR THE MEMORY OF THOSE TWO WORKING CLASS MARTYRS
IN THE CAUSE OF LIBERTY

A typical Victorian family – but Dr Pritchard had murder in mind for his wife and mother-in-law.

David Kirkwood lies injured after the 'Bloody Friday' riot in George Square, 1919.

Tanks garaged in the Saltmarket ready to quell the demonstration.

David Kirkwood and Willie Gallacher are arrested.

Arthur Thompson, long known as Glasgow's Godfather (courtesy of the Scottish *Sun*).

Thomas 'TC' Campbell smiles as he is cleared by the appeal court (courtesy of the Scottish *Sun*).

Joseph Steele, co-accused along with Thomas Campbell of murdering six people in a horrific fire. He was also cleared by appeal court judges, who deemed the case against them a miscarriage of justice (courtesy of the Scottish *Sun*).

Gangland enforcer turned author and businessman Paul Ferris (courtesy of the Scottish *Sun*).

Peter Tobin being led from court and just a split second away from assaulting a press photographer (courtesy of the Scottish *Sun*).

Glasgow's prostitutes ply a dangerous trade on the streets of the city. Many are assaulted and some have been murdered. A number of killings of prostitutes in Glasgow remain unsolved (courtesy of the Scottish *Sun*).

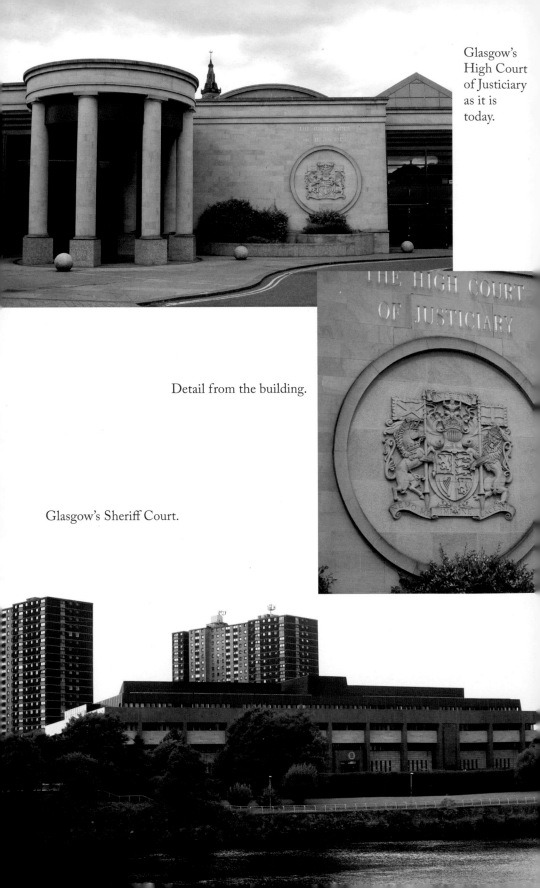

Glasgow's High Court of Justiciary as it is today.

Detail from the building.

Glasgow's Sheriff Court.

the first floor. PC Campbell climbed the stairs from street level and there he found a gang breaking into a flat. He grabbed hold of one and the others bolted into the back court, leaping over the railings into Westmuir Street. In the gloom of the back close, the two men struggled until the robber pulled himself free from the policeman's grasp, stepped back and pulled a pistol from his pocket. Then he fired twice. One bullet caught PC Campbell in the side; the other burrowed into his abdomen. As the policeman slumped down the wall, the gunman ran off.

The shots alerted residents and passers-by, who found the wounded man lying on his stomach but still conscious. He was carried into a nearby flat while a doctor was called and someone ran to the Cross to alert the officer on duty. PC Campbell provided a description of the man – between 19 and 21 years old, 5 ft 6 to 7 in. tall, dark clothes, muffler and cap – which could have fitted almost any young man in the city at the time. A man was arrested but Campbell could not identify him. He was by then failing fast and on Monday, 20 January, he died in the Royal Infirmary.

It is well known that police officers work doubly hard when one of their own is murdered and this case was no exception. Two young girls had seen a young man come flying out of the close then head towards Parkhead Cross. A man spotted on a tramcar had exhibited 'excited and nervous behaviour' just after the shooting. He was traced and cleared when it was established that his demeanour had been caused by a squabble elsewhere. Glasgow Corporation offered a reward of £200 for information, hoping to lure the killer's partners in crime into the open, but no one came forward. Three more men were arrested but there was not enough evidence for a conviction and they were released. One was remanded in custody, however, for an assault and robbery in Shotts. A further two men were arrested in Dundee but they too were cleared. It is to the force's credit that no one succumbed to the temptation to manufacture evidence.

On 23 January, PC Campbell was buried at Bannockburn, where he was born. Large crowds lined the route of the funeral procession from his Dennistoun home to Alexandra Parade. Officers and men from the force attended – including the entire night shift and half of the day shift from Eastern Division – while the police pipe band provided the suitably sombre music.

The identity of the man who killed James Campbell remains a mystery – just as the name of the man who actually pulled the trigger during the next cop killing in Glasgow is also unknown.

* * *

At around 12.10 p.m. on Wednesday, 4 May 1921, Inspector Robert Johnston sat in the front of the police van as it hauled itself up the High Street. He was on the edge of his seat, both literally and figuratively. He was crammed into the cabin with three other officers, and as part of the transport detail carrying a dangerous man from the courts in the Saltmarket to a cell in Duke Street Prison, he was tense. The prisoner was Frank J. Carty, wanted by Irish police for breaking jail. A commandant of the Sligo branch of the IRA, Carty was being taken to the prison to await extradition to Dublin, having appeared before Stipendiary Neilson, who had heard the cases two years before against the rioting sailors. Carty had lots of friends in the city and more had been arriving all the time. The police suspected that an attempt would be made to free him, so Inspector Johnston and his colleagues Detective Sergeant George Stirton and Detective Constable Murdoch Macdonald were armed. Carty was locked away in the van's cell behind them, with another man who had been charged with indecent assault.

Duke Street was by then, along with Barlinnie which had opened in 1882, the main city prison. It was not a model jail by any means and its poor reputation was reflected in some street doggerel sung to the tune of 'There Is a Happy Land':

There is a happy land,
Doon Duke Street jail,
Where a' the prisoners stand,

Tied tae a nail.
Ham an' eggs they never see,
Dirty watter fur yer tea;
There they live in misery,
God save the Queen.

At the crest of the High Street, known as 'the Bells o' the Brae', driver PC Thomas Ross touched the brakes in order to turn into the Drygate. They could see the prison, its high stone walls creating a man-made canyon with the Corporation water pumping station – an ideal spot for an ambush. There were civilians in the street but that did not concern the three groups of men who converged on the van from all sides. They came from Rottenrow, they came from the Cat's Close, a lane off the High Street, they came down from Cathedral Square. Ross ducked as his window shattered and bullets sent steam hissing from the radiator. Further rounds thudded into the sides of the van. A group of children heading home for lunch had to duck for cover as bullets whined along the street and ricocheted off the high prison walls. Inspector Johnston tumbled from his perch, the side of his head ripped off. He fell between the tramlines on the street below and tried once to rise, reaching his knees, before he slumped again and moved no more. DS Stirton leaped from the van, his gun already blasting at the attack squad. He stood over the prone figure of his colleague as if to protect it from further harm, emptying his weapon as bullets sang past him. DC Macdonald also threw himself into the street, firing all around, while PC Ross kicked and punched at anyone who tried to board his vehicle.

There was not much the officers could do to prevent the attackers from blasting at the lock in a bid to spring Carty. However, the door was made of stern stuff, for it refused to yield. Bullets bounced around the interior of the van and Carty, the other prisoner and the two police officers guarding them were in danger of becoming casualties themselves. On the outside, the would-be rescuers clawed at the metal doors, but still they held.

Meanwhile, a round shattered DS Stirton's wrist and he dropped his weapon. By this time, though, the attack force knew their moment had passed. They pulled back, splitting up and melting away into the warren of side streets. A woman ventured from a nearby house, told Stirton she was a nurse and offered to tend to his wound.

'Don't mind me any more, missus,' he said, 'go and help my chum.' Then he ran off after a group of men retreating along Rottenrow. One look at the officer lying on the road told the woman it was too late. Stirton chased the men for a time but loss of blood from his wound eventually forced him to stop.

Other attackers escaped via Cathedral Square, which was thronged with unemployed men, the feared recession having finally hit. Some of them tried to stop the fleeing gunmen but a look and a warning wave of a pistol caused second thoughts. PC Ross managed to bring the van back to life and drove into the prison yard, DS Stirton and DC Macdonald following behind. Once safe behind the huge gates, Stirton collapsed. A team of burly prison officers then managed to prise the van doors open and free the men inside, including a no doubt disappointed Carty.

Descriptions of the attackers were sketchy at best, and during the rest of the day every detective and officer hit on their 'touts', or informants, for whispers. Information trickled in, names were mentioned and raids planned. The operation centred on the East End of the city, where many Irish Roman Catholics had settled. In Abercromby Street, officers kicked in doors and hauled out several people, including a priest, Father Patrick McRery, who was arrested in the chapel house adjacent to St Mary's Church. In the street, the arresting officers found themselves faced with an angry mob. They believed the police were merely the tools of the Protestant authorities and that no Catholic could hope to receive fair treatment from them, especially in a cop-killing case. The crowd showed 'their keen indignation' by throwing insults and stones. The prisoners were taken away but the mood on the streets was turning uglier by the hour.

Police officers walking their beat had to run a gauntlet of hate.

More than 2,000 people milled about the streets of the Gallowgate. Trams were attacked and smashed, and one police officer who went to the aid of a woman hurt in an accident found himself surrounded by a gang. They kicked and battered him before he was able to escape on a passing tram.

A total of 34 people were arrested in connection with the attack on the van, and a further 12 for rioting. A detachment of soldiers surrounded the central police office, where the prisoners were held. Only 13 eventually faced trial, in August 1921, for the rescue attempt and the murder of Inspector Johnston. DS Stirton positively identified nine of them but their various defence counsel were able to prove that they had been elsewhere. All 13 men were cleared, either by not guilty verdicts or not proven. Police identification techniques, already discredited by the Oscar Slater case, were again questioned amid allegations that prosecution witnesses had been allowed to view suspects prior to the ID parade.

Carty was smuggled out of the city and back to Ireland soon after the attack, guarded by heavily armed officers of the Royal Irish Constabulary. Inspector Johnston was buried in his home town of Castle Douglas, the customary large crowds turning out at both ends of the journey. He left behind a wife and two children.

The incident prompted a crackdown in the city on persons sympathetic to the IRA. The raid on 74 Abercromby Street uncovered what was at the time the largest haul of weapons and explosives the city had ever seen. Officers emerged from the building carrying thirty-five pistols, six hand grenades, gelignite, a ready-made bomb, detonators, bullets, magazines and a bayonet. The record stood until the late 1980s, when a vast armoury was discovered in the South Side.

Curiously, DS Stirton, DC Macdonald and PC Ross went unrewarded; none of them received any kind of medal for his actions that day. It seems all the more curious given that in the years prior to and just after the murder officers were given awards for pursuing and attempting to arrest armed criminals, stopping runaway horses and, on one occasion, shooting a wild bullock.

Duke Street Prison eventually became a women's prison. It was demolished in 1958, having been closed three years before, and the Ladywell housing scheme was built on the site in the early 1960s. Only part of the boundary wall remains, but if you look hard enough, you can still see the marks made by ricocheting bullets that summer day in 1921.

CHAPTER ELEVEN

THE ROARING '20s

Prostitution, they say, is the world's oldest profession and it is prevalent in every city. Glasgow had taken many steps to try to relieve the suffering of those 'disgraced and drunken women' but, human nature being what it is, they never succeeded in driving the 'hoors' and the 'ponces' who lived off their illegal earnings out of business.

The 'honey trap', in which men were lured by the blandishments of the women in order to be fleeced by their male handlers, was well established by 1920, and in February it led to murder.

Stonemason Henry Senior had recently been demobbed and was back in his home in Govanhill in the city's South Side. On Tuesday, 3 February, he went into the city centre looking for some fun. He had originally taken £10 from his savings box but his mother talked him into leaving most of it at home, so he had a little over £2 in his pocket, more than enough for a good night. Near the junction of Hope Street and Argyle Street, the 35-year-old former soldier met Helen Keenan. The 20-year-old Aberdeen girl had come to the city two years before and was married, if only by declaration, to a Canadian soldier who had vanished to the front during the war and not returned. She wasn't particularly attractive, but then prostitutes working the lower end of the market didn't need to be. It was sex they offered, unbridled lust-sating with no questions asked and no guilt attached – as long as the punter paid up. As Ralph Glasser, in his memoir *Growing Up in the Gorbals*, recalled one prostitute saying to him, 'You can do wha'ever ye want wi' us there! And I mean tha', anything . . .' Meanwhile, her friend said, 'A' the things ye've ever dreamt aboot doin' wi' a wumman an' maybe never dared tae say!'

Perhaps Keenan, also known as Helen White, used similar words to rope Senior in; perhaps he didn't need any such promises because he already knew the score. In any case, he agreed to return with her to the South Side, to the area known as Queen's Park recreation ground. Much smaller now, it was then a large open area with very little lighting, and the ideal site for nocturnal fumblings.

Senior, his passions raging with the promise of all kinds of illicit pleasures, failed to notice that they were being shadowed by two men. James Rollins and Albert Fraser were ponces who specialised in robbing the clients of prostitutes like Keenan. Tall, pale Fraser was an Australian army deserter who had taken up with Keenan after her common-law husband had left to fight. Rollins was shorter and clean-shaven and was making cash out of another prostitute, 19-year-old Elizabeth Stewart. Senior did not spot the two men sitting nearby as he chatted with his ladyfriend on the tram. He did not see them quietly walking behind them as they stepped onto the grassy area and cut through a fence beside the railway track. He did not hear them creep up as he and Keenan began to pet. The next thing he knew, two men, one tall, the other short, were standing over them. There was a gun in the big guy's hand and the smaller one told Keenan to beat it. Without another glance at the mark, Keenan straightened her clothes and climbed back through the fence, where she waited. She had done this before and she knew the routine.

But this one was not to go according to plan. The ex-soldier knew what was happening and had no intention of giving up his money without a fight. But as Rollins grabbed him from behind and jammed a knee in his back while Fraser thudded the butt of the revolver in his face, perhaps he knew he had lost. Fraser hit him again and again until Senior slumped immobile. Keenan, watching from beyond the fence, appealed for him not to be so hard on the guy but Fraser paid no notice. Feeling that matters had turned far more serious than she'd expected, the young woman ran off into the night. The men continued to kick and beat Henry Senior until he was dead. Meanwhile, Keenan met up with Elizabeth Stewart and went to the pictures.

The body was rolled under some bushes and the two men walked away from the scene with the princely sum of six shillings. They also took Senior's coat and boots. They left the park and hopped on a city-bound tram. Later that night, they met up with Keenan and Stewart. Rollins' hands were still covered in blood and the men said they believed they had killed the man. The gun was a dummy, but, nevertheless, this was serious and they knew they would have to leave the city. They decided to head for northern Ireland, where Fraser knew of a cave where they could hide out until the heat died down.

The following morning, the murder investigation was kick-started when two young boys stumbled upon Henry Senior's body while playing in the recreation ground. Detectives soon found witnesses who had seen Fraser and Rollins carrying the overcoat and boots on the tram the night before. The descriptions furnished matched reports from earlier victims. Detectives spoke to prostitutes and their ponces. They checked pawnshops in case someone had pledged the boots and coat. They hit it lucky with one pawnbroker, who had given two men seventeen shillings and sixpence for the boots and eight shillings and sixpence for the coat. The descriptions matched. Another man told them that Fraser had often boasted of having a bolt-hole in Belfast he could use if ever he got into hot water. Further enquiries turned up two men answering the same descriptions who had been seen boarding the Belfast boat-train at Glasgow Central Station in the company of two young women. Detective Superintendent Andrew N. Keith and Detective Inspector Louis Noble set off for Belfast on 7 February.

The arrest came, as arrests so often do, through blind luck. Detective Superintendent Keith was walking along a Belfast street when he spotted two men who answered the descriptions. He decided to take a flyer and asked them for a cigarette. While the traditions of sharing a light were being observed, he studied the men more closely and told them he was looking for two blokes who answered their description for a Glasgow murder. The men said they knew nothing about it but did admit they weren't local to Belfast. Keith, though, pressed the point and asked them to go back with him to the police station. The men, seeing the officers of the RIC at his back, decided that it would be prudent to agree.

Back at the station, the men's clothing was examined and, under the lining of a jacket, they found traces of blood. This was enough to justify their arrest. On a slip of paper, the police found the address of a boarding house in the city's Lord Street. A visit there revealed the two girls. The cave on the shores of Belfast Lough had been prepared with stolen hay and cooking materials, but the men had decided on one last night in civilisation. The four suspects were taken back to Glasgow in handcuffs and on 4 May 1920 Fraser and Rollins faced trial for murder. Their erstwhile lure, Keenan, saved her own skin by turning King's evidence, as did Stewart (although she was not implicated in the murder, only as an accessory after the fact). During her evidence, Keenan collapsed as she described the attack on Henry Senior. Stewart talked of Rollins weeping over the murder and saying, 'It's awful to be the cause of death of a man.'

The judge said that the accused, like witnesses Keenan and Stewart, 'had been leading a deplorable and degrading life' but warned the jury not to be prejudiced against the accused 'in their repulsion against that form of living'. The jury took only 19 minutes to return their verdict of guilty. They did not recommend mercy. On being sentenced to death, the pair grinned at each other and shook hands. Then Fraser wiped away an imaginary tear while his partner, all remorse now seemingly gone, scowled in the direction of the public gallery and drew his hand across his throat.

On 26 May, a large crowd gathered outside Duke Street Prison to await news of their deaths. It was the first double execution in Glasgow since 1883. The two men 'walked firmly to the scaffold' and died together. Just as the lever was pulled, Fraser was heard to say, 'Cheer up, Bill.' Police, worried that a demonstration by anti-death penalty activists was in the offing, were there in force. However, the crowd dispersed shortly after 8 a.m., when the black flag was hoisted to signify that the sentence had been carried out.

In a touching postscript to the case, a few weeks after the execution, a letter arrived at the Glasgow offices of the Salvation Army. It was from Fraser's sister in Australia and said that she and her ailing mother were anxious for news of her brother's plight. They had heard he had been arrested and charged with assault but nothing more. She wrote:

> Being my only brother, I am anxious about him and I have no tidings of him. I would ask you to oblige me by trying to find my dear brother as he is all I have. I lost my only sister nine months ago.
>
> If you find him, please give him a good talking to and ask him to write his mother and I. Tell him his sister Florrie died in Sydney June 23 1919 and that his mother is in very bad health since she heard of his trouble.

The letter, from Geelong, West Victoria, was dated 1 April. It ended, 'Please give my brother this address as we were in NSW when he went abroad.'

Detective Superintendent Keith was not in the jail that day to witness the executions, for he was back in Belfast feeling the collar of a man suspected of murdering a city-centre tailor.

The body had been found in his workshop at 34 St Enoch Street. The room was filled with gas and the death was originally thought to be suicide. The man had been gassed during the war and had often complained of headaches. However, he had no business worries and no reason to take his own life. That, a fractured jaw, traces of blood outside the room and missing cash swiftly pointed to robbery and murder. A closer examination turned up a bloody fingerprint. Police experts worked out that the man had been first battered, then one end of a rubber tube thrust into his mouth with the other end fixed to a gas pipe.

The tailor, William Ross, a widower with one child, was a former soldier with an artillery unit. Using a group photo, the police tracked down each member. They learned Ross had been friendly with one of his comrades who lived in Glasgow. Robert Halliday had been with Ross on the night he died, in a pub on the corner of Sauchiehall Street and Hope Street. Ross had been drinking heavily and was quite drunk, so drunk, in fact, that he was thrown out of the bar. Outside, Halliday had hailed a taxi. According to him, he had taken the man to his workshop and left him at the foot of the stairs. He did admit to having taken his watch and chain. The Crown asserted that he and the taxi driver had battered and robbed Ross before Halliday carried him up the 91 stairs to the workshop, where he tried to fake the suicide. A post-mortem showed that the tailor had died from carbon monoxide poisoning as the gas was pumped into his lungs. Halliday then tried to avoid the police by going to Belfast but was caught and brought back by Keith on the day that Rollins and Fraser died.

The trial became a talking point. 'The frequency of sordid tragedies in Glasgow and other large cities in recent weeks has whetted the popular excitement,' said a rather disdainful *Evening Times*. Crowds turned up early on a rainy September day in an attempt to claim one of the limited places in the public gallery. Many brought breakfast with them and ignored the wet weather to eat it in the queue. Inside, the pomp of the High Court sitting began with the blowing of trumpets and the calling to order. Halliday, 22, chewed at something as he calmly waited for events to unfold. His older co-accused appeared nervous. The partial fingerprint found on a railway timetable and sent to the Metropolitan Police experts in

London – Glasgow's fingerprint department was not yet what it was to become – was deemed to have seven similarities to Halliday's. 'I have never found such a sequence on two impressions taken of different fingers,' said one of the English officers.

In the end, though, there was not enough evidence to prove that either man had actually killed William Ross. The taxi driver was found not guilty of all charges, while Halliday was cleared of murder but found guilty of assault and robbery. He was jailed for five years.

Prostitution was back in the headlines in 1921, thanks to the murder of Sarah Brookstein. She was an attractive woman, dark-skinned, dark-haired and the mother of two children. Her father, at home in Newcastle upon Tyne, knew her as Sarah Ellison and knew nothing of her marriage to Jewish tailor William Brookstein. However, the marriage had foundered and the tailor was living in London. Sarah settled in Glasgow, taking a flat at 120 Sword Street, in what was described at the time as 'a typical working class district' in Dennistoun. While her children lived with relatives nearby, she earned a living as a prostitute, using the name Sadie Brooks. Her father might have thought of her as Sarah, but she was Sadie when she died.

Her friend and fellow streetwalker Sophia Black, a Russian with very limited English, was the person who raised the alarm. She had lived on and off with Sadie but had not seen her for six days. On Sunday, 23 October 1921, a visit to the police and a door forced open by two burly Glasgow coppers revealed the 33-year-old dead in what had once been a neat little single-end. It was not neat any more. There were the usual signs of a struggle – overturned furniture, smashed ornaments – and blood, lots of it, spattered on the walls, on the floor, on the bed. The woman had been brutally beaten, perhaps with a claw hammer, and tortured. A pair of pliers was found embedded in her flesh. Her exposed skull shone through a thick layer of blood. A towel had been wrapped around her head, not to stem the blood but to stifle her agonised screams, for part of it had been thrust down her throat. There were also signs that someone had rifled through the woman's possessions, as if searching for something. Meanwhile, a pan on the stove held the congealed remains of steak and tomatoes.

Police soon discovered that Sadie was a hooker, but that did not affect their zeal for the case. This was a bad one and the killer had to be caught. The tried-and-tested murder routine slipped into gear. Her friends and associates were questioned, neighbours were interviewed. When had they seen her last? Who was she with? Had they heard anything unusual in the past week or so? Neighbours told of screams in the night, which had been put down to some local toughs who generally shouted and fought outside a nearby billiards hall. The neighbours knew of her but many disapproved of her lifestyle. She had no obvious means of supporting herself but she was always well turned out in fashionable clothing. And then there were the gentlemen callers, of course.

It was a nasty, brutal murder and naturally it caught the public's attention. Reporters visiting Sword Street found no shortage of local women, 'arms weighted by the customary loads of domestic purchases', who were willing to gossip about the case. A police officer stood sentinel in the foggy morning after the discovery and kept everyone at bay. Strangers, meanwhile, were eyed with suspicion until they revealed they were reporters or detectives.

Sadie was buried on Thursday, 27 October in Janefield Cemetery. A cluster of people, many of them fellow prostitutes, waited outside police headquarters as the coffin was carried out of the mortuary and placed in a hearse. Two coaches then carried the mourners to the cemetery, where the wreath-laden casket was lowered into the grave, the tough-talking streetwalkers bidding their last farewell to a friend who had been brutally murdered, knowing that it could have happened to any one of them.

By the following week, police had arrested a number of people in connection with the crime. By that time, though, attention had moved from the bloody events at Sword Street to another tragedy, this time at the other end of the city. On Tuesday, 1 November, the body of Elizabeth Benjamin was found in the back court of 67 George Street, Whiteinch. The victim was Jewish and, like Sadie, she had been beaten to death. There was more public sympathy for the victim this time, for Elizabeth Benjamin was a respectable girl. What was more, she was only 14 years old, although she looked much older. There was no connection between the cases, but the two victims will remain forever linked, by their shared faith, by their dying violently within days of each other and by the cases being heard in the High Court building at the same diet.

Elizabeth Benjamin had left school early to help her ailing father with his drapery business, hawking clothing around Whiteinch and Scotstoun and collecting cash from credit customers. She was a well-known figure in the area and no one had a bad word to say about her. On 31 October, she left her Clydebank home and began her customary rounds. During the following day, after her body had been discovered, more than 100 detectives and uniformed officers poured into the streets, hunting for information and clues. They searched wash houses, outhouses and back courts for anything that might lead them to the killer. They established a timeline through speaking with the women on her route and learned very quickly that she had last been seen in the late afternoon in George Street.

News of the discovery spread and as the police van arrived to cart the body to the police mortuary, George Street was thronged with people. There was anger, for word had leaked out that the victim was just a wee lassie. Many knew Elizabeth through her father's business. Her mother and sister, who had become concerned when she hadn't returned home, had the ordeal of formally identifying the body at Whiteinch police station.

When Elizabeth was found, her clothes were in disarray and her wrists tied behind her back. The rope was saturated with blood, the knot a close-hitch type used by sailors. She had been badly beaten. A small handkerchief had been stuffed into her mouth and down her throat, and a cloth had then been tied around her mouth as a gag.

Robbery appeared to be the motive, for she had not been raped, or 'outraged', as the press put it in those days. Her money was missing and the case in which she carried her father's goods was gone, although it was later found dumped a few doors away. A bag containing partially burned and bloodstained clothing was discovered in an ash pit.

The mystery, in the end, was not difficult to solve. The timeline helped police focus on 67 George Street and in particular the flat of William Harkness, unemployed shipyard worker, and his wife, Helen. Bloodstains on the stairway and outside their door consolidated their suspicions, as did the information provided by horrified family members.

On Wednesday, 2 November, arrests were made in both cases. In the west, William and Helen Harkness were formally charged, along with his brother John Harkness, with Elizabeth's murder. In the east, four people were detained in connection with Sarah Brookstein's death, although only two would ultimately face trial. The following day, Elizabeth's bereaved family laid their daughter to rest in Sandymount Cemetery in Shettleston. As in Sadie's case, the mourners followed the coffin from the police station to the graveyard, although at Elizabeth's funeral there were no flowers.

The first to come to trial was the case against the Harkness couple, although the second hearing began straight afterwards. By January 1922, the charges against John Harkness had been dropped in favour of him giving evidence against his kinfolk. There was nothing to suggest that he had been present when poor Elizabeth was murdered. His only crime had been to help move the body. He had been instrumental in leading the police to his brother and sister-in-law during the investigation.

The case had excited considerable interest and people had gathered in the Saltmarket from the early morning in the hope of securing one of the few places in the public gallery. There were 70 Crown witnesses and 11 for the defence, although none of the latter was called. Among the items of evidence were slides bearing smears of blood taken from the close and from a wash-house boiler near which the body had been stored for a time. Pieces of wallpaper and plaster from the house were also used in evidence.

The couple had attacked the young girl in their home and beaten her with a heavy drill bit, called a 'reamer', which Harkness used in his work. The most dramatic evidence came from John Harkness, who told the court that his sister-in-law had asked him to help them move the body. He and William had not spoken for some time and she had said to him, 'Surely you will help us. He is your own brother, your own flesh and blood. Surely you will help me.' He also said that she later wished they had 'got the factoress because they'd've got £50'. As it was, William Harkness said, all they got was £1 and a few shillings. Helen Harkness, who had been drinking steadily, remarked that it was 'a lousy pound'. She also said that Elizabeth was 'a strong little bugger', moaning, 'My legs are black and blue where she kicked me.' William complained that she had bitten his fingers during the struggle. John asked his brother, 'In the name of God, what made you do a thing like that?' Harkness replied, 'Johnnie, it is a thing you have never done, and once you start you have to finish it.' Remorse did not seem to be uppermost in their minds immediately after the killing.

John Harkness agreed to help them and they moved Elizabeth's body from the wash house where they had hidden her to the back court where it was discovered. 'Johnnie,' William had told him, 'you have no idea what trouble I had getting it down. I had only the help of a useless woman.' John also dumped the girl's case. Later, his conscience led him to confess his part to his mother-in-law, who informed the police.

During a break in proceedings, John Harkness found himself on the receiving end of public anger when he was attacked in the court tearoom.

It was not the beating that had killed the girl but the gag. The handkerchief had been stuffed so far down her throat that she had suffocated. The defence tried to suggest that her struggles had helped dislodge the cloth and bring about her death and that this meant the couple had not murdered her and were guilty only of culpable homicide. The accused had separate counsel and each tried to suggest that the other was the real killer. Helen Harkness, it was argued, was 'placed in the position of the wife of a man who had committed a crime and had the natural desire to cover up the traces of her husband's guilt'. The ten men and five women on the jury were not going to swallow that, however, and took twenty-five minutes to find them guilty, although they strongly recommended mercy for the female accused. Helen Harkness, who had been visibly nervous throughout the trial, wept as the judge donned the black cap and wished that God would have mercy on their souls. Her husband patted her reassuringly on the back.

The following day, the trial of a man and a woman for the murder of Sarah Brookstein began. From the start, the proceedings boasted what the *Evening Times* called 'sordid revelations of underworld life', shining a light into the 'depths of depravity in human nature which puzzles most men'. The male accused was alleged to be a pimp, his female co-accused a prostitute. The victim was a prostitute. There was bad blood between Sadie and the female accused – bad blood that resulted in her getting her 'bully', as pimps were known, to kill Sadie.

The man, who made a somewhat dodgy living in the theatrical profession, had been identified by one witness as the person he had seen in the close at Sword Street on the night Sadie was believed to have died. He had blood on his forehead and was lurking outside the door. The witness said he managed a good look at the suspect when he asked for a cigarette. However, the accused said he smoked a pipe, not cigarettes, and that the police identification system was deeply flawed. When picked out, he was standing between two policemen who looked nothing like him, while the rest of the parade was made up of 'three boys who were on a charge of stealing cabbages'. If that was so, then the Glasgow Police had not learned anything from the Oscar Slater case.

The accused was identified by other prostitutes as the man they had seen getting on a tram with the victim on the last night she was known to be alive. However, the 23-year-old man denied he had ever been in Sword Street, he denied knowing Sarah Ellison, Sarah Brookstein or Sadie Brooks, he denied living off immoral earnings. He did admit to knowing his co-accused, a known prostitute, and having some form of relationship with her, but details were very sketchy. Newspaper descriptions said he was 'a stalwart, well set-up fellow with nothing suggestive of any weakness or depravity about him'. In the dock, his black hair 'glistened after a recent toilet'.

The reporter was equally rapturous about his co-accused. She had 'a ready smile' and her dark-brown hair was bobbed in 'the look of a modern girl'. But witnesses said she had it in for Sadie and often argued with her and even threatened her. A former taxi driver, who it was alleged was a 'bully', stated that he had once witnessed a heated argument between the women in the street and that the female accused had asked him to 'go down and strike' Sadie.

No clear motive emerged for such a brutal murder. Professor John Glaister, chair of forensic medicine at the University of Glasgow, was the expert witness for the prosecution and he believed that some of the injuries were either the act of a sexual pervert or a means of demeaning the victim. The crime, he believed, had been committed by someone 'almost inhuman for the time being'.

In the end, the Crown could not prove beyond a shadow of a doubt that the male accused had murdered Sadie at the behest of the female accused. An inability to accurately specify the date, let alone the time, of death – they could only estimate sometime between 18 and 24 October – and conflicting testimony from many of the witnesses, a number of them sex workers, led to a not proven verdict for the man and a not guilty one for the woman. The murder of Sarah Ellison or Brookstein, also known as Sadie Brooks, remains unsolved.

On Saturday, 18 February 1922, Helen Harkness was told that she would not hang for the murder of Elizabeth Benjamin. The woman who had wished they'd got the factoress instead burst into tears. On Tuesday, 21 February, her husband made the short walk from the condemned cell at Duke Street Prison to the scaffold, housed in a former joiner's cupboard. He said nothing as he was pinioned, hooded and dropped. At 8 a.m., the black flag was run up to tell the crowd gathered in Cathedral Square that the sentence had been carried out. He, and Elizabeth Benjamin, died for a sum of less than £2.

Nellie Harkness escaped the noose but Susan Newell was not so lucky. The first woman to be hanged in Glasgow in 50 years, she was also the first and last woman to be executed at Duke Street and the last ever in Scotland. She had murdered young paperboy John Johnstone in Coatbridge in June 1923 and wheeled the corpse through the streets on a go-kart with her young daughter in tow. Accepting a lift from an unsuspecting lorry driver, she and her lifeless bundle reached Glasgow's East End, where she tried to hide the body in a Duke Street close. However, she was arrested soon afterwards. She tried to implicate her husband in the crime, although he was subsequently cleared. The motive for the murder was never discovered and Susan Newell held her silence until the end. She was hanged on 10 October 1923 by John Ellis, who was reportedly more nervous on the gallows that day than she. He was never comfortable when hanging women and it is said that the Newell execution and another of a woman in England helped tip him over the edge of sanity. He committed suicide some years later.

Passions run high today over crimes against children and it was no different in the first half of the last century. Anyone suspected of abusing or interfering with a child could receive rough treatment at the hands of the public. For poor Robert Stewart, a single mistake led to him being beaten to death in the street.

Stewart was a ship's cook who, along with his wife, lodged in Ibrox. Another lodger was a widower named Sinclair, whose young son John lived with an aunt in Cambuslang. Stewart befriended the young boy and saw him whenever he was in port. On 11 September 1922, he arrived unannounced with the intention of taking the young boy to see his father. He found John playing in the street and took him by the hand towards the tram stop. The problem was that he did not tell the boy's aunt or uncle. That was the mistake that cost him his life.

As the tram approached Dalmarnock Bridge, a female passenger told the conductor that she believed the boy had been abducted – and repeated the claim to Stewart's face. She had grown suspicious over the disparity in dress: Stewart was in a suit while the five-year-old boy was barefoot. She took the boy from him and began shouting 'kidnapper' and 'dirty brute'. The seaman flushed and became aware that the other passengers were staring at him. He tried to explain but the accusation had flustered him. It was true that he hadn't asked permission to take the boy from his home. Surprise among the passengers gave way to anger and hatred. This grown man had snatched the wee laddie and intended to do God knew what to him. Stewart could not find the words to cool matters down and he did the only thing his panicked mind could think of – he ran. All it did was confirm his guilt.

The conductor halted the tram and some of the male passengers pursued the fleeing sailor. They shouted what had happened to passing pedestrians and they joined the chase. Near Summerfield Street, they caught him. Stewart was dragged to the ground and the good citizens – ordinary folk, decent folk – crowded around him and kicked him until he lost consciousness. There were women there too, their faces contorted with hatred, and they, according to one witness, 'were the worst of the lot'. A police officer pushed the mob back but the damage had been done. Robert Stewart, aged 35, never regained consciousness and died the following day. He had sustained five separate fractures to his skull. Had he told the boy's family that he was taking him to meet his father, had he not lost his nerve in the face of the accusations, he might have lived. Four days later, two men were arrested and charged with the man's murder, but proving they were guilty was no easy task. They had been part of the mob, certainly, but the Crown could not establish that they were solely responsible for the man's death. The men were cleared on a not proven verdict.

It was sudden, unaccountable hatred that had done for poor Robert Stewart. It was racial hatred that led to the death of Noorh Mohammed. By all accounts, he was an inoffensive man, a Punjabi trader who had come to Glasgow to make his living peddling silks. But in one savage night of violence fuelled by lust for money and blood, he died. The case was complex and no one – then or now – could say for certain exactly what happened. In the end, one man was hanged for the murder, but there were without a doubt others equally as guilty.

Some accounts of the case state that 27-year-old Noorh Mohammed was the target of the killer all along, but that was not so. Like Robert Stewart, he was in the wrong place at the wrong time. All he did was try to protect himself, but a ravening mob is blind. He was Asian and he was there; that was all that was needed.

It began when a group of young white men visited a flat in Clyde Street, Port Dundas, occupied by Nathoo Mohammed and his white wife Louie, to trade some daggers for silk goods. Nathoo refused the deal and the men turned ugly. Early reports stated that Noorh Mohammed was in this house at the time and left to return to his own lodgings in Water Street, Port Dundas. However, subsequent testimony makes no mention of him at this stage. The initial object of the men's hatred was Nathoo Mohammed, who fled his house clad only in a silk sheet to escape them. He made his way to Water Street, a narrow road near Buchanan Street station comprising a varying array of houses, including tenements. At No. 56, he went into the second-floor flat of fellow pedlar Sundi Din and a number of other Indians, including the ill-fated Noorh Mohammed.

The white men burst into the flat, and both Noorh and Nathoo tried to defend themselves with brooms. Noorh was dragged out of the flat and at some point, either on the stairway or in the street outside, was stabbed twice in the chest. There was quite a crowd in the street at the time – one witness estimated it at about 100 strong

– but not all were in the gang. Some were there to see what all the commotion was about. Although it is tempting to ascribe the gang greater numbers, there were only about 20 or 30 real troublemakers. The remainder were potential witnesses and some lost no time in naming names, perhaps to deflect any legal scrutiny of their own involvement. Although many more were originally arrested, only four came to court for threatening assault, theft and murder: John Keen, John McCormack, Robert Fletcher and William Dayer. It was to be a sensational trial, filled with allegations of gangsterism and wife-beating, and one of the earliest High Court cases to hear about drug trafficking.

In court, speaking through an interpreter and taking his oath on the Koran, Nathoo Mohammed described how it all started. On the day before the murder, Keen and Fletcher had come to him wishing to buy a scarf, offering as payment a pistol and a knife. When he refused these, Fletcher paid up with hard cash. At around 10.30 p.m. on Saturday, 16 May 1925, Keen returned with two other men and wanted to buy more clothing. Nathoo asked them to leave and return the following day but they refused. A pistol was produced; Keen wanted to exchange it for a jumper. When Nathoo again refused, Keen produced a knife and said, 'Give me a jumper or I will kill you.' Nathoo tried to get help from a neighbour before fleeing, clad only in a sheet, to the house of Sundi Din. However, Keen and a great number of other men followed him and forced their way in. Other witnesses said that he and Noorh Mohammed tried to hold them off, but Nathoo denied this. Noorh was punched and kicked, and he fell down the stairs. At some point, he was stabbed and he died later in the Royal Infirmary of internal bleeding.

The defence alleged that Nathoo was, in fact, a drug trafficker, importing heroin from India inside hollowed-out knife handles. He admitted to one offence regarding possession of opium three years before but insisted that it had been for his own use in treating a sore chest. He strenuously denied being involved in drug dealing.

His wife, Louie, described as a 22-year-old white girl of Spanish extraction, had followed the three men to Water Street and claimed that Keen had had a knife in his hand and had shouted, 'Rush them, boys. Get ready for action.' The court heard that she had been threatened over her evidence but refused any protection. There was ill feeling against her, not just for giving evidence but for having married an Indian. However, she denied that she was the object of any such racial hatred. She stood up to a withering cross-examination by defence counsel, who suggested that her husband had starved her, beaten her and had even on one occasion threatened to cut her throat. She denied all the suggestions, saying that if he had ever taken a knife to her, 'I would have taken one, too, and we would have fought it out.'

One witness claimed he had seen Keen stab the victim in the left breast with a knife. John Stirling had once worked for Nathoo Mohammed and also knew Keen. He said that Keen harboured ill will towards Nathoo and 'would do the man in'. Keen, whether through surprise or anger, exclaimed loudly as Stirling spoke and 'looked somewhat distressed'. Stirling said he had been in Water Street when Keen told two Indians to 'send down that countryman of yours'. Then Keen and McCormack tried to break in the door. He saw both Nathoo and Noorh Mohammed defending themselves with brushes. Noorh, though, did not get back into the house fast enough. Keen stabbed the man on the left breast and he was dragged out of the close by others in the gang. Stirling's sister Jeanie also said she had seen Keen wield the blade.

Later, when word reached the gang that the police were looking for him with regard to the 'row' at Water Street, Keen was heard to say, 'It is always the same; they are always looking for me for everything.'

Richard Stephen had been at a dance nearby when he heard about the disturbance. At the close mouth, he recognised John Keen and saw him pass a knife to a man called Robert Purdon. Purdon confirmed that Keen had passed him a knife, saying, 'What do you think of this?' Purdon then handed the weapon to another acquaintance, Joseph McCall. This man said he heard someone say, 'Give it to McCall and he will put it in the canal.' However, McCall stashed the blade in the chimney of an old building near the canal. Later, he and Robert Purdon's brother retrieved it and took it to the police.

Bloodstains were found on Keen's jacket and trousers, while McCormack had similar marks on his trousers and the soles of his boots.

The charges against Dayer were withdrawn, as the evidence supported his claim that he had not taken part in the assaults and had, in fact, tried to convince the other accused to leave.

Keen, who had appeared jaunty at the beginning of the trial, gradually became more and more nervous. He wept as Noorh Mohammed's death was described, and as the jury returned to deliver their verdict, his lips twitched until, finally, tears burst through again. In the end, only he was found guilty of murder, while Robert Fletcher was convicted of culpable homicide, and Keen and McCormack were found guilty of intimidation. The theft charge was found not proven. Fletcher was given seven years and McCormack nine months. The murder verdict was unanimous, the judge told the shocked and despairing Keen, and he hoped that during his short time still to live in this world he would 'endeavour to recover as much courage and peace of mind as would enable him to cross to the next world without any fear or misgiving whatever'. Then, as sobs punctured the breathless silence of the courtroom, he laid the black hat over his wig and sentenced Keen to death. The young man sat back in his seat, unable to believe what had happened.

As he was being led below, Keen called out, 'I want to ask Your Lordship a question. I am not getting justice in this case at all, my Lord. If I had got into the witness box, I could have cleared myself. I don't think there has been any justice at all. I ask for justice.' He continued, 'Why were witnesses dropped who would have spoken on certain things had they been called, such as the other dagger? Instead I was picked up alone. Why should I be the only one to suffer? I thought there was justice in the High Court, but now I know there is none. I have been called a hooligan and a gangster, but this I never was.' His plea fell on deaf ears and after a final, pained glance around the courtroom, he began to descend the stairs into the cells below the court. Onlookers in the public gallery called out, 'Cheer up, John,' but by that time he was gone.

Whether John Keen did or did not strike the fatal blow, he paid the price. There were many people around Noorh Mohammed that night and any one of them could have plunged the dagger into his chest, as the defence insisted. The weapon was then passed from hand to hand until it reached Joseph McCall. There was some doubt as to when the deadly wound was administered – on the landing or in the street – and, as one lawyer said, 'they all knew what Glasgow gangs – in fact, the gangs of any city – were, and there might have been several in the crowd who wanted to vent their spleen on the dead Indian and who delivered the blow'.

The jury had recommended mercy and a hefty petition of names called for the sentence to be commuted, but all to no avail. On Thursday, 24 September 1925, John Keen was escorted from the condemned cell in Duke Street Prison and walked briskly the eight or ten paces to the death chamber. Among the official witnesses was, for the first time, a woman: Depute River Bailie Mary Bell. Earlier, she had spoken to Keen in the cell and he had asked if he could shake her hand. In the death room, she watched as he was led to the scaffold, his arms pinioned and the white cap drawn over his head and eyes. The executioner, looped the noose around his neck and someone said to Bell, 'Close your eyes.' However, even before she could do so, the lever was pulled and Keen's body jerked through the trapdoor.

Around 2,000 people had gathered in Cathedral Square and beyond but they did not see any black flag fluttering up the mast and no bell tolled to announce that the final penalty had been paid. The authorities had decided to dispense with these traditions in a bid to discourage 'the morbid curiosity of that section of the public for whom an execution exercises an attraction'. The crowds, mainly young men and women, faced the prison walls as the appointed hour came and went. They kept their voices low and their demeanour sombre. Then, at just after 8 a.m., mounted police moved slowly forward to disperse them. An hour later, an unobtrusive notice was pinned to the prison gates.

Later, Mary Bell told reporters:

> Many people urged me not to attend the execution, but I wanted to prove that a woman is fit to take her place on public bodies. When I took the oath as a Magistrate, I undertook to carry out the duties of a Magistrate, without having the option of picking and choosing. We women in the civic body of a city like Glasgow are pioneers of the women's movement, and we have to show that we are fit to take the unpleasant with the pleasant.

She also said that 'there was really nothing to upset any woman possessed of ordinary nerves'.

* * *

The Clyde played a vital role in the city's development, and in return the city played the major part in the river's destruction. Sewage, waste and other filth was for centuries poured into the grey waters, until the river all but died. Although far purer now than it has been for centuries, the Clyde remains a dumping area for criminal detritus. Guns, knives and other evidence have been dropped off the banks and bridges to settle in the silt and never be seen again. Bodies have also been thrown in with a view to disposal, while desperate people have chosen to end it all by jumping in. However, it may be Judgement Day before the sea gives up its dead, but the Clyde is less possessive. Currents and tides send corpses and body parts bobbing to the surface, leaving police with the grisly task of identifying the dead person and finding the killer, if one exists. For many years, the Geddes family of the Glasgow Humane Society specialised not only in saving lives but in helping to drag the sorry remains of the dead out of the river. And on 15 October 1927, George Geddes senior found something particularly gruesome.

It was eight in the morning and he was helping tow a barge up the river to Polmadie Bridge when he saw a white parcel lying at the water's edge about 150 yards upstream from the King's Bridge on the Glasgow Green side. He hauled the bundle aboard, cut the string with his knife – and found inside the head, the legs sliced off below the knee and the left arm of an elderly woman. The flesh bore severe burn marks and the woman's ring finger had been cut off. It was later found tucked away in the folds of the paper.

Forensic experts told police that the parcel had not been in the water very long and that their initial estimate was that the woman had died up to two weeks before. Officers conducted door-to-door enquiries in nearby streets, asking if anyone knew of an old woman who had not been seen for days. They soon found a woman who identified the head as that of her mother-in-law, Agnes Arbuckle. Independently, worried neighbours in Main Street, Gorbals, had reported that the 60-year-old had apparently vanished. The man in charge of the case was Detective Lieutenant Stirton, who had earlier in his career bravely faced up to the IRA gunmen attempting to spring Carty from the prison van in the Drygate. He called at the home of Mrs Arbuckle's only remaining son, 40-year-old James McKay, in Thistle Street.

A joiner to trade, he was well known in the area. He had been a prisoner of war, sent to work in German salt mines. He suffered from malaria, contracted while in India. He was intelligent and articulate but known locally as 'the mad hoodjee' because of his habit of 'hudging', or hunching, up against the cold during winter. He was found sitting beside his fire 'cool and sober' and 'interested in a newspaper containing photographs of the spot where the body had been found'. Unhappy with some of the answers he received, the officer cautioned McKay and charged him with murder. McKay replied, 'She is dead. She died about ten days ago. I put part of her in the Clyde; the rest is in the bunker.' In his pocket was a sheet of paper bearing attempts at forging his mother's signature.

The police took McKay to his mother's room-and-kitchen apartment, where the prisoner said, 'It is in there, and the saw is in the room.' Stirton opened the bunker and shoved some coal aside to reveal a bundle containing the right arm. They waited until the arrival of forensic expert Professor John Glaister before investigating any further. Then they hauled all the coal from the bunker and uncovered three more parcels, containing the woman's chest, lower body, right thigh and right arm. The entire investigation lasted 25 hours.

With a suspect now in custody, police found a man who claimed McKay had offered to sell him the dead woman's false teeth, while there was evidence that McKay had sold items of his mother's furniture. Meanwhile, footprints left in the river mud were compared with McKay's shoes and found to match.

Professor Glaister's examination of the body parts led him to believe that the work had been done by an unskilled person with no knowledge of anatomy, using a fine-toothed saw. It would have been bloody and time-consuming. Cause of death had been loss of blood, which meant the woman had been alive when McKay began his hacking. There had been an attempt to burn the remains.

McKay claimed that he had found his mother dead in the house. He was drunk at the time and his addled brain had reached the conclusion that he would be blamed for her murder, so he decided to dispose of the body. The prosecution version was that the mother and son had argued over money and in his drunken temper McKay had beaten her to death then, to cover up the crime, hacked the body to pieces with a saw and a razor. The jury believed the Crown case and James McKay was sentenced to hang. When he heard his fate, he waved to his wife in the courtroom and told her, 'Cheer up.' On 24 January 1928, he went to his doom in Duke Street Prison, the *Evening Times* reporting that he 'expiated his crime with the same nonchalant charm which has characterised his demeanour since his arrest'. The same newspaper said that the usual 'large crowd of morbid onlookers' was attracted to the prison gates.

The last person to be hanged in Duke Street was George Reynolds, on 3 August 1928, for the murder of bakery stoker Thomas Lee in what was known as 'the Bakehouse Murder'. The 41-year-old seaman had met his victim in a Glasgow poorhouse two years before. On the night of the killing, they had been drinking together and Reynolds accompanied Lee to Lang's Bread Company in Wesleyan Street. At some point, the two argued and Reynolds, the Crown argued, beat Lee to death with a shovel. Reynolds insisted that it was in self-defence, that Lee had attacked him with the shovel because in his drunken state he had come to believe that Reynolds was after his job. Dr John Glaister, the son of the learned professor, believed that the cause of death was a blow from a branding iron, not a shovel.

Whatever happened, it was a sad, meaningless little tragedy that was made no better by Reynolds' own state-supported death. He died on a dull August morning and there were few people gathered to await the news. Also not in evidence was Glasgow magistrate Alexander Brown, who had been due to form part of the official witness party. He had watched James McKay walk to his death and had expressed a desire never to witness such a spectacle again. It had affected him so much that he was now a declared opponent of capital punishment. His place was taken by Bailie Robert McLellan.

CHAPTER TWELVE

THE SLASH MY FATHER WORE

The image we have of Glasgow in the 1930s is grey. Grey buildings bordering grey streets walked by grey men under grey skies. It was not quite like that, of course; we have that impression as much because of the monochrome photography of the time as anything else. There was colour – all too often blood red – and not every day was overcast. But life was not easy. The industrial boom of the previous century had led, perhaps inevitably, to the bust of the late 1920s. The city had prospered through the manufacture of arms and ammunition, as well as shipbuilding, steelworks and other traditional industries. With the end of the war, the call for weapons was muted, while the famed Clydeside shipyards found themselves in competition with cheaper yards in other countries. By 1923, their output had tumbled to 180,000 tons from 760,000 tons 10 years before. The industry rallied briefly before the Great Depression hit the developed world, but the shipyards produced only 66,000 tons and 56,000 tons in 1932 and 1933 respectively. Yards closed and men found themselves out of work, on the dole and on the street. Other industries – building steam trains, cars, steel production – were similarly hard hit. Although cotton weaving was 'in poor shape', as Charles Oakley put it, hosiery manufacture prospered, along with 'printing and paper-making, and the preparation of foodstuffs, drink and tobacco'. However, the number of names of the needy on the books of the City of Glasgow Society of Social Service exploded in the 1930s.

Glasgow's police had grown into the second-largest force in the country after the Metropolitan Police. It boasted a strength of 1,500 men and women; it was, however, far from overwhelmingly popular. The actions of the police during the 1919 strike and again during the General Strike of 1926, when they had to deal with rioting workers in the East End, the city centre and Maryhill, alienated many working-class folk. During these incidents, batons were drawn again and mobs were charged. Most of the casualties came from the strikers' ranks, and although police historian Douglas Grant writes that 'it is doubtful whether the police at any time before or since have been held in higher esteem by the public', they were not universally admired. Some strikers remembered the events of Bloody Friday with bitterness and saw the police actions of May 1926 as a repeat performance. And, naturally, the city's gangsters had nothing but contempt for the forces of law and order.

A street gang known as the Norman Conks tried to make something out of the general unrest and injure police officers. They doused the street lamps in their home base, Norman Street, and strung a rope between two posts. A call was made regarding an imaginary crime and police arrived. The first two officers on the scene sensed skulduggery afoot and called for reinforcements. Colleagues turned up mob-handed in a lorry and drove straight through the rope. The Conks surged from their hiding places and surrounded the van, but to their surprise around 20 police officers tumbled out primed for action. The resultant street battle ended with a number of injuries and three arrests.

As the depression bit and the jobless figures rose, the Government cut unemployment relief. On 1 October 1931, thousands massed in Glasgow Green to hear speakers protest at the cut in the dole. A march to George Square followed and a further rally was planned for the Green that night. Jittery police chiefs decided that the night-time rally should not proceed. However, some men and women ignored the order and massed on the Green as planned. Mounted officers charged and six of the leaders were arrested. When the demonstrators tried to rescue them, the mounties and foot officers charged again. As women screamed and men yelled, the police line broke up the large knot of protesters and within minutes had the Green secured. In the Saltmarket, the mob gathered again and was herded towards Glasgow Cross, breaking shop windows as it went. The tinkle of breaking glass was accompanied by the cracking of skulls as the police dealt with the problem in a direct fashion. Only three people were arrested during these riots and the outbreaks of violence that followed throughout the night, but untold numbers of men and women were injured. The police response to the demonstrations was raised in Parliament and senior officers were denounced. This did not stop the hierarchy from ordering another charge when demonstrators, emboldened by the seeming support from Westminster, took to the streets again the following night. A party of protestors was dispersed in Jail Square only to reconvene in the Saltmarket. Again a strong police force piled in with batons raised and again the streets around Glasgow Cross witnessed violence, vandalism and looting. The attacking officers were bombarded with every sort of missile the rioters could lay their hands on, while police vans roamed the streets looking for trouble. This time, 51 people were arrested during the disturbances, and once more the police were heavily criticised.

Two months later, Glasgow had a new chief constable, arguably the most famous in its history. The police committee had decided to ignore a number of applications from local men in favour of an Englishman with a colourful past. Captain Percy Joseph Sillitoe had already proved himself to be a tough guy in Sheffield, where under his leadership his men had smashed the seeming stranglehold that street gangs had had on that city. Prior to that, he had risen through the ranks of the British South Africa Police in Rhodesia, chasing killers through the veldt with a gun on his hip. During this time, he had a liaison with a local woman and fathered a child. In

Africa, he had learned some tough lessons: never show fear, never let them see you blink. It was that sort of two-fisted approach that the city fathers wanted to see in action in Glasgow, for the street gangs were in the process of becoming more than just a bunch of hoodlums looking for a rammy.

There is an impression that Glasgow did not have gangs until the early part of the twentieth century, but in fact the city had known organised bands of street ruffians for decades. Thieves had swarmed out of their slumland hives almost since their construction, staging muggings, assaults and pocket-picking, while rival gangs had kicked, punched and stabbed each other over religious differences, over territory or sometimes for no more reason than because it was something to do. In the mid-nineteenth century, a group of Glasgow criminals known as the Fancy extorted cash from stallholders and bookies at Paisley races. Earlier, a sandbank in the middle of the Clyde was seen by thugs from the Gorbals and their counterparts from the city as a no-man's-land on which to stage fights because they believed that officers from the two police forces had no jurisdiction there.

There did seem to be a tendency in the city for disaffected young men and women to band together under a collective name. It was a tribal instinct, a need to belong to something larger than themselves, and a way of gaining safety in numbers. It is generally accepted that the first recorded Glasgow street gang was the Penny Mob, which had its roots in the Townhead area in the late 1880s. Its leaders were named chairmen, and it levied a fee on members to help with payment of fines, hence the gang's name. Its coffers were further enriched by robbery and extortion; shopkeepers were prevailed upon to pay a fee in return for not having their premises trashed and their persons injured.

Around the same time, rival mobs included the Drygate Youth and both the Big and Wee Do'e Hill. As the century waned and a new one began, so the number of gangs grew and the names became more picturesque: the San Toy Boys and their rivals the Tim Malloys, the McGlynn Push, the Mealy Boys, the Hi-His, the Baltic Fleet, the Hazel Bells, the Village Boys, the Gold Dust Gang, the Black Hand Gang, the Cowboys and the Redskins. The last name referred to the number of livid scars on their faces, which they bore like badges of honour. The Redskins adopted the old Glasgow Fancy speciality of targeting racecourses. They became one of the most potent gangs in the city, boasting a membership of 1,000, until the police decided to crack down. Former detective chief superintendent Robert Colquhoun observed in *Life Begins at Midnight* that two gangs in particular, the Cheeky Forty and the Black Diamonds, who both operated out of the St Rollox area,

> were street corner thugs, who fought one another in head-on clashes a hundred strong or more – though they usually preferred it if some unsuspecting rival gangster strayed alone into their territory and could be 'done up' in the appropriate tradition. Sometimes girls attached to a gang would provide the necessary lure to achieve the catch.

Weapons were invariably edged and efficient. Firearms were a rarity. The closest thing to hand was often a bottle, which could be used as a club until it shattered, when it transformed into a nasty weapon for slashing and gouging. Knives, bayonets, pickaxe handles, hatchets and sharpened bicycle chains were all popular. Often, female affiliates of a gang – known as 'queens' – carried the weapons for their men. Blades were sewn into the men's soft cloth cap that was then in vogue so that the cap could be wielded as a weapon during a rammy. Curiously, although the mobs became known as 'razor gangs', razors were not popular, according to Sillitoe. 'It was easier to stun an opponent with a beer bottle, knock him down and kick him in the face,' he wrote in *Cloak Without Dagger*. Decades later, former gang member and criminal Thomas 'TC' Campbell dismissed the open razor as 'hopeless'. He said that the majority of times the user would cut his own fingers with it when it closed over. However, he did admit that it was useful in a tight spot:

A razor's handy if you get attacked in a house. People get a hold of your neck, someone's hitting you with a bottle, someone's trying to stab you at close quarters and you've just got to touch them with a razor. No matter where you touch them with it, it's like a sharp sting. And they let go.

Battles could be bloody – faces were opened, bones were shattered, skulls were lacerated – but fatalities were few. In 1924, though, the long-standing enmity between the San Toy and the South Side Stickers led to hostilities breaking out between the Parlour Boys and the Bridgegate Boys, two smaller outfits with allegiances to the big boys. Jim Dalziel was the leader of the former gang, which had as its headquarters the Bedford Parlour Dance Hall in Celtic Street in the East End. It was their custom on entering to wipe their feet and say they knew the boss. This tipped the cashier off that they were gang members and they were allowed through without paying. Once inside, Dalziel scorned dancing with any of the queens, much preferring to take to the floor with another male member. In his mind, it was effeminate to be seen dancing with a woman.

On 2 March 1924, Dalziel, known as 'Razzle Dazzle', was on the dance floor when members of the Bridgegate Boys streamed in from the rainswept street. They were affiliated to the San Toy, while the Parlour Boys were associated with the South Side Stickers. Although the newcomers had declared they knew the boss, they had forgotten to wipe their feet and a member of staff alerted the local crew. This incursion onto opposing turf was not to be tolerated and soon there was blood on the dance floor. Bottles were wielded and thrown. Knives were drawn and plunged. Dalziel, 26, was killed after being stabbed in the throat, and a youth named Collins was subsequently charged with and cleared of the murder. He did, however, go down for 12 months for affray.

Four years later, members of the South Side Stickers were involved in another fight that ended in death. It began with an injury to a female gang member and a challenge to meet on Albert Bridge to settle the matter. Five members of the Stickers faced up to a similar contingent of the Calton Entry gang, one of whom, James Tait, was stabbed. The combatants were all aged between 15 and 17. Two were sentenced to one year, a third to eighteen months while a fourth, who put his hands up to mobbing, rioting and culpable homicide, was given five years.

By 1931, the gangs were well established and proficient both in fighting each other and in furthering their criminal enterprises. Sir Percy Sillitoe later wrote that the city was 'overrun by gangsters terrorising other citizens and waging open war between themselves in the streets and I, with my experience of Sheffield, was thought to be capable of dealing with them'. He was unimpressed by the calibre of the average gangster, dismissing most such criminals as 'very violent and unpleasant hooligans . . . weak-willed, not over-intelligent products of slums and unemployment'. He wrongly believed that the Glasgow gangs came into being after the First World War, stating that they were formed by 'young men who had lived through the war without seeing action and older "scoundrels" who were reluctant to settle down to a peaceful life'.

One of these was Peter Williamson, a legendary figure in the annals of Glasgow gangdom. He was a powerful figure, both physically and in the respect he commanded. His followers called themselves the Beehive Gang, the spawn of the older Beehive Corner Boys. Unlike the vast majority of gang members, Williamson seems to have come from a respectable family and was, in Sillitoe's words, 'well enough educated'. He was no slouch in dishing out the violence but was canny enough to drop his fists and weapons at the first hint of a police presence and would then be seen 'tearfully appealing to the brawling gangs to behave themselves'. His power over his followers was such that on one occasion a senior member of the gang went down for an assault that had been committed by Williamson and Dan Cronin, a hard man associated with the Beehive Gang but, Sillitoe said, never a fully fledged member. Cronin was greatly admired by the people of the Gorbals and his funeral in 1950 was attended by hundreds of locals. His reputation lived on and he became the kind of tough guy that the likes of Jimmy Boyle venerated, even though, Boyle admits, Cronin was dead by the time he was six. Williamson and his coterie branched out into safe-blowing and armed robbery, and it was that path that he trod on his return to civvy street following the Second World War.

William Fullerton was another gang legend. He was a Fascist and the 'King of the Billy Boys', a rabid Protestant gang from Bridgeton whose arch-enemies were the Roman Catholic Norman Conks, under Bill 'Bull' Bowman, whose territory was just a few streets away. Fullerton was a hardened street fighter, but his gang took its name not from him but from William of Orange, 'King Billy', whose victory at the Battle of the Boyne is a touchstone for Orangemen. The fights between these two forces were given an added edge by religious hatred and they never missed a chance to wind each other up.

On 19 January 1932, Bowman used a march organised by the National Unemployed Workers' Movement to stage an incursion into Billy Boy territory. He and 300 of his fellow Norman Conks merged with the procession and steered it into Abercromby Street, where Fullerton and his boys were waiting. A frank exchange of views took place, followed by the inevitable violence. Pickaxe handles were swung and ordinary workers fled the scene as the two sides clashed in the street. Police accompanying the marchers found themselves in the middle of a bloody battle. Sergeant Daniel McKay was hit in the face by a pickaxe handle when one Billy Boy's cry of 'God Save the King' provoked a flurry of blows. Another officer had his fingers broken when he tried to stave off a strike at his face. Arrests were made and fines duly paid, some from gang funds, swollen from the levy on members, but mostly from a collection among local shopkeepers who knew better than to decline to pay up on demand.

The Billy Boys regularly returned the compliment by invading the Conks' territory. They had their own flute band, known for swaggering into Norman Street on saints' days. Naturally, the presence of the Orange-sashed musicians playing martial sectarian tunes provoked outrage among the Conks, who showed their displeasure in the time-honoured fashion. Bottles and stones were fired from windows while men steamed into the lines, their pickaxe handles striking out a less regular beat than the Billy Boys' drums.

It was precisely this behaviour that Percy Sillitoe addressed, the achievement for which he is best known in Glasgow. He recognised that appealing to the men's better nature was useless, for many of them did not have one. He understood that arrest and fine, or even imprisonment, was not a sufficient threat to divert them from their violent ways. He adopted the approach that had served him well in Sheffield: law and order would be upheld by the boot and the baton. Justice was swift, it was tough and it was often bloody. He selected the biggest and the hardest of his men and gave them a simple order. As one officer later put it, they were to go out and 'batter the living shite out of every ned who scratched his balls without permission'. As a police technique, it perhaps leaves something to be desired, upholding the law by breaking the law, but it was certainly effective, although not perhaps quite as effective as Glasgow legend, and Sir Percy himself, would have us believe. According to legend, the batter squads became known as 'the Untouchables', after the gang-busting team formed by Elliot Ness to bring down Al Capone. Like the Chicago outfit, the Glasgow men became the stuff of legend and their exploits, and effectiveness, exaggerated. In fact, it was Sillitoe's intelligence-gathering techniques that proved particularly successful. Heavy sentences dished out by the courts also played a major role in dampening the gangs' volatility.

They came down on the Billy Boys and the Norman Conks like a ton of bricks. Whenever the two sides engaged in a rammy, Sillitoe's Untouchables waited until most of the juice and ginger was out of them and then piled in mob-handed to mete out their own particular brand of justice on the last men standing. One legend has it that on one occasion a Billy Boy musician, Elijah Cooper, escaped a beating and incarceration by hiding in his huge bass drum until the trouble had passed. Each time gang conflict flared up, the police were there.

Fullerton was finally arrested when he took a drunken poke at a police sergeant who was not prepared to take any nonsense. The sergeant drew his baton and gave Fullerton a few punishing taps before hauling him away. The gang leader was sent down for 12 months.

Sillitoe liked to think that he and his techniques quashed Glasgow's gang fever for good. Of course, that wasn't the case. Many of the gangsters went away to fight in the Second World War, including Williamson and, perhaps surprisingly, Fullerton, who had been one of Oswald Mosley's Blackshirts. Many of them served well, their natural aggression and love of a scrap finding some focus and purpose in the military. When they returned, Williamson forsook his street-fighting ways for mainstream crime, while Fullerton seems to have settled down and gone straight. He went to work in a shipyard and died in 1962. His coffin was followed from Bridgeton Cross to Riddrie Cemetery by 600 to 1,000 people. Orange flute bands played his beloved sectarian tunes, as well as 'Onward Christian Soldiers'. His bigoted Billy Boys live on in a song that can still occasionally be heard on football terraces where fans refuse to let go of the city's sectarian past:

> Hello, hello, we are the Billy Boys.
> Hello, hello, you'll know us by our noise.
> We're up to our knees in Fenian blood,
> Surrender or you'll die,
> For we are the Brigton Billy Boys.

The gangs did not surrender nor did they die. Sillitoe's methods did have an effect but failed to stamp them out. Young men still banded together in groups and sought out violence. The older men gravitated towards mainstream crime and more violence. Steel still glittered in the night and blood flowed into the gutters from opened faces and sliced flesh. The law of the boot and the blade remains in force today.

* * *

Sillitoe did more for the city than crack down on the gangs. He streamlined the force, partly because the authorities required cuts in expenditure but also because he recognised that it had become a somewhat unwieldy and inefficient behemoth. It was the second-largest force in the nation but it was collaring too few criminals. Detection rates were down and officers were performing too many menial duties, becoming almost like the watchmen of old. He wanted to see the number of city divisions reduced and the number of police stations cut. In their place, there would be more police boxes, 323 in all, plus 10 telegraph pillars. Each box was, he said, like a miniature police station. Not only was there a telephone behind a grille allowing the public to contact divisional HQ, there was enough space for a beat officer to write up reports, conduct interviews and even hold a prisoner for a limited period of time. He could also pause there and eat his sandwiches. The number of senior officers was reduced – many were older officers who had qualified for their pension – and the CID was transformed. More policewomen were taken on and the promotion system was cleared of the nepotism with which it was riddled. A fingerprint and photographic department was formed – Detective Sergeant Bertie Hammond being transferred from Sheffield to take charge – and a new system of mobile radio cars introduced.

Sillitoe became convinced of the necessity of these newfangled patrol cars after meeting FBI chief J. Edgar Hoover in Chicago in 1933. Sillitoe used the New York radio patrol cars as a template for his Glasgow scheme, which many home-grown politicians and ranking police officers insisted was unworkable. He bought a radio unit in New York for $15 and brought it back with him. He showed the naysayers that it was indeed possible and saw to it that Glasgow became the first British force to have equipment in vehicles that could transmit both Morse code and speech. The vans housing the equipment were called 'Q Vans', and later the intelligence-gathering squads using the new technology became known as the 'C Specials'. These became very handy in the fight against the gangs, enabling the police more efficiently to pinpoint trouble spots.

It was Sillitoe who introduced the black-and-white checked band for his officer's peaked caps. This made them more easily identifiable at night and the pattern, later adopted across the country, became known as 'Sillitoe Tartan'. He reduced the number of police officers on traffic duty, helping to usher in traffic lights at busy intersections, and cracked down on licensing laws, drink being seen as the cause of much of the city's lawlessness.

His work brought him into conflict with many of Glasgow's councillors and bailies. It was a dishonourable tradition in local government that a contract could be awarded for a financial consideration, or a promotion gained in the ever-increasing council industry in return for a backhander. The nod-and-wink school of government was endemic in the grand corridors of the City Chambers. Such corrupt working practices were to be the chief constable's next target.

His seeming crusade to root out graft in Glasgow Corporation began in 1933 when a female market trader told one of his detectives that she had been offered a better spot for her stall if she paid £25 to one of the bailies sitting on the City Markets Committee. Such practices were well entrenched in Glasgow, and no doubt in every city in Britain, but Sillitoe was determined to eradicate them. Marked bills were given to the woman and a meeting arranged in a city-centre café, during which two men were arrested. One was subsequently convicted but the other was acquitted. A third man was tipped off about the police involvement and kept well away. The incident prompted the Secretary of State for Scotland to order a public inquiry into civic government but it fizzled out as witnesses declined to come forward to give evidence. The suggestion was that threats had been made to keep them away from the committee. So sleaze still existed in the city council, and the issue came raging back eight years later, when the war was in full swing.

It began in 1941 when Sillitoe formally objected to the renewal of a liquor licence for the Beresford Hotel. There had been what he called 'a minor infringement of the licensing laws' – alcohol had been sold to persons who were not guests – but it was enough for him to oppose the renewal. The managing director of the hotel was Councillor Hugh Fraser, and while he might not have taken too kindly to the chief constable of a force under the control of his council interfering in his business affairs, he was outraged when Bailie Hugh Campbell, who was on the Licensing Committee, suggested that the whole thing could be smoothed over if Fraser was willing to 'see the boys right'. He had friends on the committee and for a consideration of £120 they could ease the renewal through. The boys, it seems, were looking forward to what Campbell called 'the happy hunting ground at the April Licensing Court', which suggests that more than one bung was in the offing. Councillor Fraser kept his outrage to himself and listened politely, then went straight to the police. This was not the first time he'd been approached in such a manner and he had decided that this time something should be done.

Two detectives, Ewing and McIlwrick, gathered the sum required in marked £5 and £20 notes and a meeting was arranged between Fraser and the corrupt bailie at the hotel. Fraser's office was bugged and the two officers stationed themselves in the room directly above. Then, Murphy's law kicked in: the listening equipment developed a glitch. Campbell was due to arrive for the meeting at any minute and a technician was called to pull the gear apart and find the fault. The boffin fiddled with the equipment but could not make it work – and they had run out of time.

Then someone had a brainwave. Fraser had an intercom system on his desk and if they left it on and linked a telephone extension to it, the police officers could listen in upstairs. Disaster averted, Ewing and McIlwrick settled down again to await the arrival of their target. Their troubles were far from over. When Bailie Campbell arrived, he asked to be taken to Mr Fraser's room. The porter made a mistake and led him to the Frazer Room – the very room in which the two officers were sitting surrounded by listening gear. Campbell took fright and decided to make himself scarce. Fraser intercepted him in the foyer and tried to assure him that there was nothing sinister in what he'd seen, that it was merely workmen trying to repair the telephone system. But Campbell was no fool; he sensed something was not right and he told Fraser so. However, his greed outweighed his concerns and he agreed to talk to Fraser in his car, where he took possession of the £120. Then the air-raid siren sounded and he drove off, leaving Fraser to scuttle back into the hotel to tell the detectives that the bait had been taken.

Police obtained a warrant to search Campbell's house, even though they did not really expect him to be so stupid as to hide the money there. However, it never pays to overestimate the intelligence of a greedy man, and they found the marked bills stashed in a bedroom chimney. Campbell was arrested, stood trial and was sentenced to six months for receiving cash in return for using his influence to renew the hotel licence. Hugh Campbell was not a hardened criminal, although he was a crook, and life inside was not kind to him. The money, he insisted, had not been for him; he was merely an intermediary. Sillitoe and his men already knew that there was not just one bad apple in the council barrel and they interviewed him in jail to enlist his aid in reaching the core of the corruption. Eventually, he burst and provided them with enough dirt to build cases against three other local politicians: round-faced Thomas Wilson, who sat on the housing, public assistance and transport committees; defender of the working man and champion of justice Joseph Taylor; and Alex Ritchie, who had been found not guilty in the 1933 case.

Campbell told them that in 1939 he had been a member of the council's Gas Committee, which was to award a contract for the reconstruction of the Provan Gasworks. In the course of their research, he and other councillors travelled to Portsmouth to view similar works constructed by a company in the running. During the visit, Campbell claimed, Councillor Alex Ritchie said to him, 'Here we are, walking round with an order of a quarter of a million in our pockets and there seems to be nothing doing.' The inference Campbell took from that was that Ritchie and others were looking for a backhander from the company in question. Campbell was no fresh-faced young newcomer. Although only in his late 30s at the time, he had been in local government for 20 years and could tell a nod from a wink. He knew his colleagues had their hands in the till but had done very little about it, despite his claim that he had gone into local politics in order to help clean it up. That idealistic stance changed and, in his own words, he 'fell from grace'.

Campbell was the man nominated to drop a quiet word in the company chairman's ear that the councillors would 'require to be squared'. The figure of £2,000 was mentioned, to be shared between Campbell, Ritchie, Taylor and Wilson. 'Old Tom' Wilson as he was known, was to receive only £200, as he was drawing his pension. At first, the chairman wanted nothing to do with the matter, but business was business and later he gave Campbell a down payment of £100, on the understanding that more would follow.

In court, Campbell defended his decision to blow the whistle by saying that he had to clear his conscience. 'It took my arrest to bring me to my senses,' he said. 'I received my just deserts and have no ill will towards anyone connected with my case. I wish to clear up the mess of corruption I know exists in Glasgow Corporation.'

The graft ring was not yet complete, however. The fifth member of the grasping crew was not revealed until a public baths attendant said that he had been told that he would be promoted – as long as he paid £30 to none other than Bailie Robert Young Gemmell, who in addition to being on the committee that controlled the city's public baths was convenor of the Police and Fire Committee, and therefore Sillitoe's boss in some respects. On 21 August 1941, Gemmell was sentenced to twelve months and disqualified from holding any kind of public office for five years.

The following month, Old Tom Wilson, fiery Joe Taylor and slippery Alex Ritchie appeared on charges of receiving a total of £225 from the gas company. Wilson was jailed for fifteen months, the other two for eighteen months each. In addition, they were all disqualified from local politics for seven years. A minor official, Neil Shaw, was sentenced to six months for receiving ten pounds for using his influence as a member of the Licensing Committee.

Sillitoe was told by the Right Honourable Tom Johnston, Secretary of State for Scotland, that if any more officials were caught with their snouts in the trough, the Government would dissolve the Corporation and put a commissioner in its place. No further dirty councillors were found, and Sillitoe was knighted in the New Year honours list of 1942, the first Glasgow chief constable to be so honoured.

In February 1943, he resigned to head up the new Kent constabulary, formed out of nine local forces. He later became chief of MI5, taking up the post just as the Cold War was at its frostiest and Britain was about to become embroiled in one spy scandal after another. He spent seven years with the spooks and mandarins of Whitehall and became the first security chief to write his memoirs. After he left the security service, he returned to Africa at the request of diamond company De Beers to staunch the flow of gems being smuggled out of South African mines. His methods were characteristically blunt, and it has been suggested that the notorious Bureau of State Security (BOSS), the brutal secret weapon of the apartheid state, had its origins in a security network he set up later. Sillitoe died in 1962, the same year as Billy Fullerton.

CHAPTER THIRTEEN

THE HARD MAN AND
THE PETERMAN

The outbreak of the Second World War caused much the same
kind of problems as had been presented by the start of the Great
War. Glasgow police officers volunteered or were called up, leaving
the force considerably depleted. In addition, there was a new threat
– air raids. It was believed that the blackouts would be a godsend
for the night stalkers and skulduggers of the city, while the lighting
restrictions themselves would require to be enforced. That duty fell to
Superintendent James A. Robertson, later to become chief constable,
who headed up the new Air Raids Precautions (ARP) service. To
help bolster the depleted force, Sillitoe established the First War
Reserve, 350 ex-officers who were fit enough to return to active duty
on the city streets. He followed that with the 770-strong Police War
Reserve, made up of men who elected to police the streets of home
rather than fight abroad, and the Women's Auxiliary Police Corps,
220 female officers who would take their place behind the wheel,
on the radio and behind canteen counters. In addition, almost 2,000
special constables were to patrol two nights a week each and car owners
volunteered to be on call every night to help respond to crime. While

the armed forces took on evil abroad, Glasgow Police continued to tackle the everyday menaces of burglary, rape, theft and murder. They also had to guard the city's infrastructure against attacks by saboteurs, so they were issued with firearms and stood watch at power stations, gas plants and docks.

The feared onslaught of enemy paratroopers did not materialise, but the air raids did, although Glasgow suffered far less than other cities. A daylight raid in July 1940 saw German bombers over the city for the first time; then, in September, the city centre, in particular George Square, was targeted, with little damage resulting. A cruiser docked at Yorkhill was hit and burst into flames, the threat of exploding ammunition prompting the evacuation of the immediate area, including the Royal Hospital for Sick Children. On 13 March 1941, the shriek of sirens marked the beginning of the first devastating onslaught. First the East End, then the centre and finally Clydebank were pummelled by the heavy bombardment. Over the next three nights, the Luftwaffe bludgeoned Clydebank, killing 1,083 people and seriously injuring 1,602. Among the dead were ten officers of the Glasgow Police and the War Department Constabulary. Three died while guarding the Dalmuir ordnance factory. Further raids on Clydeside, in April and May, killed another 400 people and injured a similar number. Police and civilians collaborated in digging the dead and the wounded from under the rubble of ruined tenements and houses. In Clydebank, wrote Charles Oakley, only seven houses were left undamaged. Officers who performed well under these trying conditions were rewarded with medals of honour.

Afterwards, figures revealed that of the 339 Glasgow police officers who had served in the armed forces, 30 had been killed and 10 rewarded for bravery. Criminals had also served their country, but no one knows how many died or whose gallantry was recognised. No one keeps those figures.

Peace, of a kind, broke out across the world in 1945. And back in Glasgow, it was business as usual, for one of the first big cases to hit the headlines marked the resurgence of an old problem: street gangs. This time, though, it was not just a case of brawling. This time, it was big boy's stuff. This time, it was murder.

John Brady was only 19 years old when he died. Home from navy service, he had been at a dance in the City Halls in Candleriggs on 20 October 1945 when he walked into trouble as he made his way home. A gang from the South Side, including John Lyon, Alexander Crosbie, his brother Hugh and John Lennie, had crossed the river to Washington Street in Anderston in search of trouble. They were looking for a rival team, known as the Dougie Boys because they hung about on the corner of Douglas Street and Argyle Street. Local youth Joseph Smyth heard the interlopers shout, 'Where are the Dougie Boys?' as they swaggered across the road towards him. When one of them pulled a bayonet from inside his jacket, Smyth decided he had to 'blow'. He tried and failed to jump onto a tram, then a scream from a bystander made him turn around and the sight of one of the gang behind him spurred him to greater speed. He did not want to be 'done up', he said later. However, the thugs pursued him into Brown Street, where he heard one snarl, 'Give him the message.' He knew then he was in for a kicking.

The trouble was only beginning. One Dougie Boy later heard that the Crosbies were in the area looking for a fight. He said that 'a wee burd' had whispered it to him, so he went along to see what was going on. He saw one of the other team stepping forward waving a bayonet and shouting, 'Here's your man.' The witness grabbed a blade from someone else and took up the challenge, shouting back, 'Here's your man.' Another youth then ran past, swinging a bayonet and at the cry of 'Wire in!' all hell broke loose. The gangster who'd run past said to the witness, 'If you're game enough, you and I are for it.'

Later, the Dougie Boy picked out two or three young men in a police ID parade because he'd seen them before. He insisted he could not identify anyone as being present that night because he'd only seen the backs of their heads. This led to an unusual attempt at identification in court when the four accused were ordered to stand and turn away from the witness box. The witness still could not identify them.

John Brady stepped off the tram from the city centre at around 10.30 p.m., along with his sister, his father and a girl. They found his mother in the street, worried about her other son, Joseph, who was a member of the Iona Boys, yet another street gang. She was worried that he had become embroiled in the warfare. John told her to go home and that he would bring Joseph back. He wandered into the thick of the fighting and was stabbed to death. In the words of the charge, he was 'cut and stabbed repeatedly on the body, head and face with bayonets or similar weapons'.

The Crosbie brothers, Lyon and Lennie were all arrested and appeared in court on the murder charge and assault charges. They each lodged special defences of alibi – producing witnesses who testified that they were nowhere near Anderston on the night of the murder – but the jury did not believe them. The case excited huge interest, not just because it was a throwback to the heady days of gang warfare in the 1930s but also because Alexander Crosbie was under 18. If he was found guilty, he could not be sentenced to death, as he had not yet reached his majority. However, he was due to turn 18 on Saturday, 15 December – and that was the very day on which the jury found him guilty, freeing the judge to pronounce the death sentence. As he was led away, the cocky youth waved to the court and shouted, 'Happy New Year!' John Lyon and John Lennie were also found guilty and sentenced to die. Hugh Crosbie was given a not proven verdict for the murder but sentenced to three years for the assault on Smyth.

Their appeals were heard and dismissed, and efforts were then made to have their sentences reduced to life in prison. For Lennie and Crosbie, those efforts were successful; four days before they were due to die, their sentences were commuted. That left only 21-year-old John Lyon to face the noose. His family and 20-year-old wife did what they could to generate public support for him. A petition was raised and garnered thousands of signatures. His brother Robert threw himself into the effort on his return from military service in the Middle East. He sent a telegram to the King on John's behalf, begging for mercy. On Wednesday, 7 February 1946, his young wife sent an emotional letter by express post to Buckingham Palace, pleading with the King to intercede. However, there was to be no respite for John Lyon, and he became the first man to hang in Barlinnie Prison. On Friday, 9 February, at 8 a.m., he was led out of the condemned cell and walked the few paces into the area known as 'the hanging shed'. He said nothing as they pulled the hood over his head and placed the noose around his neck. The rope ran off into a hole in the ceiling and safety wires were attached to harnesses worn by the two warders who accompanied him. The trapdoor sprung and his body plummeted through.

Outside the dark walls of the Victorian jail, a crowd of about 30 people waited for news. They were kept 100 yards or so away from the main gate, down a small hill. Among them was a man with a black greyhound on a lead and a number of women. At around 8.15 a.m., the small doorway set into the larger gate swung open and two prison officers came out to tack a typewritten notice onto the door. The crowd were allowed to come closer then and an old woman sobbed, 'It's his young wife who's left.' Then they melted away into the misty February morning.

The night before, John Lyon had had a final visit from his family, during which he handed them a piece of prison notepaper on which were his final words: 'Everything is all right. Don't worry yourselves. I don't want you to hold a grudge against the Secretary of State for Scotland, Mr Westwood. He is just doing his job and it just happens to be me.' There was nothing about being sorry for having been part of a group that had taken the life of a young man.

John Lyon's claim to infamy is as the first man to be put to death in Barlinnie. Patrick Carraher's is that he beat one murder rap before he was hanged for another.

The Celts love a good scrap, but inferiority complexes and the accessibility of liquor are also at the back of the myth of the Glasgow hard man. Even in 1889, the city had a fearsome reputation thanks to alcohol and the fighting mentality of some of its citizens. One observer, Sir John Hammerton, quoted in Charles Oakley's *The Second City*, wrote:

> Glasgow was probably the most drink-sodden city in Great Britain. Many of the younger generation thought it manly to get 'paralytic' and 'dead to the world' . . . there were drunken brawls at every corner and a high proportion of passers-by were reeling drunk. At the corners of the darker streets the reek of vomit befouled the evening air, never very salubrious. Jollity was everywhere absent: sheer loathsome, swinish inebriation prevailed.

Hard-drinking, hard-living and ready, willing and able to take on all comers with fist or boot, the Glasgow hard man became notorious throughout the world. Examples of the type could be seen on street corners and in pubs in all parts of the city. Often small men, their faces scarred with memories of previous encounters, they could be taciturn or garrulous, likeable or despicable, affectionate or cold. The most dangerous were the silent ones who seemed peaceful but inside whom a demon lurked. Many were drunks who would round off a night's carousing and brawling with a spot of wife-beating and child abuse. Others were hard-working family men who liked nothing better than to celebrate the end of the week by getting bevvied in the local pub or shebeen and then indulging in a 'square go'.

Others, the chib men, disdained their fists in favour of something more lethal: the blade. Patrick Carraher was such a man, an alcoholic with a persecution complex, a thug who rejected the gang life for the way of the loner. His criminal record was lacerated by acts of violence – assaults, robberies, batterings, slashings, hackings. He was good with a blade and he used one often, developing a reputation as 'a fast draw', pulling his weapon free in the blink of an eye and sending it out in a bloody, painful arc. He had few friends but was insanely loyal to those he had. That loyalty eventually led him to the gallows.

As far as is known, he killed his first man in August 1938. Carraher, drunken, staggering, but still dangerous, became involved in an unseemly tug of war over a woman in a Gorbals street. He had wanted information about another woman he had been seeing but this girl refused to give it to him. Her boyfriend, 19-year-old window cleaner James Durie, took exception to him manhandling his date and fought back. Carraher did what Carraher was good at – he pulled a knife. Durie ran off but returned later with his brothers, catching up with Carraher in Ballater Street. The young man, ashamed that he had lost face by running away, threw down the gauntlet of a square go. Carraher declined to pick up the gage, saying he was in no condition to fight.

Things might have ended there with a promise of further action at a later date had not James Sydney Shaw come by. The 23-year-old soldier was also somewhat the worse for drink and joined in the general name-calling. Carraher told him to back off and Shaw derided him for 'speaking like an Englishman'. A policeman happened by then and broke the tumult up. As the Durie clan went to go, they heard a scuffle. When they turned around, Carraher was gone and Shaw was swaying in the lamplight, his hand to his neck, blood streaming through his fingers. He staggered to the corner of Thistle Street, where he collapsed, then hauled himself up and stumbled to Gorbals Cross. Finally, he slumped to the ground outside a cinema. A policeman reached him and tried to stem the blood pumping steadily from his throat, but the young man died soon after being admitted to the Royal Infirmary. Peter Howard, who had been with the Durie boys, was arrested for the murder. He had been spotted by police in the area and was the only person who had tried to help the stricken man, leaving him with blood on his clothes.

Carraher, his sense of honour rising to the surface, resolved to hand himself in for the killing. 'I'll not let Peter Howard swing for it,' he said bravely. However, that sense of honour sank like the knife that he threw into the Clyde. He didn't give himself up, but Howard was freed by the police, who were satisfied that he had not struck the fatal blow. Carraher's name was carried in the wind as that of the real culprit and he was arrested in his Florence Street flat by Detective Sergeant John Johnstone. However, with no one able to say that Carraher had beyond a shadow of doubt stabbed the victim, and his drunken state suggesting that any act was done with recklessness rather than malice, the jury found him guilty of culpable homicide rather than murder. He was sentenced to three years in Barlinnie.

The war came and many of Carraher's contemporaries went off to expend their violent energies against the various enemies. Carraher, on being released, was deemed unfit for service thanks to a chronic stomach complaint and a weak chest. However, his stabbing arm was still as fit as a fiddle, and he lost little time in proving it. Along with Daniel Bonnar, the brother of his latest flame, Sarah, he was soon up to his old tricks and in February 1943, he was given another three years for assault.

On the streets again in 1945, he came to the aid of Bonnar, who had had a run-in with a group of brothers called Gordon. The encounter had not ended well for Bonnar, who decided to exercise the better part of valour and took to his heels. Word reached Carraher, who was swilling drink at a party, and he set out to help his pal. Bonnar, meanwhile, had rediscovered his courage and had sallied forth again to find the Gordons. This time, he had an axe in his hand and, curiously, had pulled on a woman's jacket to keep out the November cold. Carraher, having decided that a woodcarver's chisel was 'the very tool for them', met him as he hunted for his quarry. At the intersection of McAslin and Taylor streets, they found John Howard Gordon and Duncan Revie. Gordon, like his brothers, was a bonny fighter but no criminal. He was on demob leave after serving for 20 years with the Seaforth Highlanders. Revie was a deserter on the run.

Revie closed with Bonnar, who turned and ran again. His opponent took after him, leaving Carraher and Gordon to slug it out. Carraher, though, was not likely to have a square go with anyone, and it was not long before Gordon slumped to the ground, his neck punctured by the chisel that had appeared like magic in Carraher's hand. The soldier, like the previous victim, died in the Royal Infirmary. The knife-man melted into the night, but this time he had been seen delivering the death blow. Knowing he was being hunted, Carraher forced a man to dispose of the murder weapon by breaking the wooden tool in half and slipping it down separate drains in the High Street. In the early hours of the following morning, John Johnstone, now a detective inspector, lifted Carraher for the second time on a murder charge. This time, it was to stick. There were witnesses; even his pal Daniel Bonnar would turn against him. The man the press called 'the Fiend of the Gorbals' was to hang. On 6 April 1946, he became the second victim of Barlinnie's hanging shed.

Only Sarah Bonnar cried.

* * *

Not every Gorbals criminal was a thug who thrived on violence. Scotland had a name for turning out safe-blowers, known in the underworld as 'petermen', who travelled the country opening safes and depleting the coffers of banks, post offices and insurance firms – anywhere there was cash. They did not crack safes – the use of stethoscopes and the painstaking efforts to hear the tumblers fall are largely fiction – they blew them. Robert Colquhoun described these experts as 'commonplace in Glasgow', continuing:

> In fact, if I was asked to name the type of specialist criminal most often produced by the city, I would plump for the safe-blower. There's a strong suggestion that a school for safe-blowers, where novices can learn their trade from experts, has more than once been organised in the city.

The best-known Glasgow-based peterman was Johnny Ramensky, whose life and exploits are the stuff of legend.

He was born Yonas Ramanauckas in Glenboig, Coatbridge, in 1905, four years after his father and other miners were shipped in from Lithuania to help break a strike at a local fire-clay pit. The future peterman first came to the Gorbals at the age of ten after his father had died and his mother had lost an arm in an accident. There, his unwieldy Lithuanian name simplified to John Ramensky, or Ramsay, he took the usual route to a life of crime: petty misdemeanours leading to borstal and finally, aged 19, the big house for theft. He was a sturdy, agile, likeable sort of bloke. Good looking in a James Cagney kind of way, he had an unassuming nature that made him popular with men and women alike. Although he had done time for a minor assault, he was not aggressive. He could handle himself when it came to it – life in the Gorbals streets as a young tearaway did teach him a few things – but his subsequent career was marked by an aversion to violence. Over the years, he became known as 'Gentle Johnny' by crooks and public alike. Forensic expert Sir Sydney Smith, who gave evidence against him more than once, said that 'even the police, with whom he had waged war since boyhood, regarded him with some respect and even affection'.

He married in 1931, under the name Ramsay, and for the sake of his young wife, Margaret 'Daisy' McManus, he tried to go straight. But by that time, criminality was too deeply ingrained in him, and in 1934 he and his brother-in-law blew the safe of an Aberdeen bakery. It is said that he cut his explosives teeth during a spell down the mines and learned his trade from another criminal legend, James Muirhead, known in peterman circles as 'Scotch Jimmy'. It took great skill to blow a safe properly. Too little gelignite and the safe would not yield its goodies; too much, and the safe and its contents could go up in smoke. The most common way was to fix the gelignite over the keyhole with putty, attach a detonator and fuse, then cover everything with cushions and other materials to soften the noise. If the peterman did his job right, the lock would be blown and the safe swing open. If too much explosive was used, the ballast from the safe, partly made up of sawdust, would go everywhere.

The bakery job was smartly pulled off but the bad luck, or sloppy planning, that dogged Ramensky's career saw the two men being nabbed at Perth railway station as they tried to return to Glasgow. They had left a piece of a ten-shilling note at the scene of the crime and a fragment found in Johnny's pocket matched. Sawdust was also found in the turn-ups of his trousers, while his partner in crime had managed to leave a heel print at the scene. Johnny gallantly claimed he had led his brother-in-law into a life of crime, admitted his own involvement and was thanked for his honesty by being sentenced to five years in the forbidding hell that was Peterhead Prison.

It was here that the legend of Johnny Ramensky began to take shape, when he staged the first in a series of jailbreaks. They say he did it because the authorities refused him leave to attend his wife's funeral, but that may not be the case. Perhaps it was merely an insatiable desire for freedom that forced him to do it. Whatever the reason, he picked a lock, climbed a high gate clad only in his underwear, dropped to the other side of the wall, swam a freezing river – and was caught having managed to travel only a few miles.

His wife's death freed him from his promise to go straight and when he got out he resumed his old ways, blowing safes up and down the country. In 1938, he was caught again, this time for robbing an Aberdeen laundry, and he found himself back in Peterhead. It was during this five-year stretch that he was approached by the War Office with an unusual request. Britain had need of his special skills to help them break the safes of the Third Reich. However, he had to complete his sentence first. Once released, an army jeep picked him up and took him off for training. It is possible that the tale of Johnny's wartime career grew in the telling. It is possible that he merely trained special-forces soldiers in the skills needed. However, the legend has it that Johnny himself underwent commando training and was parachuted behind enemy lines to open the safes of top Nazi officials, including Hermann Göring.

His patriotic duty done, on his return to civvy street he went back to his old ways. Naturally, his luck being what it was, he was caught and imprisoned. Another Peterhead stretch saw him escape again in 1952, his memoirs tucked under his shirt. He wanted to get them published but the authorities were having none of it. He was at large for a day and a half before he was caught at roughly the same spot as before.

In 1955, he was married a second time, to a woman named Lilly Mulholland. However, he was soon back in the arms of the law and in court, this time facing Lord Carmont, said to have been an indifferent lawyer but by then one of the toughest judges on the bench. In the 1950s, he waged war on the lawbreakers of Glasgow, his stiff penalties giving rise to the phrase 'copping a Carmont'. Ramensky, caught red-handed on the roof of a garage, was seen by him as a menace to society and sent to prison for ten years. The public was by this time very much on the veteran crook's side, encouraged no doubt by his almost quixotic escape attempts, of which he made three during that sentence alone. Two songs were penned about him, one, 'Let Ramensky Go', by the actor Roddy McMillan, the other 'The Ballad of Johnny Ramensky' by the Labour MP Norman Buchan. He even featured in a series of supposedly self-penned articles in the *Evening Times* detailing his daring escapes.

By the early 1960s, he was wearying of his life. He always kept himself fit but the only honest work he could get was digging roads. The straight life was not exciting or rewarding enough for him and he returned to crime – and to jail. In 1964, he blew the safe of Woolworths in Paisley, and every window in the shop along with it. Naturally, this drew the attention of the police, and he was arrested again. This time, he got two years. In 1967, he botched another caper. Aged 62, he decided to blow the safe of a Rutherglen bank. However, again, he used too much gelignite and the resulting blast was heard as far away as Bridgeton Cross. Two uniformed cops chased him as he lugged a bag of half-crowns, all he could grab, across a rooftop. On being caught, one of the officers claimed, Ramensky tried to resist arrest by punching him in the face. Johnny, as usual, admitted blowing the safe, but he denied the assault charge. For once, his reputation went in his favour, for the charge was dropped, although he was still sent down for four years for the robbery.

In 1970, he tried to break into a Stirling office. However, he was not the man he once was and he fell. After being hospitalised for fourteen weeks, he was sent away for two years. Then, in 1972, came his last job. He was caught on the roof of a shop in Ayr, without any swag. Sentenced to another year inside, he died in Perth Prison that year.

The Glasgow criminal world has precious few heroes. The man known variously as Yonas Ramanauckas, John Ramsay and Johnny Ramensky stands head and shoulders above all others. 'Gentle Johnny' might not have been as successful a crook as his legend would suggest – his prison sentences prove that he was not – while his wartime record may have been exaggerated. But he was that rarity: a good crook admired by all. Perhaps the judges and lawyers who opined that, with his abilities, he could have earned a living in some other way were right (to Sir Sydney Smith, his criminality was 'a pity, for he seemed essentially a good fellow'), but if he had, we would have been deprived of a real character.

CHAPTER FOURTEEN

TRIGGER HAPPY

The expected wartime crime wave failed to materialise, but when hostilities ceased it was a different matter. The country was awash with refugees and military personnel from the Continent. Then there were the Allied soldiers, sailors and airmen. And some of the demobbed boys returning home still had some pent-up aggression that needed to be expended. Additionally, many crooks had gone off to do their patriotic duty, like Ramensky and Fullerton, but now those who had not deserted were ready to get back into criminal harness.

With police leave cancelled all over the country to help combat this fresh tide of lawlessness, the main headache was the increasing use of firearms. Even the city of the blade and the boot was not immune to this new menace, as pistols and rifles slipped out of kitbags and onto the underworld market. It was weapons such as these that ended up in the fists of two deranged killers.

* * *

It was 15 days before Christmas 1945 that death came to Pollokshields East station. Thick, greasy fog filled the streets, clogging the light and sliding down throats. Somewhere, street musicians could be heard playing Christmas carols, the joyful notes muffled and flattened by the yellow vapour. In the station, down a steep flight of steps from the main road, porter and clerk William Wright, clerkess Annie Withers and porter Robert Gough huddled around a coal fire, chatting happily. It was Gough who saw it first, just the merest hint of a face at the soot-encrusted window, and then it was gone. Then the door burst open and the man stood there, wrapped in a light linen coat, a soft hat low over his eyes, a wispy suggestion of ginger or fair hair between the rim and the coat collar, a pale face staring at them. But it was the gun that commanded the most attention.

'This is a hold-up,' was all he said before he started firing. Annie rose involuntarily to her feet, a scream building in her throat when he pulled the trigger. The bullet punched through her left arm and buried itself in her left thigh. Then the gun swivelled towards the men, the muzzle coughing bullets. One sliced through Robert Gough's right arm and ended up in his abdomen, another grazed William Wright's side. As he fell, the clerk could still hear the woman screaming as she lay on the floor. But the screams stopped when the gunman stood over her and calmly shot her twice more. The first bullet caught her on the chest and exploded out of her left armpit, the second erupted through her stomach and blew a hole in her back.

The man rifled the station's drawers looking for cash before he ran off into the fog-filled night. All he got was a packet containing a signalman's wage. Then William Wright heard a train puffing into the station. He staggered out to tell the guard that there had been a shooting but the man thought it was a joke and signalled the train to pull out. In the gloom, he didn't see the blood at Wright's side, or the shape of Robert Gough lying on the platform where he had dragged himself. The clerk raised the alarm by phone, and ambulances and police were swiftly on the scene. Miss Withers was still clinging on to life but it was too late for her. The 36-year-old woman died on her way to hospital. Robert Gough, only fifteen, died two days later. Their killer took their lives for four pounds.

No one had seen the gunman arrive or leave. Only William Wright was left to identify him if he was caught. And for ten months, he evaded capture, despite appeals in the press, despite a city-wide manhunt, despite the offer of a £1,000 reward by the *Sunday Express*. The hunt slid from the front pages and was relegated to inside columns. Finally, with nothing new to report, it vanished altogether.

Other crimes took up police time, other guns. In March 1946, a woman returned to her flat in Whitehall Street, Dennistoun, to find that someone had broken in by firing a bullet into the lock of the door. The following week, another woman surprised a man in her home in Golfhill Drive, also in Dennistoun, as he rifled through her jewellery. He pulled a revolver on her and got away. All she could tell police was that he was in his early 20s, about 5 ft 6 in., slim with a pale face and was wearing a grey overcoat, a white scarf and a cap. The only clues the police had were the bullet pulled from the door of the first house and a solitary partial fingerprint left at the second. However, within a day of the second break-in, the young burglar was about to graduate to the big time.

At around 8.30 p.m. on Tuesday, 26 March, James Deakan and his wife, Annie, were returning from the cinema when they noticed a light on at their house at 524 Edinburgh Road, High Carntyne. Mr Deakan, known as Lawrie, tried to turn his key in the lock but found it blocked, so while his wife went off to look for other help, he went next door to fetch his friend James Straiton, a former detective sergeant with the Glasgow Police. Now 58 and working for a furniture firm, Mr Straiton paused only to pull on his shoes and grab his baton before joining his neighbour at the rear of the house. There they found a scullery window lying open and Mr Deakan climbed in. The former cop went round to the front where he met Mr Deakan at the door.

'I think the birds have flown,' he said, just as two young men came running down the stairs. The man in front was older than his crony and was wearing a white scarf. He had a gun in each hand. A shot rang out, the bullet just missing Mr Deakan.

'Put down the guns,' ordered the former officer.

'If you don't get out of the way, I'll let you have it,' snarled the young man.

James Straiton did not think twice; he launched himself at the gunman, while Mr Deakan grabbed hold of his younger accomplice. During the struggle, the would-be gunsel was hit on the head with the heavy police baton but it did not fell him. He grunted once and sagged a bit but remained on his feet. He took a step back, levelled one of his guns, a .45 automatic, and fired again. Mr Straiton dropped his baton and stumbled back, shouting, 'Lawrie! Lawrie!' And then he died.

In court, Mr Deakan described the scene. 'He was staggering in the pathway and I caught him in the act of falling down heavily. I laid him down the best way I could and they ran out of the gate, where I heard another shot fired. My wife was calling me.'

Annie had just returned with a bus conductor whose bus she had stopped on the road. The two young thieves erupted from the garden and the older one yelled, 'Get out of the road or you'll get the same!' He fired another two shots, one narrowly missing Mrs Deakan and the other going into the ground. The crooks ran off down Edinburgh Road, the killer, with his white scarf, clearly visible. The bus driver tried to follow them in his vehicle. However, they gave him the slip by turning into a side street. As he had fled the garden, the killer had thrown away the second gun, a pistol belonging to Mr Deakan.

There were similarities between the Deakan break-in and the previous two in nearby Dennistoun, so police, using their recently established cross-referencing card system, pulled the records of all the young criminals who fitted the description provided by Mr Deakan and who had a similar MO. These could then be further cross-referenced with the partial print found at the second break-in. It was a laborious process in those days before computers, but it paid off. A sharp-eyed young detective constable spotted similarities between the thumbprint of a known felon and the partial print from the Golfhill Drive job. The print belonged to 20-year-old Bridgeton man, John Caldwell, an army deserter later described in court as 'well away from the normal'.

A prison doctor testified that he was 'an unusual sort of person in the nonchalant attitude he took with regard to his offences'. He went on to say that he was more likely to be rash in his actions than a normal person and to feel little or no remorse. 'He appreciated intellectually what he was doing, but he did not appreciate to the same extent emotionally. He was definitely below the moral standard.'

However, Dr Angus McNiven, of the Royal Mental Hospital, said that even though he did not believe that Caldwell was normal, the accused was responsible for his actions. There was, however, 'something very peculiar' in his attitude to his offences and their consequences.

His accomplice, a 15-year-old boy, was deemed 'mentally defective' and no action was taken against him after the initial charge. Caldwell, despite the best efforts of his defence team to show that he was psychologically disturbed, died on the Barlinnie rope on 10 August 1946.

Two days before, police investigating the Pollokshields East station shootings called at the South Side home of one Charles Templeman Brown. He was a railway fireman and they had received a tip-off that he was in illegal possession of a Luger pistol. He was not at home at the time and they left a message with his mother for him to get in touch with them. The next day, a police officer on points duty at Newlands Road in Cathcart was surprised when a fair-haired 20-year-old man approached him and confessed to the Pollokshields job. The man was Charles Templeman Brown and he had with him a 1918 Luger and a box with 13 rounds of ammunition. He'd tried to kill himself that morning when he learned that police had tracked him down. When charged, he said, 'I didn't mean to kill anyone but once you start shooting you can't stop.' However, a note found inside his book of railway regulations, meant for a friend, said, 'I am not sorry for anything I did, only for the things I did not do.'

Brown's fingerprints matched those found in the station. William Wright identified him as the killer; his was a face he would never forget. The gun Brown handed over was the same gun that had fired the deadly bullets. For the police and the prosecution, it seemed like a classic open-and-shut case. Surely Brown was destined for the hangman's noose. However, although the defence could not deny that he had pulled the trigger, they could use Brown's psychological make-up to avoid the ultimate penalty.

Lawyers had tried it in a limited way with John Caldwell, but Brown's team were determined to make a braver stab at it. Writer Bill Knox, then a young reporter, said that the technical terms spouted by the learned witnesses stretched journalists' shorthand to the limit. Only one, he said, a newly demobbed soldier by the name of Douglas Malone, managed to catch the full gist and was able to supply it to his press-room colleagues. 'But then,' Knox commented in his book *Court of Murder*, 'how many shorthand writers know the outlines for such terms as psychasthenia or dementia praecox?'

The defence maintained that their client was a hopeless dreamer, a young man so obsessed with Frank Sinatra that he dressed like him, travelling 500 miles to buy a jacket similar to one worn by the singer. He was also interested in Joseph Stalin and Adolf Hitler, suffered mood swings and would often remain silent for hours. Doctors argued that he was mentally unstable, suffering from a form of schizophrenia called incipient dementia praecox. However, they fell short of declaring him legally insane, and the jury found him guilty of murder. Brown sat unmoved as the judge, Lord Carmont, donned the black cap and sentenced him to death. However, there was mercy in the air for the double killer. Four days before he was due to die, Charles Templeman Brown was told that his sentence had been commuted to life.

He was released on licence in 1957 and found work as a travelling salesman. Three years later he had a third and final encounter with his date of destiny. He had committed his murders on 10 December 1945; his trial began on 10 December 1946. And on 10 December 1960, he was killed when his car left the A9 near Dunblane and smashed into a wall.

* * *

The increasing incidences of gunplay in the city did not mean that the more traditional blades, boots and bottles had been superseded. On Monday, 30 October 1950, Paul Christopher Harris was hanged in Barlinnie for the murder of Martin Dunleavy in the back court of a tenement in Neptune Street, Govan. The 38-year-old man had been battered with a bottle 'or similar instrument' and then kicked to death. The problems had begun in an Orkney Street pub, where a man had his face slashed with a broken glass, spread out to the house in Neptune Street, where allegations of wife-beating led to assault, and then ended with the death in the back court. Harris, his brother Claude and Walter Drennan were charged with assault and murder. Paul Harris, aged 28, and Drennan both claimed they had acted in self-defence. Drennan was found not guilty of killing Dunleavy, but the Harris brothers were both found guilty and sentenced to die. The court was satisfied that one or other of the men had inflicted the fatal blow. In the end, only Paul died, having taken the full guilt on his shoulders, allowing his 30-year-old brother to be reprieved.

It would not be long before guns blasted their way back into the headlines once again, with two crimes that left the city shocked. Both involved robbery, both involved young men, both are tragic in their own way.

* * *

Postmaster James Plenderleith knew the two men were trouble as soon as they walked into his Tollcross Road post office in the East End. Maybe it was the way they looked around the empty shop before approaching. Maybe it was the way they wore their wide-brimmed hats pulled down low, like gangsters in the pictures. His gut feeling was confirmed when he found himself staring the wrong way down a gun and one of the men snarled, 'Hold your tongue or I'll shoot.' The second man had stepped behind the counter and was wrenching the safe door open, thrusting money into his pockets. Then he ran out, making his escape in a taxi, leaving the gunman still holding Mr Plenderleith at bay. But not for long.

Bravely, the slightly built GPO employee launched himself at the 6-ft-tall raider, making a grab for the pistol. The robber grasped the fifty-two-year-old war veteran by the throat and the two of them struggled for possession of the weapon. The postmaster knew he was fighting for his life. Finally, Mr Plenderleith pushed the man away, but as he made a dash for the door he heard the gun go off and pain seared across his left leg. A passing postman rushed in and came face to face with the business end of the gun. He and the limping postmaster managed to dive out of the shop and hold the door closed with the aid of John Neilson, who worked in the grocer's next door. They had trapped the gunman inside and must have thought the worst of it was over. But the drama had only begun.

Evening Citizen reporter Archie McCulloch and photographer Jack Hill were heading out on a job when they drove straight into the middle of the commotion. It was Wednesday, 2 October 1952 and the 28-year-old photographer was on his first assignment for the newspaper, a routine photograph at Motherwell swimming pool. But he and McCulloch never got there. Jack was examining the camera he had been given, trying to get used to it before they reached their destination. As they were driving along London Road they saw a man rush out in front of them, aiming what looked like a gun through the windscreen. The reporter wrenched at the wheel, halting the car as a mean-looking crowd began to gather round the gunman, who was backing away from them, panic rising in his face.

They had held the gunman in the shop as long as they could. As Plenderleith and Neilson gripped the handle, they heard the furious robber swearing and banging at the door. Then the wood splintered around them as he blasted away at it with his gun. Across the road, a woman cried out in pain when a ricochet nicked her. Everyone ducked for cover as the young man burst out of the post office, gun held high. A passer-by threw a newspaper billboard at him, but he deflected it and kept moving. Someone shouted to the would-be hero that the guy had a gun.

'Fine time to tell me!' said the man. 'He might've blown my brains out!'

A street sweeper also tried to stop the fugitive, throwing his brush at him, tripping him up. But the fleeing villain jumped to his feet and continued running. A shouting crowd pounded after him, picking up whatever weapons they could find, chasing him into Maukinfauld Road . . . where he found his hostage.

Sixty-five-year-old Catherine Fleming had been shopping in London Road that afternoon and was waiting for a tram to take her to her Rattray Street home when she found herself in the centre of a real-life thriller. She saw the young man, wearing horn-rimmed glasses, running towards her but thought nothing of it, until he whirled round and grabbed her from behind, whispering in her ear, 'Save me, ma. Those men are after me. I have just drawn some money from the post office and they are out to get it.'

She could tell he was American by his accent. As he held her, Mrs Fleming could feel his body trembling. For all she knew, his story could have been true. But when the howling mob halted some distance away, she felt the barrel of a gun pressed into her back. And then the police arrived.

Constables Alfred McNiven and Bernard Watson were walking their beat when they heard about the hold-up. They went first to the post office, where witnesses filled in the details, pointing in the direction the chase had taken. The uniformed officers set off at a run, arriving at the scene just as the gunman took the old woman hostage. The man towered over the 5 ft 1 in. grandmother, who was still holding her shopping bag.

Jack Hill was trying to get the best possible pictures of the dramatic scene, moving as close as he could, armed only with an unreliable camera. The gunman saw him and snarled, 'Have you ever had a bullet in your guts?' The unarmed officers carefully moved closer, talking softly to the young American as he edged away, still using the woman as a shield. The cat-and-mouse scene continued for about 100 yards until Mrs Fleming's captor found himself with his back against a wall. A police car swerved onto the pavement and detective inspectors Murdo McKenzie and John Asher jumped out along with Constable William Logue. Together, they closed in on their quarry, soft words urging him to give up the gun and let the old woman go, just hand it over, son, and it'll all be over, don't do anything silly, lad, just hand it over and let her go . . .

And then, amazingly, he did.

The gunman was 18-year-old Albert Field and his unhappy home life had led to what was described in court as a psychopathic personality. His father had been captured by the Japanese during the war but had died when the ship transporting him to a POW camp was torpedoed by a US submarine. The youngster had then locked himself in his room, refusing to talk to anyone, becoming moody and uncommunicative. After the father's death, his mother in South Africa and his American grandmother had waged a legal war for custody of the boy. The grandmother won. In October 1951, Field had visited his mother in Johannesburg and in August 1952 had begun the return trip to the States, but he had run out of cash while in London, where he fell in with the man he would subsequently accompany to Glasgow.

His grandmother borrowed money to allow her to come to Scotland for the trial in December 1952. The day before he was sentenced, she paid a tearful visit to him in Barlinnie Prison, hoping he would be deported or receive probation. The judge, though, was Lord Carmont and he was seldom in a mood to be lenient. He told Field, 'You have pleaded guilty to a series of charges which can only be described as carefully planned, deliberate gangsterism.' And then he sentenced him to seven years. In the public gallery, Mrs Field gasped.

The following year, PCs McNiven and Watson received the British Empire Medal for their efforts in talking him down. Jack Hill was highly praised for his photographs, although he always insisted he'd only done what any other photographer would. And Field's accomplice, who got away with the £148 haul, was never caught.

One month earlier, at the other end of the city, another young man staged a more successful robbery. Had he played it clever, he might have got away with it but his unrequited love for a young woman brought tragedy. And death.

Edwin Finlay was described as 'a pleasant unassuming boy, a typical banker, well-groomed and neat'. The 18-year-old 'quietly respectable' youth lived with his family in Broomhill, a tidy area of red sandstone buildings in the west of the city. He was known for tending to his ailing father, helping him downstairs into the garden at the rear of their home, where he sat talking with him on sunny afternoons. But behind the respectful demeanour of this pimply-faced Sunday school teacher, something else lurked. He had few friends and was incredibly moody. More sinister was his fascination with weapons and desire to go to war to kill people. He might have got that wish, for he was due to take up National Service and the war in Korea was still raging, while the following month the British government declared its intention to stamp down on the Mau Mau terrorists in Kenya. However, Finlay had other plans.

On Saturday, 30 August, the former pupil of Glasgow High School failed to turn up for his job as a banking apprentice at the Kelvinhaugh branch of the British Linen Bank in Argyle Street. Soon after, the manager discovered that £1,220 was missing and with young Finlay nowhere to be seen, suspicion fell on him. The young man had taken the money and flown to Dublin. Had he stayed there, he might have evaded capture. Had he stayed there, he might be alive today. But there was something festering in his brain, something dark and dangerous, something that told him he must return to Glasgow. And return he did, but not empty-handed. In Eire, he had talked a gun dealer into selling him a .22 Beretta automatic by telling him he was home on leave from Korea and wanted a decent weapon to take back with him. This joined the long-barrelled .38 Webley revolver and a smaller, antique .22 Spanish revolver he already owned. In addition, he bought a supply of ammunition to be carried in wrist and body bandoliers. And back he came, armed and dangerous.

Why he did so is a mystery, although one theory is that he came back for love. He had developed feelings for a teenage schoolgirl but she did not return his affections. Police believed he returned to kill her. He flew back into Glasgow, booked a hotel room, put the rest of the money into a left-luggage box in St Enoch Square and, amazingly, phoned the girl's home. He must have known the police would be hunting him but still he got in contact. The teenager, luckily, was out but her mother then phoned Finlay's family to tell them he had been in touch. Finlay's mother, who just wanted her boy safe, told the police he was back in Glasgow and looking for the object of his unrequited love.

The girl was a member of the Western Lawn Tennis Club in Hyndland Road, so officers were sent to the area to see if they could spot him. They were not expecting any trouble from the lovesick Sunday school teacher and were unarmed. They knew nothing of the bristling array of weapons on his person, of the ammunition belt around his waist, of the smaller one strapped to his wrist. They knew nothing of his psychological make-up. They did not know that he had met up with an acquaintance earlier that day and boasted that he had stolen 'a cool thousand' from his bank and vowed, 'I am not going to be taken.' The young man he said this to did not take him seriously because Finlay had made boasts like that all his life, saying that if he was ever in trouble he'd never let them take him, that he'd save the last bullet for himself. Even though he showed him the guns, the young man still did not know whether to believe him.

On Thursday, 4 September, at just before 8 p.m., PCs John MacLeod and Thomas MacDonald spotted Finlay in Hyndland Road, near Great Western Road and very close to the tennis club. They blocked his path and PC MacLeod said, 'Excuse me, a police officer would like to talk to you.' Finlay said nothing. What was going on in his brain we will never know. Maybe he thought of his boast that they'd never take him. Maybe he wanted to go out in a blaze of glory. Maybe he thought he could impress the object of his affections with a show of machismo. Whatever it was, he stepped back a couple of paces and pulled his hands from the pockets of his light-coloured raincoat, revealing a gun in each fist.

'Stand back!' he cried and then blasted away. The first shot caught PC MacLeod in the chest and careered through his body to lodge in his spine. He really did not have a chance. The second slug sent a lunging PC MacDonald spinning out of the way. The bullet snapped into his arm but he still tried to prevent Finlay from escaping. The young man let loose another round, this time hitting the officer in the body. Finlay then took to his heels, for he could hear a police whistle shrieking and saw a uniformed copper running towards him.

PC Charles Hill was walking his beat when he heard the shots and saw PC MacDonald spinning and falling. He blew his whistle sharply and loped after the dark-haired gunman, who was running into Westbourne Road. Finlay let loose a shot but PC Hill kept coming until his quarry swerved into Westbourne Terrace Lane South, a service lane between two streets of tall terraced houses. PC Hill could hear him slamming against the high wooden doors leading into the gardens, but none were unlocked. The lane was a dead end. Finlay swiftly loaded his gun again and whirled round to face the police officer, who ducked behind a wall as a fusillade of shots peppered the brickwork. Resident Robert Hamilton poked his head out of his gate and the cop tersely told him, 'Get inside.' The man did so, but not before he saw Finlay beginning to move forward, guns at the ready. He thought he would wait in hiding until the youth came level, then he would try to jump him. At the very least, he thought, he could keep the policeman company.

'You'd better stop shooting,' the officer shouted from behind the wall. 'It's all up.'

'I'll get you anyway,' replied the gunman.

PC Hill poked his police cap over the wall and Finlay let loose another barrage of shots. The cop was playing for time. He knew other officers were in the area, he could see them working their way round behind Finlay. If he could just hold him off for another few seconds, then perhaps they could nab him. Finlay, though, had other ideas. He had spotted the reinforcements arriving and knew his day of glory was over. As they burst out of a garden behind him, he put a gun to his head and pulled the trigger. PC Hill, hearing the final muffled shot, risked a look over the wall and saw officers surrounding the body of the young man.

At 9.30 that night, PC John MacLeod lost his battle for life. The thirty-one-year-old Stornoway man, the father of a four-year-old son, had been on the force for six years, having previously served in the navy. The body of the highly commended officer was taken by train to be ferried back to his island home. His brother, Murdo, was a sergeant in the Metropolitan Police, while another brother was on board ship travelling to New Zealand. He was informed of the death by radiogram. The dead officer was posthumously awarded the Queen's Commendation for Brave Conduct. PC MacDonald, from Carluke, was seriously ill for a time but recovered from his injuries. Both he and PC Hill were awarded the British Empire Medal.

CHAPTER FIFTEEN

THE MONOCLED MAJOR
AND THE DANDY

The 1950s saw the beginnings of one of the city's most far-reaching transformations. The nation had come through its second devastating major conflict of the century against a foreign evil and now it was time to deal with domestic evils, one of which was poor housing. Every city had slums but Glasgow retained its reputation for having the worst of all. The tenements in many areas had been allowed by uncaring landlords and even the Corporation to deteriorate to a level not seen since the great purge of the late nineteenth century. In the so-called modern age, there were still families who shared a 'stairheid lavvie'. Rats were known to crawl from the festering ash pits into the homes. The conditions were insanitary, overcrowded and decidedly unpleasant.

In 1954, local authorities across Scotland drew up plans to clear their cities of slums. Glasgow had paved the way a year earlier with the opening of the first high-rise blocks at Moss Heights, near Hillington. The grand notion was that the old crumbling tenements would be cleared away and brand-new 'skyscrapers' would grow from the rubble like a shining phoenix heralding a golden age of housing. The slums of the Gorbals, Springburn, Maryhill and other areas were hauled down to give tenants a taste of high living. Even before the war, the city had begun building the 'dream schemes', housing estates on the outskirts that were to offer inner-city dwellers the chance of clean air, an inside toilet and, luxury of luxuries, both a front and a back door. The war halted the programme but it began again in the 1950s and new homes began to spring up in Castlemilk, Carntyne and Drumchapel.

However, things did not work out as the planners had hoped. The new schemes lacked even basic amenities, while the houses were often poorly constructed and some were soaked with damp almost at once. The high-rises fared little better, for in clearing the old streets of the dark sandstone buildings, the planners had also destroyed the sense of community, the sense of belonging, and the old problems of sectarianism, gangsterism and what we would now call antisocial behaviour persisted.

In crime, the more things changed, the more they stayed the same. The new-found hopefulness of the city fathers carried little weight in the underworld. For the crooks, business went on as usual and was, as usual, booming. Shebeens continued to attract customers. Illegal gambling dens still raked in the cash. Moneylenders still held their interest. The gangs, despite Lord Carmont's draconian sentences, still fought and hacked and slashed and kicked their way through the night. Extortion and armed robbery were still lucrative for the thugs and plugs. And, of course, murder, assault and rape were ever present.

Garnethill, a residential area of close-packed terraces that runs behind Sauchiehall Street, remains relatively untouched by the urban improvements of the 1950s and 1960s. In 1952, it was the scene of one of the saddest mysteries in Glasgow's history. It was on Friday, 10 October 1952 that the sexually assaulted and suffocated body of little Betty Alexander was found in the yard of the Royal Hospital for Sick Children dispensary in West Graham Street. The four-and-a-half-year-old girl had been missing for three days. The search for a missing child now became the hunt for a child killer, the first of its kind since the Susan Newell case.

From the beginning, detectives believed that the killer was local, for only someone who lived nearby would know that the yard was entered only once a week. The large wooden door was taken away for scrutiny by forensics experts, and on it they found a partial fingerprint. Checks were made against prints on record but no matches were found. Public feeling ran high. This was an innocent who had died needlessly – and the monster who did it was still walking the streets. Suspicion of any locals seen as 'different' turned ugly, while anyone questioned more than once by police found themselves an object of hatred. Clearly, a dramatic step was required, and the police were about to take it. Detectives wanted to stage a mass fingerprinting exercise for the first time in Scotland. They wanted every male over 17 years of age who lived in the area to have his prints taken. Later, this was extended to any man who worked in the vicinity.

Meanwhile, little Betty was buried in Cadder Cemetery. Unprecedented crowds stood in the soft autumn rain to watch the little white coffin go by, for the case had touched hearts all over the city. Among the flowers was a large floral cross with a card reading 'To Bunkum – our dear wee Betty, from Daddy and Mummy'. It was a sad day, the atmosphere accentuated by the weeping clouds, but there was anger, too – and when someone tried to abduct a 15-month-old boy, that anger burst. A woman was spotted picking the boy up outside a shop. The police were called but the news flowed with the rain through the streets. Police managed to get the woman into the back of a van but the mourning crowd, now an angry mob, battered the sides and screamed, 'Lynch her!' The woman was later charged with plagium, the ancient name for child-stealing.

The fingerprinting exercise continued but no match was found. Suspects were lifted, questioned and released. No explanation was ever put forward as to why the little girl's feet and socks were soaking wet but her clothes were dry. Nor was it ever ascertained why the brooch pinned on Betty's clothing by her grandmother before she vanished had been replaced by another.

And the killer was never found.

The murder of little Betty Alexander is one of the city's most enduring mysteries and almost 60 years afterwards it is still felt that someone, somewhere might know the truth of what happened in those damp few days in October.

* * *

Three years later, a major bank robbery raised its own mysteries. In many ways, it mirrored the Union Bank robbery of 1811: it was committed during the Glasgow Fair by a gang attracted from down south, the subsequent police hunt excited tremendous public interest and in the end it was not clear exactly who was behind it. Unlike the Union Bank job, which happened overnight, it took a mere 60 seconds of spirited action to pull off what was described in court as 'the most audacious crime of the century'.

The two men had been waiting in a telephone box for the bank van to arrive. It was 9.45 a.m. on Tuesday, 19 July 1955 and they watched as the red vehicle pulled up outside the British Linen Bank in Ibrox's Gower Street. They watched as driver Gilbert Tait climbed out of the cab and walked round the back. They watched as he accepted two bags from Lindsay Currie, his partner, and walked into the bank. Then they moved, out of the phone box and across the road, their long, tan-coloured dustcoats flapping slightly in the summer breeze. They looked as if they might've come off a cattle drive, but these two men had more in common with Jesse James than a cowpoke. They climbed into the front of the van as two more men, similarly dressed, walked round the back. Mr Currie had just enough time to be aware of movement behind him before he was coshed. The van screeched away from the kerb just as Gilbert Tait emerged from the bank. He saw the rear doors being hauled shut as it tilted round a corner and a money bag tumbling out. Without thinking, he flagged down a lorry and asked the driver to follow that van, but they lost it very quickly.

The raiders had made off with a total of £44,000, making this – for the time being – the biggest haul in Scottish criminal history.

Later that day, the warden of a boys' home in Dumbreck Road heard a noise from the garden of the deserted villa next door. When he went to investigate, he found the semi-conscious Mr Currie bound and gagged in the rear of his van. The 56-year-old had tape plastered over his eyes and mouth, and the hair on the back of his head was matted with blood. By that time, witnesses had told police that they had heard the men speaking with London accents, so all roads leading south were blocked. Vehicles were stopped and searched but nothing was found. There was a good reason for that: the gang had fled north-west, specifically to the Rob Roy Roadhouse near Aberfoyle, which they had been using as a base.

It was when the staff there alerted the police that they first heard about the man who became known as the 'Monocled Major', the leader of a group of seven men posing as gamblers, in Scotland to make a killing at the country's racetracks. He was tall and well-spoken, his grey hair and moustache, his flannels and blazer and his monocle making him the epitome of the retired army officer. After the raid, staff saw piles of cash in one of the rooms, while the major had paid the various bills with a wad of notes. Perhaps the men had been lucky with the horses. Perhaps not.

The news that the major was the apparent mastermind of the raid caught the imaginations of newspapers and their readers. He became, for a short time, something of a folk hero – the leader of a league of gentlemen, down on their luck, who used their military training to plan and execute a daring robbery with precision. No one had been seriously hurt and there were many people who hoped the gang would not be caught. It was suggested that they might also have been the gang behind a £250,000 bullion blag in London the year before.

A car abandoned in a Perth car park provided the law with the first break. Two of the dustcoats worn by the raiders were found inside, as well as keys to rooms at the Rob Roy. And fingerprints – a big mistake for such a professional mob. Members of the Rob Roy staff were whisked off to Govan police station to leaf through the face books of known felons. They picked out six men. On Monday, 25 July, television was used for the first time in a police investigation, to broadcast images of the recovered coats to the nation. An AA patrolman reported that one of the coats had been stolen from his van in Fulham. As the car had also been nicked in the Smoke, Scotland Yard's Flying Squad used their considerable influence and tough-guy investigation techniques to trawl for information among the big city 'faces'.

Two men were subsequently lifted in Dublin, one of them while on his honeymoon, and four more were arrested around Britain, including in London and Glasgow. None of them proved to be the major. They came close a couple of times, though. In August, a police officer questioned the owner of a black Rover outside a hotel in Killin, Perthshire. The man said that his name was Ian Stewart, that he was from Bath – and promptly slipped out the back while the officer was checking his details by phone. In the man's room were found £240 in 10-shilling notes and a monocle. The following month, five police officers chased a black car that they thought was similar to one seen leaving the Dumbreck Road villa after the robbery. Their vehicle collided with an armoured lorry near Dunblane and the car sped away. All five officers were injured. All this fed the legend of the Monocled Major, but the facts were about to get in the way. In October, a petty thief named George Grey was arrested in Yorkshire in connection with a series of burglaries. It turned out that this 56-year-old Australian was, in fact, the Monocled Major and he told police where, near Callander, they would find twelve of the stolen bank bags. However, all they found was a threepenny bit and a penny.

In January 1956, the six other men arrested for the robbery faced trial in Glasgow. Three of them received between six and eight years in jail, but the other three were released after the cases against them were found not proven. George Grey did not appear, as he had already been sentenced to seven years in an English court for other crimes and under the rules of the day he could choose not to appear in Scotland. Moves were made to amend that law, and in November 1957 George Grey stood in the dock of the High Court at Glasgow and was sent down for six years as an accessory after the fact. The Crown could produce no evidence that he had taken part in the raid, and police were satisfied that this small-time crook and gambler was not the real mover and shaker behind it.

The identity of the real master criminal behind the British Linen bank raid of 1955 remains a mystery. Only £6,000 was recovered during the arrests. Whoever planned the crime got away with £38,000.

* * *

If there is one name from the story of Glasgow's 1950s that stands out, it is that of a cold-eyed, boastful, cocky little man who murdered his way into the criminal history books. Peter Manuel was not the country's first serial killer, nor the last, but he is perhaps the most notorious. He slaughtered two families in their homes, he killed two young women in a frenzy, he may well have murdered more. Before he was caught, the man who broke into the Burnside home of the Watt family and shot three women dead was known as 'The Top Twenty Killer' because the youngest victim, Vivienne Watt, had been listening to Radio Luxembourg's hit parade prior to her death. Attempts have been made of late if not to rehabilitate his name then certainly to offer a medical explanation for his deeds and to question the legality of his ultimate death sentence. The age-old legal question regarding diminished responsibility hinges on whether the accused can tell right from wrong, and in Manuel's case he knew most certainly that what he was doing was wrong. He lied about his actions, he tried to avoid punishment, he even tried to put the blame onto others.

One of the men he tried to blame was a Glasgow crook called Samuel McKay, whose smart appearance and manners gained him the nickname 'Dandy', although an underworld figure later said he was known to his pals as 'Hooky', thanks to his nose. Manuel had kicked around the underworlds of Glasgow and Lanarkshire for years but was never accepted in either. He was not an unintelligent man – his performance while defending himself in court would prove that – but his self-delusional nature, his need to impress his peers, did alienate the more down-to-earth among the area's criminals. That did not mean that men like McKay would not use men like Manuel when they needed to, and Dandy most certainly knew the dead-eyed would-be gangster, having met him during a turn in Peterhead Prison in the late '40s. However, Manuel had been incarcerated for a sex offence and would therefore have been beneath McKay's contempt.

In January 1958, in a dingy little police interview room in Hamilton, McKay and Manuel met again. Manuel had been arrested under suspicion of murdering the Smart family – mother, father, little boy – in their Uddingston home. He had been found with banknotes that could be traced back to Mr Smart. Manuel had told police that Dandy had given him the notes in return for helping him case the home of a bookmaker.

The cops questioning Manuel, Detective Inspector Thomas Goodall and Detective Superintendent Alexander Brown, did not believe a word of it. They knew Dandy McKay to be a crook, but not a killer – and certainly not the kind of man who would slaughter a family in their beds. The 33-year-old Gorbals-born gambler was one of the city's most prosperous and successful criminals and had been on the police radar since he was 14 years of age. Although from a decent family, he followed the traditional route of borstal and prison before being called up to the army, from which he twice deserted. Tall, fit and well groomed, he eschewed the path of the hard man, although he could handle himself when necessary, to follow the more honourable profession of peterman. In 1948, he blew the safe of the Dennistoun post office and netted a grand total of twenty-five pounds and four years in jail. While doing his time in Peterhead, he was convicted of assaulting a prison officer and given a further 18 months. He was then sent to Inverness jail, which he hated, so he asked a pal in Glasgow to spread a rumour that a jailbreak was in the offing in order to be sent back to Peterhead, where security was tighter but inmates had more privileges.

McKay got out in 1952, a non-smoker – he had taken to swapping his tobacco ration for soap – and very near a teetotaller. From then on, he apparently kept his nose clean, or at least ensured that he was never caught. On the face of it, he was a successful gambler. He co-owned two gaming clubs, including the Gordon Club in the city centre and the Cuban Club in Paisley Road, which was little more than a betting shop. It was in the former that he met his Irish-born wife Mary, and together they set up a home in a plush bungalow in Clarkston. He had, he insisted, given up his old ways and was making a healthy living from games of faro, poker and chemmy. He also bet on the horses and dogs.

In that grimy, bare little room in Hamilton police station, the well-dressed, well-spoken Dandy McKay was brought face to face with the diminutive, cunning, arrogant Manuel, who told him that he had been forced to come clean about the money. McKay's blue eyes turned icy cold as he stared at the lying killer. McKay was no giant, only 5 ft 9 in. tall, but he looked on Manuel as a little man. This was the little man who had terrorised his city. This was the little man who had killed innocent people in their beds, shocking the most hardened of crooks. This was the little man who had managed to forge the unthinkable, an alliance between the underworld and the hated Glasgow Police, for it had been information from criminal sources that had helped steer the cops to Manuel's door. Now he was trying to drop McKay in it by suggesting that he was responsible for three motiveless murders – and one of the victims a child. This was the little man who had made the biggest mistake of his life, and McKay told him so.

He told Manuel, 'You'll swing for this,' and the show was over for the killer, for Dandy proceeded to sing like the proverbial fat lady. He felt no guilt about breaking the code of silence, for Manuel had proved to be a liability and a monster. The smartly dressed crook told the cops about being with Manuel on a visit to Florence Street in the Gorbals, where Manuel had collected a parcel from a contact of McKay's. The parcel had contained a Berretta, the same gun that had killed the Smart family. Manuel had claimed that he had been in the Gordon Club one night and McKay had handed him the gun. McKay told them the truth and repeated it in court later that year. On Friday, 11 July 1958, Dandy McKay's prophecy was fulfilled when executioner Harry Allen pulled the lever on Manuel in Barlinnie's hanging shed.

It was not the last Glasgow would hear of Samuel 'Dandy' McKay.

* * *

The prison break could only have been more traditional if a file had been concealed in a cake. The prisoner sawed through the bars on the window of Barlinnie's hospital wing, then, dressed in pyjamas and slippers, slid down a rope made of bed sheets. Someone had left one end of a clothes rope tied to a small gate, the other end led up and over the jail's 30-ft walls. The inmate hauled himself up the rope while pals on freedom's side held the other end. Then he slid down and into their waiting arms on the service road that separated the prison from football pitches. A fast car idled nearby, waiting to speed him away.

It was a daring escape, brilliant in its simplicity, and Dandy McKay must have had inside help to enable him to pull it off. His fitness regimen stood him in good stead for the gruelling scaling of the wall. The long-standing nasal complaint from which he suffered, for which he had already travelled to London in order to see a specialist, proved to be a blessing, for it got him into the less secure hospital wing

The escape was discovered early the next morning and roadblocks quickly ringed the city but by that time McKay was long gone. Docks, airports and railway stations were watched but they were too late. Pictures and descriptions were circulated to police forces all over the country but no one saw him. Clubs, pubs, shebeens, brothels and other criminal haunts were raided but the cops came up empty-handed. The *Queen Mary II* was searched while at berth in Rothesay when a man answering his description was spotted but it proved a dead end. Plain-clothes officers followed his blonde wife and her friends to Butlin's holiday park in Ayr in the hope that McKay was enjoying the delights of camp life but they hit another brick wall. Samuel 'Dandy' McKay was in the wind.

He had been arrested in June 1959 in connection with the April robbery of the Shettleston branch of the Clydesdale and North of Scotland bank. It was the second time in weeks that intruders had managed to get in. The first time, they had left empty-handed. This time, though, almost £40,000, a payroll for local teachers, had been taken from the safe overnight. The safe had not been blown and the locks had not been picked. The raiders had used duplicates of two of the three keys needed to open it. The third key was not in use at the time. Police knew that there must have been an inside man. The robbers had taken the booty in twenties, fivers and single notes, the serial numbers of which were not recorded. They left behind other cash that could be more easily traced, and more than three grand on the floor outside the safe. It was later suggested that a peterman was supposed to move in behind the gang and make it look as if the safe had been blown in order to protect the inside man and give the others a chance to establish alibis elsewhere. However, the cleaner had varied her usual routine and the safe-blower was unable to get in. The crime, the *Evening Times* breathlessly reported, was 'one of the most baffling the police in Glasgow have been up against in many years'.

The inside man was a young bank apprentice and he was the first to crack during the intensive police probe. He handed himself in and told detectives about his connection with local bookie Alexander Gray, how visits to his betting shop and queries about a job had led to meetings in city-centre pubs and plots to rob the bank. He told them he'd been promised £100 and a cut of the take for palming the keys needed and making impressions of them in plasticine held in a soap dish. He told them that the first break-in had been little more than a dress rehearsal. He told them about the other people involved, including Samuel McKay, who had helped introduce Gray into the gambling world.

Police tailed the various suspects, often being none too subtle about their presence to try to rattle them. Later, the accused claimed that officers had plagued them while wearing ludicrous disguises, including false moustaches, dark glasses and bowler hats. In court, a detective quipped, 'I might as well have worn a policeman's helmet if I had.' At one point, McKay complained to Chief Inspector Tom Goodall about the heavy police presence wherever he went and threatened 'to do something about it'. Neither he nor any of the other suspects knew that the young bank clerk had burst like a wet paper bag – and Goodall used that to his benefit. He decided to smoke McKay out by getting the young man to phone the Gordon Club to complain about not receiving his end of the cash. With his ear to the receiver as the young man made the phone call, Goodall noted the conversation.

'Who's speaking?' asked McKay.

'Bill, Alex Gray's friend.'

'I know you now. What do you want? You shouldn't phone me here.'

'Alex has let me down with my holiday money.'

'How did you get my name?'

'A fellow in Gray's club told me it.'

'I can't talk here. Where are you speaking from?'

'Provanmill 5200.'

'Right. I'll telephone again in five minutes. What's the number again?'

'Provanmill 5200.'

'I'll phone you right away.'

McKay hung up and in the phone box Goodall endured an anxious three minutes. Had McKay suspected something? Would he phone back? Had he overplayed his hand? Was the man on the run even now? Then the phone rang.

'Is that you, Bill?'

'Yes.'

'What's wrong, Bill? Has Gray not seen you?'

'No.'

'Did he give you the £30 I gave him for you?'

'I never got any money.'

'That man is in a terrible state. He is being followed all the time,' McKay reportedly said. 'Deal with me from now on and don't go near him. Has he never seen you or contacted you?'

'I saw Chris [another witness] once or twice. He told me I can't get no money just now.'

'Are you being followed?'

'At first I was, but not now.'

'That's good. Now just deal with me and no one else. Forget about Gray. What do you want for your holiday?'

'One hundred pounds.'

'That can be arranged.'

'Can I see you then?' asked the young man.

'Yes.'

'Can I see you tonight?'

'Yes, sure.'

'Whereabouts then?'

McKay asked, 'Do you know St George's Cross?'

'Yes.'

'Well, come out of the subway at eight o'clock and walk down Great Western Road on the left-hand side. Do you know what I mean?'

'Yes.'

'Right. I will point you out to a woman who will give you the money. It will be Bank of England fivers. She is about 30 years old but looks like 25. She has blonde hair and is a good looker. She will put her hand up to her hair so you will know her. Do you know what to do now?'

'Yes.'

'There's another place, wait till I think . . . no, that's OK, eight o'clock, Great Western Road. And be sure you are not followed.'

'I'll watch.'

'Right, eight o'clock. Remember to deal with me only.'

Naturally, the area around St George's Cross was swarming with plain-clothes officers for the meeting that Saturday night, 27 June. They watched for the young man coming out of the subway station and followed him. Two women officers sauntered up the opposite side of the road. At Burnbank Terrace, Dandy was spotted along with two others, a man and woman. McKay had told no lies: she was blonde and she was a looker. They shadowed the young man from the opposite side of the broad street. The young man stopped at a news vendor and bought a copy of the *Evening Times*. At that point, the cops saw McKay hand the woman a package and nod towards the young man. She crossed the road and spoke briefly to him, then handed the envelope over. That was when the police moved in. A detective had worked his way round behind McKay and pounced on him from the mouth of a close, while a colleague nabbed the male accomplice. The woman was lifted by the policewomen. Inside the envelope with the £100 was a note said to have been dictated by McKay which read, 'Your cut of the money is safe and will come to you when the heat dies down. Don't contact me or the other chap for three months.'

Charged in connection with the robbery, McKay was noted as saying, 'Nothing to say just now. I must think things out and I may speak to you later.' When he was searched, an envelope containing an invoice was found with a set of drawings or diagrams drawn on it. To the police, it looked like a rough map of the location of the Shettleston bank. In court, though, the judge, Shettleston-born Lord Wheatley, knew the area well and stated that it could have been any road junction anywhere. As a piece of evidence, it was not helpful. Later, Chief Inspector Goodall said he had another conversation with McKay during which the man tried to bargain his way out of trouble. 'You can never get that money back except through me,' he supposedly said, 'and the only way is to guarantee me my freedom 100 per cent. Let me go free and in two days you will have thirty thousand pounds.'

When the police would not give him his freedom, McKay decided to take it, and one month later, while awaiting trial, he staged his daring prison break. The first thing he did was phone his wife. He then laid low with a pal in the city for a couple of days before being smuggled off to London. He hung around the Smoke for 16 days before taking a well-worn route for Glasgow criminals on the run: he sailed for New York. There were rumours during his year at liberty that he was in America for plastic surgery to alter his features. He did in fact have surgery in New York; he finally had his old nasal complaint fixed. He stayed in the USA for around three months, travelling between the Big Apple, Connecticut and Miami.

Back in Glasgow, Tom Goodall knew for a fact that McKay was in New York – because someone sent him a photographic negative. When printed up, it showed two men walking on East 54th Street and Fifth Avenue. One of the men had his hand up to his face, but it was clearly Dandy McKay. A note with the negative said, 'I think you will find the enclosed of interest to you. I managed to get this from New York. I believe the man to be Samuel McKay.'

By November 1959, his nose fixed, McKay was back in London. He'd not had much fun in America. 'When you are on the run, there is always a certain amount of worry about it,' he said later. His old pal Danny Hynds, who had broken free from jail himself, echoed this when he told the *Evening Times*, 'It's not fun being a hunted man, I can tell you. You reach the stage where you'll jump at shadows – always on the alert.'

However, that did not prevent Dandy from pulling another daring stroke on his return to the UK: he hired a car and drove back to Glasgow. He knew his face was familiar to the cops in the city and that grasses were always ready to trade on his name, but he missed his wife and his two young daughters. He pulled up outside his Nethercliffe Avenue home, picked up his family, then headed back to London, where they stayed until February 1960 under the name Fraser. They then moved to Killiney, near Dublin, where he had a second home. He remained at large until June, when Dublin police swooped and carried him off to the city's Bridewell Prison. Tom Goodall flew to Ireland to escort him back, and in the swanky Killiney home he found a print of the same photograph that had been sent to him. He believed that McKay himself had sent the negative in order to goad him.

McKay said that he'd escaped from jail because he'd believed his wife was being threatened. She had been receiving sinister phone calls from Glasgow heavies who had thought he had been involved in the robbery and wanted a piece of the action. He had reasoned that if he escaped, it would force the police to keep watch on his home and so keep his family safe. However, he denied having profited from the robbery, saying that he had merely acted as a go-between for Gray and the young bank clerk. He also claimed that Gray had asked him to launder £5,000 of the stolen money. He admitted trying to strike a bargain with Goodall, but said that had only been so he could get to Gray and convince him to give back what was left of the loot.

By the time McKay appeared in court in November, Alexander Gray was already serving ten years and another man had gone down for a stretch for resetting (fencing) the cash. There was talk that someone had tried to silence Gray forever with poison but the pill had been slipped to the wrong man. Two other accused persons – the blonde woman and her husband – had been released, while the young bank clerk, in return for giving evidence, had not been charged. McKay's own trial had been delayed when witnesses went missing. When it did finally begin, the police took no chances. They were a conspicuous presence inside the courtroom and in the corridors. Uniformed officers stood by all the doors and in the street. They surrounded him with blue serge as he was transferred to and from Barlinnie Prison. In a letter to Danny Hynds, McKay dismissed it all as mere showmanship designed to influence the jury – a claim that would be made by other men in other high-profile cases.

Dandy McKay was sent down for eight years for the robbery and two for his escape. In court was William Watt, the husband, father and brother-in-law of three of Peter Manuel's victims. The Glasgow baker had been suspected of murdering his wife, daughter and sister-in-law, and had spent too many long hours in Barlinnie. During the investigation, he had come face to face with Manuel in a bizarre interview in a city-centre restaurant, organised by a lawyer. The cold-hearted killer said he had information about the culprit; his intention seems to have been simply to taunt the grieving businessman. Why Mr Watt was in court to hear McKay being sentenced is not known. All he would say was that he had a 'special reason'. Perhaps he felt a kinship with the man who had helped bring down the decade's biggest bogeyman. Perhaps he felt that McKay had been more involved in Manuel's crime spree than was known and wanted to see him punished.

As a Glasgow crook who kept violence to a minimum, Dandy McKay was a dying breed. The swinging '60s were around the corner, and criminal life in the city was about to get bloodier.

CHAPTER SIXTEEN

BULLETS, BLADES AND BOMBS

They say that guns don't kill people. They say people kill people. And in the 1960s people were killing people a lot.

The steps leading to the columned portico of Glasgow's High Court had never witnessed anything as undignified as the events of November 1961. A man had just been found not proven of the shooting of a Glasgow taxi driver in the Castlemilk scheme on the South Side. The accused, who already had a criminal record, had a high-powered legal team fighting his corner and in the end the evidence simply was not there to link him satisfactorily to the murder. It was as he walked free from the court that an unseemly spectacle marked the beginning of the craze for lionising criminals that endures to this day.

Oscar Slater, of course, had attracted press interest but his was a notorious case. Johnny Ramensky was also a press darling but he was a character and something of a folk hero. Newspapers had always reported criminal cases but not until Walter Scott Ellis stepped onto those stone steps a free man did a new-found fascination for crooks and crime really manifest itself. The gathering reporters and photographers mobbed the bemused man, pulling and hauling in a bid to snatch him exclusively for their publication. Punches were thrown and kicks were aimed as each hack and snapper struggled to ensure he came out the victor. The steps were slippery and many a body came a cropper as Ellis was yanked back and forth. Finally, one reporter snatched defeat from the jaws of victory when he manhandled Ellis into the back of a car he thought was his, only to be left stranded on the pavement as the rival vehicle sped off with what he had thought was his prize in the back.

Ellis subsequently pocketed £100 for telling his story and enjoying his 15 minutes of fame. He was known as the man who had cheated the gallows, but he was not guilty of the crime, he said. The victim, John Walkinshaw, must have been murdered by a madman. The incident taught the city's pressmen a lesson: from then on any deal for such a story would be made ahead of time. Ellis's criminal career continued and in 1966 he was sent down for 21 years following an armed robbery on a Pollokshields bank during which the manager was wounded. Other convictions followed, while new criminals became fodder for the front pages.

Jimmy Boyle would become a media darling, although not until after he had served time for murder. A pal of London's Kray twins, whom he met while dodging the law in London, he became 'the man they couldn't hang' after he beat two murder raps in the High Court. Known as a 'baby-faced thug', he learned his vicious trade in the streets of the Gorbals, graduating through the street gangs that many believed Percy Sillitoe had stamped out. They were still there, though, and Boyle developed a taste for the blade and the boot while running with the Wild Young Cumbie from Cumberland Street. Gangs also proliferated in the many schemes on the outskirts of the city, most notoriously in Easterhouse. Later in the decade, considerable media attention would focus on the area thanks to the intervention of singer Frankie Vaughan, who organised a weapons amnesty.

Boyle's criminal skills were honed in the finishing schools of borstal and prison. Gradually, petty crime gave way to more serious stuff and he gained something of a reputation for being a handy man to have on your side. He became an enforcer for the 'tallymen', loan sharks who practised the age-old trade of lending cash at usurious rates of interest. Anyone who failed to keep up the payments, or tried to pull a fast one, had to deal with someone like Boyle. Boyle has claimed that reports of violence meted out by the moneylenders have been exaggerated, and there may well be some truth in that. The tale that a man was crucified by having his hands nailed to a wooden floor seems to be an urban legend. However, the loan-shark racket was not as rosy as he might like to think. Like pushers, the tallymen played on people's need and misery, and they were certainly not averse to doling out physical punishment to keep recalcitrant customers in line.

The big man behind the tallymen was Gorbals-born Frank 'Tarzan' Wilson. The blond-haired hard man was known simply as 'the Boss' and he had come up through the ranks of the Cumbie and big-time crime. He had the scars to prove it. His face was criss-crossed with the tracks of violent encounters. One scar was received during a brawl with an Irish labourer who wielded a broken bottle with some expertise. He had also lost part of his left ear in a fight in London in which his opponent, a large black man, bit it off. His criminal record began when he was 11, when he appeared in court on a malicious mischief beef. From then on, it kept growing, filling up with acts of theft, housebreaking, assault and receiving stolen goods.

By the late 1960s, though, he was the epitome of the wise guy on the make. He sported fancy suits and he liked expensive food. He had a succession of pals drive him around in a flash motor. He was loyal to his friends and remorseless with his enemies; he had his own twisted sense of honour. At the age of 29, he saw himself as the Glasgow version of the Sicilian crime bosses, a Mafia don meting out largesse and punishment in equal measure. He read *The Honoured Society*, Norman Lewis's account of the Cosa Nostra in Sicily, and did what he could to live by the Mafia's tenets. Perhaps he even had dreams of creating a Glasgow version of the crime organisation, a Scotia Nostra. But despite his lofty ambitions, he stayed in the 'old neighbourhood' and only moved from the Caledonian Road tenement in which he was born to a room and kitchen in Parkhead with his young girlfriend shortly before his empire crumbled.

Tom Goodall was the nemesis of both Wilson and Boyle. Boyle had heard about him while he was growing up in the Gorbals and knew him to be a tough, no-nonsense cop. 'Goodall,' he later wrote, 'was spoken of with fear.' While Boyle was rising in the criminal hierarchy, the pipe-smoking police officer was the top man in Glasgow's CID, and veteran police officer Joe Jackson, who became a 'plainer' and then a detective under his aegis, speaks of his superior's detestation of bent coppers and crooks. Bill Knox wrote of a piece of doggerel he saw scratched into the door of a cell beneath the High Court that read:

Hang down your head, Tom Goodall,
Hang down your head and cry.
Hang down your head, Tom Goodall,
You'll never catch [name unprinted].
It will never be tomorrow,
It will never be today.
Lay off your men, Tom Goodall,
For he's far, far away.

Knox said the name he removed was that of a well-known city criminal and it's tempting to imagine that it was Boyle who wrote those words when he was in the process of avoiding jail or the death penalty for the first two murder charges. There was insufficient evidence for the first case to proceed, while in the second the charges were reduced. It is important to note that Boyle maintains his innocence of both charges.

Goodall and his men brought Boyle to book in 1967, following the stabbing of small-time crook and pimp 'Babs' Rooney, who had committed the unforgivable sin of falling behind in his payments by around a fiver. Again, Boyle denies that he killed the man, but this time the charges stuck. Again, the trial was marked by allegations of intimidation. One witness had a gelignite bomb thrown through his window. Boyle, aged 24, was sent down for 15 years to life.

But now the cops had Wilson's organisation in their sights. He was into a lot more than moneylending, so a special team of hard-nosed cops, known as 'The Tightrope Squad', was set up to bring him down. David McNee, later to become chief constable, was at the head of the six-man secret task force, which included surveillance experts and disguise specialists. One member, Detective Sergeant Stuart Waldman, was a former commando, while Detective Sergeant Jack Beattie was known to crooks and cops alike as 'the Flea' because he was always jumping about. Tarzan Wilson, John 'Bandit' Rooney and lawyer James Maxwell Latta were found guilty of plotting to have Boyle and another man cleared by inducing witnesses to give false evidence and provide bogus alibis. They received twelve, four and eight years respectively. Wilson was the real target, with 24-year-old chauffeur and legman Rooney being described by the judge, Lord Grant, as having 'a walk-on rather than a speaking part'.

Family man Latta's fall from grace was public and dramatic. He had been a successful solicitor but was not content to sit behind a desk and push paper while his investigator, or precognition agent, interviewed witnesses. He wanted to get out on the streets and defend his clients to the best of his ability. 'It was his duty to prepare the case and ascertain from witnesses what evidence was available and what evidence they would give,' said Lord Grant. 'But this is very different from putting statements into witnesses' mouths.'

The problem is, the dark side of life can be very seductive. The lawyer became too pally with some of his clients. Good solicitors keep matters on a business footing – they call their clients 'Mr' and the neds return the favour. But Latta was known to meet with clients and witnesses in pubs and clubs, including the Hi Hi Bar in the Gorbals, where, it's been claimed, he discussed the nobbling of witnesses, perjury and bribery over a convivial glass or two of the barkeep's finest. Meanwhile, a heavily disguised Jack 'the Flea' Beattie was sitting nearby listening to every word. He had a knack for such undercover work and even visited make-up experts to find out how best to apply fake scars and facial hair. He later became the head of the drug squad. The 39-year-old lawyer was ruined. His heavy smoking and the stress of the trial had brought his childhood asthma back with a vengeance and he sat in the dock a nervous, drained little man.

The man credited with helping the Tightrope Squad to topple Wilson from his throne was an aquarium salesman known as 'the Fishman'. In court, he claimed he had vowed vengeance on Wilson and his boys back in 1961 when he was stabbed while a pub manager in the Gorbals. He claimed to have infiltrated their organisation in order to help smash them, and when he was induced to become part of the conspiracy, he saw his chance. He blotted his copybook slightly when he tried to sell his story to the highest bidder – he said he needed money to get far away from the city – but after the trial he was highly praised by the police for his courage.

Meanwhile, Jimmy Boyle was banged up inside. He had never been what you would call a model prisoner, and his rage at the system stepped up a gear. Violence and dirty protests were the norm, and this behaviour led to him becoming one of the first inmates in the experimental Special Unit in Barlinnie Prison. The unit adopted an enlightened approach in which the dehumanising treatment of other prisons was replaced with respect and a certain amount of trust. Inmates were allowed to prepare their own food and pursue artistic pursuits and were allowed a level of freedom they'd never known on the inside. Boyle found a new life as a sculptor, artist and author. He published two books and collaborated on a play. He became the prime example of the bad boy made good. Towards the end of his term, he married a psychiatrist whom he met in the Special Unit, and after his release in the early '80s he continued to stay on the right side of the law. He now lives on the Continent.

Boyle had one more brush with the courts, in 1994, in tragic circumstances. On Friday, 13 May, his 27-year-old son, James Boyle junior, was stabbed to death in an Oatlands back court. The younger Boyle, who fluttered around the edges of crime and drug addiction, had been having a relationship with the former girlfriend of Gary Lane Moore, a very tough customer from the East End schemes. The two had argued over the girl and Moore pulled a knife when he thought Boyle was reaching for a gun. Boyle lunged forward and, the court heard, the knife went in accidentally. Moore, charged with murder, eventually received eight years for culpable homicide.

During his first two murder trials, Jimmy Boyle senior sat in the shadow of the noose. His third took place two years after the death penalty was temporarily abolished in 1965. It was not done away with permanently until 1969. They might have called Boyle 'the man they couldn't hang', but another young Glasgow man had no such luck.

* * *

In 1920, James Rollins and Albert Fraser went to the gallows for murder born out of a honey trap in Queen's Park recreation grounds. In 1960, two Glasgow youths, James Denovan and Anthony Miller, saw to it that history repeated itself. They, too, had a honey trap but theirs had a new wrinkle. They did not use a prostitute to draw punters into the shadows; instead they preyed on the homosexuals who used the same dark corners and quiet grasslands. The 16-year-old Denovan acted as the lure for the often ageing men, while Miller provided the strong-arm stuff. The marks were attacked and robbed, but they were gay and homosexuality was illegal in Scotland until as late as 1980, so they did not report the crime to the police.

On 6 August, it all went wrong. Petty crook John Cremin went with Denovan into the playing fields but did not return alive. When he was found, it was believed that the 50-year-old had collapsed and died from natural causes. However, the cap he wore concealed the true cause of death: he had been battered on the head and had succumbed to a massive subdural haematoma. Whoever killed him got away with his bank book, watch, a knife and £67 in cash.

Denovan and Miller were regular customers of the Cathkin Café at the top of Victoria Road, a short distance from the recreation grounds. They were amateurs and blabbed about what they got up to at night, and in particular the attack on Cremin. They flashed his bank book and spent his cash. Miller showed off a press cutting regarding the crime to friends. Denovan even pointed out the spot where the crime had taken place to pals, where, in his words, Cremin had 'flaked', and suggested that they all observe a two-minute silence. In court, Lord Wheatley asked if this was 'the callousness of youth or the callousness of a boy who had become a fairly hardened criminal before his time'.

It was Denovan, being questioned on another matter, who burst and told police about the attacks they had carried out. He said his partner was Tony Miller. Together they became known as the Glasgow Park Bandits. After that, everything fell into place and the police had their men. Hanging was going out of fashion – the 1957 Homicide Act had outlawed the death penalty for certain types of murder – but this was still a capital crime. Bespectacled Denovan, who had confessed first, was only 16, so he would not face the noose. Tony Miller, if found guilty, ran the risk of being hanged. He was only 19.

Although there was no doubt that the young men had committed the crime, there was some question over who had actually dealt the killing blow. Denovan insisted that it was Miller. Miller did not give evidence on his own behalf, a fact that unfairly went against him in the subsequent appeal. Both were found guilty, and Miller was to hang. He listened to the verdict with his thumb tucked in the waistband of his trousers, seemingly uncaring. Earlier, a reporter had noted, he had joked with his co-accused, but the younger man had kept his head down. The same reporter said that he saw a 'hard smile' come to Miller's lips when he heard the sentence of death.

The news devastated his parents, decent, respectable people, but they campaigned vigorously to have the sentence commuted. Petitions were circulated throughout the city in clubs, pubs and factories. A stall was set up in the city centre to rally public support for their cause. Over 30,000 names were scribbled on sheets of paper and sent to Secretary of State for Scotland John Mclay. They did not do any good. The politician sent his regrets but he was unable to find any grounds to justify advising Her Majesty to 'interfere with the due course of law'. A telegram was sent from Glasgow to Buckingham Palace but it was no use. Tony Miller was to be put to death.

He had killed, or at least been involved in a killing. But his judicial execution would not bring back the dead. The Crown was about to do in cold blood what he had done in stupidity. His lawyer, Len Murray, wrote years later in *The Herald* that 'the barbarity and the futility of it all were inconsistent with our claims to be a civilised society'. He went on:

> Not only were they going to destroy a life that should be saved, a life that did not belong to them, but in addition a punishment far greater than any other that man could ever possibly devise was being handed out to two innocent individuals – the parents of the condemned boy.

On Wednesday, 21 December, Tony Miller met with his parents, 49-year-old seaman Alfred and Marie, and his brother Paul for the last time. At eight the following morning, he took the fateful eight steps from the condemned cell into the Barlinnie killing chamber. The hangman put the white hood over his head, hiding from the witnesses the once well-oiled hair and the thin, sallow features, and pulled the lever. By 8.02 a.m., it was all over.

Glasgow had hanged its last man. Never again would the trapdoor clanging open echo through the halls of Barlinnie Prison. Never again would a body be thrown into a hole in the ground behind the hanging shed and covered in quick lime and earth. Never again would a dead man's initials be scratched into the brickwork of the wall. Scotland's final execution took place at Aberdeen's Craiginches Prison three years later.

On 21 December 1964, MPs voted 355 to 170 in favour of abolishing the death penalty, if only as an experimental measure.

The depth of feeling – and the size of the majority – meant it was unlikely that the House of Lords would oppose it. Finally, almost exactly five years later, on 18 December 1969, the House of Lords accepted the 1965 law on a permanent basis.

* * *

Tony Miller, despite his place in the history books, is no household name in Glasgow crime. He does not rank alongside the Peter Manuels and the Jimmy Boyles. But during the 1960s, another big name began to rise from the shadowy depths of the underworld. He became arguably the city's best-known gangster, staying at the top for the next three decades. Acres of newsprint have been dedicated to him and he became known, wrongly, as Glasgow's 'Godfather'. Arthur Thompson was a powerful and a dangerous man, but he was not the supreme criminal in the city's crooked empire. No one has been, is or will be.

He was born in 1931 and his family settled in the notorious Blackhill area in the north-east of the city. Crime beckoned and Arthur was banged up for the first time in 1949, on an assault charge. Further spells of prison came over the next few years, on charges ranging from robbery to reset. He also did three years for blowing the safe of the Commercial Bank in Beauly in 1955, a job pulled with Paddy Meehan, another name that would become very familiar during the '60s. Well built and handy with his fists, Thompson was, like his contemporaries, no stranger to violence. In the late '50s, he was working with Glasgow bookmakers and gamblers and rubbing shoulders with the likes of tough guy Teddy Martin.

Martin was a guy who could charm the ladies with his good looks, although his fair complexion was marred by the inevitable scars, while he could also put the fear of death into men with his fiery temper. He was called 'The Terror of Blackhill', although, like many nicknames, this may have been a press invention. Big Arthur, never a matinee idol, did not have Teddy's way with the ladies but he was equally vicious when circumstances demanded it. There were, though, strict rules of engagement in those days (although, of course, rules are there to be broken). Women must never be touched. You never went after a guy when he was with his family. Civilians were to remain unharmed wherever possible. And unlike the Young Turks who would follow, they did not court media attention, much preferring to work under the radar.

In 1955, Teddy Martin made the first wholly successful escape from Peterhead Prison. Johnny Ramensky might have gone over the wall on numerous occasions, but Martin was the first to make a clean getaway. And he owed much of its success to his pals Thompson and Paddy Meehan, whom he had known since approved school. Martin had been sent down for shooting at a man in Blackhill and had then been hit with another 12 months for assaulting a prison officer. On 13 March, he was part of a small work detail sent to paint the harbour wall in the Admiralty Yard on Keith Inch, an island connected to the prison by two bridges. Martin seized his chance while the guard was in a hut and went over the fence. Meehan and another man were in a car waiting to pick him up, while Thompson laid a false trail for police to make them think that the running man was hiding out in Glasgow. The gang had obtained a prison uniform and had Martin's number placed on the collar. A quick anonymous call to the police had them speeding to the 'dunny' (the bottom floor) of a Townhead tenement, where they found the uniform. The getaway car was later found abandoned. Police focused their hunt on the city, leaving Martin and Meehan free to travel through the Highlands and on to Ireland.

Appeals were made through the press to bring 'Scarface' Martin to justice but he remained at liberty for a month before cops swooped on a holiday hut near Cumbernauld and found him sleeping in bed. His lawyer argued that the charge of having 'conceived the felonious intent of defeating the ends of justice by escaping from legal custody' had no precedent under Scots law and that he should have been punished for a breach of prison discipline. However, the submission was dismissed by the judge and Martin had another 15 months added to his sentence, while Paddy Meehan went down for 15 months. Thompson was never charged.

In 1961, Martin and Thompson had a falling out. They had been planning a job in London that would require a considerable amount of bankrolling if they wanted to pull it off. Martin wanted them to speculate to accumulate and Thompson agreed. However, when he put up a £100 note, Martin took the hump. He felt that such a large note must have been part of the proceeds of another robbery and would be easy to trace. If true, such a rookie mistake could be devastating to their heist plans. He questioned Thompson's motives, suggesting that he was being tight with a buck, and Thompson took offence. On 25 March 1961, in Paddy Meehan's flat, Thompson pulled a gun and shot Teddy Martin right in the middle of his scarred face. He might have finished his old pal off if Meehan's pregnant wife had not rushed in and the gangland rule of not dishing out violence in front of a woman come into play. Martin survived and the robbery went ahead with Meehan but without the wounded Martin and Thompson. The plan was to rob the Co-operative store in Edmonton, north London, but the new gang was not as adept with the gelignite as Meehan. He told them that they had used enough explosive to blow up the whole building and was in the process of unpicking some of the charges with a knitting needle when the police arrived, acting on a tip-off. Meehan was subsequently given eight years' preventative detention.

In addition to robbery and illegal betting and gambling, another big money-making racket for the Glasgow boys was extortion, and Arthur Thompson was in it up to the scars on his face. Rivalries were also common – over turf, over betrayals, over insults – and it was Thompson's feud with the Welsh family that made him a household name, depending on the kind of household you were in. In 1966, he was called to defend the honour of one of his protection customers who had been slighted by Patrick Welsh and his pal James Goldie. Thompson ran the men's van off the road and killed them. The whole thing was witnessed by two off-duty cops, Joe Jackson and his brother John, and they were able to identify Thompson as the man behind the wheel. The two police officers were later told that some heavies were going to pay them a visit in a bid to change their minds about testifying, and Joe Jackson spent a tense, angry night being guarded by his colleagues while his wife and young child were taken to a safe location. In the end, no one tried to pull anything, which was just as well, as Jackson was ready to fight fire with fire should a gangster show face at his door.

In the end, Thompson beat the murder rap then held true to the code of the underworld by refusing to implicate anyone at the trial of three members of the Welsh gang who were accused of planting a bomb in his MG. Thompson had been slightly injured in the blast but his mother-in-law, Maggie Johnstone, had been killed. All three accused were cleared.

Thompson's criminal empire continued to grow, unimpeded by his receiving a two-year sentence for robbery in 1968. He did not court the press but they knew of him nonetheless. He was a friend of the Kray twins, often lending them Scottish muscle as well as providing aid and succour to London crooks on the lam. In return, just as they had harboured Jimmy Boyle, the twins looked after any associates of Thompson's who needed to lay low for a while. Thompson began to increase his interests in legitimate concerns, not always, it was claimed, through fair means. He became a partner in pubs, clubs and restaurants. Timber outlets, betting shops, car salerooms and scrap-metal dealers all became part of his money-making, or money-laundering, empire.

His home in Provanmill Road was a monument to the garish tastes of gangsters the world over. Decorated in pseudo-ranch-house style, it became known first as The Ponderosa. As times changed and the gun-toting *Bonanza* gave way to the oil-rich *Dallas*, locals took to calling it South Fork. Thompson had holiday homes in Spain and on the Isle of Bute. He was no social climber. He enjoyed simple things: watching *Coronation Street* on the telly with his wife, a quiet drink in a local pub. If there was any trouble, and a man like Arthur

Thompson could attract it, punters soon had their drinks refilled or replaced, with apologies.

They called him 'Big Arthur', but at 5 ft 10 in., not because he was a giant of a man. He was Big Arthur because he was a powerful man, a dangerous man, a big fish in the Glasgow crime pond. He once said that he had been accused of many things but had not served time in 20 years. There had to be good reasons for that. Either he was no longer the man everyone thought him to be, or he was incredibly slippery, managing to keep a distance from his involvement in crime. There is a third scenario, but one for which there is no evidence: that he had befriended police officers and over the years those friendships paid off. Such alliances are a part of underworld tradition – some may say myth – but police vehemently deny they have ever existed. However, when known crooks like Thompson seem to lead a life unfettered by interference from the law, eyebrows are naturally raised. On the other hand, there were no doubt many buffers insulating him from any nefarious activity on the streets, and it was perhaps very difficult to link anything directly to him.

Big he might've been, powerful he was, but that did not mean Thompson didn't have enemies. However, he also had some very hard-worked guardian angels, or maybe demons. He narrowly missed being blown to bits by the car bomb in 1966 and later assassination attempts also failed. He was shot on a number of occasions but each time he bounced back. In March 1993, he confounded everyone when he died in bed, having already paid a heavy price for his lifestyle. His daughter died before him, having suffered a drug overdose, while his son, Arthur junior, did not have the old man's luck: he was gunned down in the street outside South Fork.

In his later years, Big Arthur came to the aid of his old pal Paddy Meehan. In 1969, the veteran safe-blower was accused of a brutal murder he did not commit and although freed from jail after seven years, he continued to campaign to have his name cleared.

The murder, which took place in Ayrshire, reverberated in the streets of Glasgow when a crazed gunman went on a shooting spree

– and it began an astonishing chain of violent death that ultimately claimed seven lives.

* * *

In the early hours of Sunday, 6 July 1969, 67-year-old bingo-hall owner Abraham Ross and his 72-year-old wife Rachel were undergoing a brutal ordeal at the hands of two masked raiders in their Ayr home. Robbery was the motive and the two Glasgow men, who called themselves Pat and Jim, gave Mr Ross a severe beating with an iron bar to force him to part with the keys to his safe. They knew he had money and when the old man finally gave in they found £4,000. They left the couple bound and gagged, promising to alert the police. But they didn't make the call. The couple lay all day and all night untended until their cleaning lady found them on Monday morning. Mrs Ross subsequently died but her husband, despite the horrendous beating, survived. The crime was sickening, disgusting and unnecessarily violent. But all the niceties of the old crooks were being swept away by the late '60s and, to paraphrase former prime minister Harold Macmillan, we'd never had it so nasty.

Meehan was hoovered up for the crime. Police had been tipped off that he was in Ayrshire at the time and as one of the men had been called Pat, it was reasonably assumed that he could have been responsible. Mr Ross picked him out of a line-up, but only because of his voice.

The Glasgow peterman insisted that he was never called Pat. He later claimed that the tip-off had come from MI5, who had tapped his phone. He believed that they had been monitoring his movements since he had tried to warn them that the Russians were going to break spy George Blake out of Wormwood Scrubs. The KGB had arrested former Communist Meehan while he was in Eastern Europe, on the run after breaking free from his preventative detention, and had questioned him about the Scrubs. On his return to Britain, Meehan said, he'd tried to warn MI5 about the plan but was either not believed or deliberately ignored. Sure enough, Blake escaped in 1966 (Meehan believed that he was allowed to do so) and from then on the Glasgow crook believed he was the man who knew too much. Yes, he had been in Ayrshire that night, but he'd only been passing through, on his way to Stranraer with a buddy to case a motor taxation office. He had not committed this terrible crime. He was a safe-blower, not a murderer – and he had been fitted up by the security services. It all sounds so plausibly implausible that it just might be true.

The man with him that night was James Griffiths, a 34-year-old petty crook from Rochdale with a wicked temper and a self-destructive streak. He had met Meehan in Parkhurst Prison on the Isle of Wight, where they had shared a cell with another Glaswegian, Roy Fontaine, a conman later to achieve notoriety when, using the name Archibald Hall, he killed five people, including his own brother. Griffiths was not in the Glasgow men's league, but he wanted to be. He impressed them when he walked off a work detail and onto a ferry. Still wearing his prison uniform, he made it to the mainland, where he shared a train compartment with a prison officer and his wife, remaining at large for several weeks before he was nabbed and sent back.

Meehan and Fontaine had spoken about Glasgow so much that Griffiths wanted to see the place for himself, so on his release he moved his base of operations to an attic flat in Holyrood Crescent in the West End. He had learned a thing or two from the smooth-talking Fontaine and he posed as a Mr Douglas, an antique dealer. He then exercised his skills as a thief, lifting antiques, fast cars, firearms, all the time looking for the big score. He met up with Meehan again, believing that the experienced old hand could help lead him to it.

When Meehan was arrested for the Rachel Ross murder, Griffiths knew that his pal was innocent. He wanted to help him but could not do so without firing himself in for a crime. Honour among thieves was one thing but he did not relish the thought of going back inside. He did everything he could, bar turning up at a police station. He contacted reporters, he even spoke on the phone to Tom Goodall, who urged him to give himself up. Finally, under pressure, Meehan gave up his partner's name and address, and on Tuesday, 15 July, a posse of police officers was ordered to bring Griffiths in.

And that was how the shooting started.

Griffiths had always boasted that he would go down fighting. He was a violent man – on one occasion in Blackpool, he'd hacked at two guys with a bayonet, almost chopping off the fingers of one man's hand – and his unbalanced mind now tipped over the edge. He had stolen a number of weapons during his time in Glasgow and when the cops came calling he met them with a shotgun. Detective Constable William Walker took a blast in the back and had to be carried to the home of a retired doctor while other officers laid siege to the flat at 15 Holyrood Crescent. But Griffiths wasn't going to wait it out. He knew he had more weapons and ammo in his car, which was parked in Great Western Road, and he came running out of the terraced house, his shotgun booming. He sprinted to the car and loaded himself up with a high-velocity rifle and telescopic sight, throwing a bandolier of ammunition over his shoulder before dashing back to his flat, pumping his shotgun at anything that moved and screaming, 'You won't take me!'

Police reinforcements arrived and immediately came under fire. Windscreens cracked and shattered, a detective fell back, a round nicking his neck. Griffiths had already wounded a number of passers-by. The street was cordoned off. A police marksman stood ready to bring the gunplay to a halt. Men in bulletproof vests hid behind walls and cars. Even the army was contacted for reinforcements if needed. Tom Goodall took personal charge of the situation and ordered up tear gas. But when the bark of gunfire from the attic window ceased, he knew instinctively that Griffiths had managed to escape. He'd gone through a skylight and dashed along the rooftops before dropping down into a lane. He was at large in the city and he was armed to the teeth.

In Henderson Street, Griffiths commandeered a dark-blue Anglia, wounding the driver, and sped off through the North Woodside area to the Round Toll at Possil. The police had stormed his flat by then and found it empty; now they were fanning out in a bid to bring him down before anyone else was hurt. Griffiths crashed the car and burst into the Round Toll Bar, where he calmly ordered a drink. The few customers in there at midday stared in amazement as the short, stocky, wild-eyed man with an English accent stood before them, a rifle in his hand, a shotgun hung on his shoulder and an ammunition belt crossed over his body. No one moved, no one breathed. They could hear the wail of the sirens outside and they knew the law was coming for him. He seemed crazy, his eyes flashing, his breathing erratic, and they knew that it wouldn't take much for him to start blasting; all it would take was for someone to move.

Then someone moved.

William Hughes was a regular at the pub, a 65-year-old news vendor. All he did was twitch his hand towards his glass but the jumpy Griffiths whirled round, the rifle up, the barrel spitting twice. The poor man fell back. Both bullets had found their target and blood pumped from wounds that would kill him five days later. Owner James Connelly seized the chance to grab the gunman and throw him bodily out of the bar. It was a brave act, perhaps a stupid act, but Connelly was used to all kinds of tough guys and he wasn't having this lunatic shooting his bar, not to mention his customers, to pieces. As Connelly reached for the phone, Griffiths came roaring back in, the rifle jerking once. The bullet went wild and Connelly ducked for cover; then Griffiths was gone again, spooked by the screeching tyres of the police as they converged on the area.

Outside, a young man named Ian Shaw tried to capture Griffiths and was shot for his trouble. A lorry was hijacked but a taxi driver kept close tabs on it and was able to keep police informed of the route Griffiths was taking. His driving was as erratic as his mind: he skidded round corners, ran red lights and sent motorists swerving. The rifle lay on his lap and every now and then he poked it from the cab of the lorry and fired it with one hand. He reached Springburn and swerved into Kay Street, not knowing it was a cul-de-sac. Still firing, he leaped from the cab and ran up the short street towards the Corporation baths at the far end, then ducked into the close mouth at No. 26.

Police moved quickly to clear the street, for they knew that Griffiths would start shooting again once he found a vantage point. He had pounded up to the top floor of the tenement and blown the locks of a door. From the window, he could see the street and he sent bullets raining down on the police. He did not see the little child in the pram directly below him, but the police did. The baby's parents wanted to run out and grab the child, but that duty fell to a volunteer officer who carefully crept up the street, his back pressed against the sandstone walls, until he reached the pram. The child was carried to safety. Griffiths might not have been at the window during the rescue. After letting loose with a few rounds, he had moved down to the first-floor landing to check the rear of the building. From there, he took potshots at children in a playground, hitting an eight-year-old child, an eighteen-year-old newly wed woman and another man. The woman's young husband had to be wrestled to the ground to prevent him racing towards the window to get to the man who had put a bullet in his wife's leg.

But Griffiths' time was running out. In one hundred and five minutes, he had loosed off more than one hundred rounds and had wounded nine men, two women and a child. Now back in his top-floor sniper's nest, perhaps he knew there was no hope, but as he had vowed before, he wasn't going to go down without a fight. He was no Edwin Finlay; there was no self-inflicted bullet to the head for him. He still had ammunition and he still had the will to use it.

The end came when he heard the creak of a letterbox being pushed open behind him. He turned and saw eyes watching him from the landing outside. With a bellow of rage, he charged towards the door. A pistol barrel was thrust hastily through the letterbox and the trigger pulled.

The bullet hit him in the shoulder, but bullets are unpredictable things. Rounds can bounce from bone, glance off sinew and change direction. In this case, it surged downwards through his body to career off his ribs, then tore through organs and flesh and blood to end its trajectory in his heart. He fired once more as he hit the floor but the shot went wide. By the time the police forced open the barricaded door and carried him none too gently down the stairs to the streets, the gunman was dead. He was the first man in Scotland to be gunned down by police officers in the line of duty.

Chief Superintendent Malcolm Finlayson was the man who had pulled the trigger that put 'Mad Dog' Griffiths down. He had not meant to kill, but kill he had. 'That's not something I will readily forget,' he said later. Both he and Detective Sergeant Ian Smith, who had been with him as they crept up the stairs, were honoured for their gallantry, as were James Connelly, Ian Shaw and ambulanceman John Preston, who braved the bullets to bring aid to the wounded.

Meehan spent the next seven years in self-imposed solitary confinement, protesting his innocence. In court, he claimed that the crime had been committed by Ian Waddell, a career criminal with a record for housebreaking and violence. The son of a slaughterhouse sheep-killer, Waddell had been a troubled youth – he'd once assaulted his primary school teacher – and had been in and out of jail on a variety of charges. He had been in the frame for the Ross job from early in the investigation but the Meehan tip-off had deflected the heat from him. That didn't prevent him from telling a Scottish newspaper that he was the real killer. Meehan's advocate, Nicolas Fairbairn, and author Ludovic Kennedy campaigned to have the case re-examined.

The break came when Glasgow crook William 'Tank' McGuiness was found unconscious in a Parkhead gutter in March 1976. He had been kicked near to death and police sat by his bedside for 13 days waiting for word about who had attacked him. Tank, though, died without breathing a word. However, his passing did free lawyer Joseph Beltrami from the chains of client confidentiality. McGuiness had confessed to him that he and Waddell had pulled the Ross robbery and murder. Beltrami, who also represented Meehan, was now free to kick-start the process that would clear an innocent man. Waddell was arrested and charged with the Rachel Ross murder. He returned the favour by lodging a special defence of incrimination – he didn't do it, Paddy Meehan did. The case was found not proven.

The man who police believed had given McGuiness his fatal tanking was another Glasgow crook, John 'Gypsy' Winning, also known as 'the Great Escaper'. The Romany blood in his veins and his love of freedom and the open air led him to make a total of eight escape attempts from jail or police custody. But his dislike of confinement did not prevent him walking the crooked path, for he had spent only four years as a free man since the age of twenty. Now he faced life inside for murder.

Tank had been an old friend. In fact, they had both escaped from Barlinnie in 1960, using the tried-and-tested method of bedclothes fashioned into a rope, followed by a real rope over the wall. 'You can't get closer to a man than that,' Gypsy said. However, the prosecution insisted that Tank had for some reason been condemned to death by the underworld powers that be (McGuiness had been acting like a marked man for some weeks and his home had been broken into by a gunman) and that Gypsy was the man who carried out the sentence. Either that, or the two old pals had fallen out and, in a fit of anger in Springfield Road, Winning had methodically beaten and kicked McGuiness to death. They supported their theory with bloodstains on Gypsy's coat that matched the victim's rare grouping.

Winning denied the charge. Tank was a pal and he had no reason to harm him. He'd met him that night, sure, but he hadn't killed him. If he had given him such a kicking, surely there would be blood on his shoes? The blood on his coat was easily explained and his account backed up by a witness. McGuiness had got into a beef with another man during which his nose had been burst open and Winning had gone to help him, getting the blood on his coat in the process. When he had last seen Tank, he had been hale, if not particularly hearty.

The prosecution might have won their case had procedure not been badly screwed up. The blood sample taken from the dead man had not been properly recorded and therefore could not be lodged as evidence. They could not legally establish that the sample lodged as evidence was, in fact, McGuiness's blood. Therefore it did not matter that it was rare and that it matched the spatters found on Winning's coat. And without that sample, they had no case. The jury was directed to find Gypsy Winning not guilty, giving him his last, narrow escape. He died, aged 51, during a brawl in Dunfermline in 1991.

In May 1982, Ian Waddell and another crook named Andy Gentle got involved in a neighbourhood row in which Mrs Josephine Chipperfield died. She had complained about her 16-year-old daughter being allowed to get drunk at a house party in Buchlyvie Street, Easterhouse. In retaliation, Waddell and Gentle forced their way into her home and stabbed her to death. Afterwards, they hid out in a flat in Springburn's Blackthorn Street, their threatening manner forcing the resident to flee. But Gentle began to fear that Waddell would fire him in for the murder in order to save himself. He throttled the 44-year-old crook with a curtain wire and buried the body in a shallow grave in the back court.

Gentle had an extended list of previous, including an eight-year stretch for culpable homicide in 1969, and was sentenced to a twenty-year minimum for the two murders, although he claimed that Waddell had killed Mrs Chipperfield and another man had done for Waddell. He hanged himself in prison. His suicide marked the end of the chain of death that had begun all those years before in that little Ayr bungalow.

Meehan was pardoned but never gave up his fight to completely clear his name and prove that he had been fitted up by the authorities. Three months after Waddell died, Lord Hunter's report into the case failed to exonerate him. 'The theory of an initial assault by Ian Waddell and "Tank" McGuiness with a follow-up by Meehan and gunman Griffiths to open the safes believed to have been in the house,' it concluded, 'is a possibility that cannot be ruled out.' In 1994, throat cancer claimed Paddy Meehan.

Tom Goodall, who had helped trap Peter Manuel and had put the fear of death into Jimmy Boyle, fell victim to a heart attack on 12 October 1969. He had been in charge of Glasgow's CID since 1963. The underworld he had policed had always been violent, but it was changing, and not for the better. Increasingly, the robbers were spurning the old-fashioned skills of the peterman, and the hoodlums rejecting the edged weapon, in favour of the firearm.

In 1966, the country was shocked to hear of the callous murder of three police officers in London. PC Geoffrey Fox, DS Christopher Head and DC David Wombwell had been carrying out what they believed was a routine stop and search in Braybrook Street, west London. The crescent-shaped street lies on the edge of Wormwood Scrubs, the common land that gave its name to the prison. The jail itself sits at the end of Braybrook Street, at its junction with Wulfstan Street. On 12 August, the three officers spotted an old, rusting blue estate car with three men inside. The officers wondered what this dilapidated vehicle was doing so close to the jail and decided to investigate. A few minutes later, they were dead. As they spoke to the driver, John Witney, another man pulled a gun and shot DC Wombwell in the face. The gunman was Harry Roberts, and he and a third man piled out of the vehicle and killed the other two officers. The third man was Glasgow-born John Duddy, who shot PC Fox as he sat behind the wheel of the police car. The blue car jerked forward and ran over DS Head, who had been shot in the back by Roberts.

The three men, petty criminals setting out on a job, fled the scene. Witney, who was using his own car, was scooped up within hours and he swiftly named his accomplices. Harry Roberts, the former soldier whose twitchy trigger finger had started the bloodbath, used his evasion skills to remain at large for months, hiding out in Epping Forest. He and Duddy had buried the guns on Hampstead Heath before splitting up. Duddy scuttled back to Glasgow.

John Duddy was born in 1928 in the Gorbals, one of eleven children. His father, Bernard, was originally from Ireland and had been a city cop for three years before becoming a mason's labourer. In the tough streets of the Gorbals, the young boy, like so many others, drifted into crime, earning his first conviction at the age of 13 for housebreaking. Despite the events of August 1966, he was a crook with a soft heart. During one burglary, he surprised the female resident of a house and was shocked to see her slump in a faint. He helped her up, made her a cup of tea and ensured she was all right. She wanted to drop any charges but her husband was of a different mind and Duddy was duly sentenced. His last conviction was at the age of 19, for stealing a car. After that, he tried to go straight. He'd married a good-looking local girl and wanted to put his youthful transgressions behind him. He joined the army and served in Malaya, as did his future co-accused Harry Roberts. On leaving the army, he and his young wife moved to London to find work. As the 1960s dawned, they were back home for a spell but soon moved back down south, where he thought he could make more money. It was while driving lorries that he met John Witney and the crime bug bit again. They teamed up with Roberts, who was coming off a four-year stretch and had vowed never to go back inside. Witney and Roberts had already been nicking lead but now they graduated to sticking up shops and robbing rent collectors.

Back in Glasgow, Duddy told his family what had happened. His father was on holiday in Ireland at the time and was unaware that his son was a wanted man. Later, the old man said, 'John has brought shame to my family and myself. I go to church every day and pray for him. There is nothing else I can do . . . after all, he is still my son.'

A massive manhunt had been launched to track down the two killers and Duddy's family urged him to give himself up. Duddy agreed but could not take that final step. He was a nervous wreck, on the move constantly and afraid to show his face in the street lest he be gunned down by a cop with revenge on his mind. Tom Goodall spearheaded the hunt in Glasgow and his men were never more than a few steps behind.

Five days after the shootings, Duddy's brother Vincent led Goodall and his men to a small flat in Stevenson Street, Bridgeton. It was rented by a night-shift worker who had showed typical Glasgow hospitality by allowing Duddy to spend the night. He didn't know who he was; he'd only been told by a mutual acquaintance that the man needed a bed for the night. The night before, Duddy had told his family to do what they had to and Vincent did it. Later, he said he had not acted like a Judas but had simply wanted to ensure that his brother was arrested safely. He and the cadre of armed officers crept up the dingy staircase to the first-floor flat and Vincent knocked on the door. Then he pushed the door open and threw himself on top of his brother as he lay on the bed, putting himself between John and the police. There were guns all around that room and he didn't want any of them going off. Duddy, probably relieved that it was all over, went along quietly.

Roberts remained at large until November. By that time, Witney and Duddy were already on trial and the proceedings were halted to allow Roberts to take his place beside them in the dock. They were all sentenced to life, with a minimum of 30 years.

Duddy's wife vowed to stand by him. She had separated from him ten days before the shootings because she was unhappy about his new lifestyle. It was clear he deeply regretted what had happened. Before his arrest he'd told his family, 'I will be punished, for what I have done is wrong.' He was grateful for the support his wife gave him. He wrote from prison, 'No matter what happens to me now I will always be grateful that I, at least, had a wonderful wife. Even in here I can feel her love.'

Even so, his wife eventually divorced him and he planned to marry again, this time to a prison visitor who had fallen for him. John Duddy died of a heart attack in Parkhurst Prison in February 1981.

* * *

Three years after the London shootings, as the swinging '60s were dying, Glasgow saw its own cop-killing tragedy.

On 23 December 1969, Archibald Ross McGeachie was reported missing from his home at 62 Craigie Street in the South Side. The 21-year-old was a partner in a fruit and vegetable shop at 57 Allison Street. His Triumph 2000, bought in July of that year under a hire purchase agreement, had been left by him at a local garage for repair, but on 30 December it was found in Craigie Street, near Allison Street. Police later discovered that it had been parked there by a relative. In the early hours of 1 January 1970, it was removed to the police garage at Pollokshaws police office to be examined by officers of the Identification Bureau, the force's forensic experts.

But of McGeachie there was no sign – and police really wanted to speak to him. It was unusual for them to become so concerned over the whereabouts of an adult who had been missing for only a week. But then, these were highly unusual circumstances.

Archibald McGeachie had been implicated in the robbery of the British Linen Bank in Williamwood on 16 July. Three men had walked into the bank in Eastwoodmains Road and politely asked the staff to hand over cash. They had backed up their request with ammonia and firearms, and they got away, driven by McGeachie, with £20,876. The press later dubbed them 'the Gentleman Raiders'. Even that was not the full reason for the police's interest in McGeachie. On 30 December, three men had robbed the Linwood branch of the Clydesdale Bank. He had not been one of them, having vanished seven days before, but subsequent events in a cramped little flat in Allison Street had brought the missing man's name to police files. When suspicious cops had questioned gang leader Howard Wilson, he had pulled a gun and started blasting, killing two.

What made matters worse was that Wilson had once been a cop himself and had received chief constable's commendations for zeal and efficiency. However, he left the force after ten years to go into business with McGeachie. This did not prove as successful as he had hoped and he convinced three friends – one also a former policeman, another a former prison officer and the third McGeachie – to take up a life of crime. One quick score was all they needed to pull themselves out of the financial mire, and so the Williamwood job was duly pulled. But it wasn't enough for Wilson. They had carried it off with ease and got clean away. The cops couldn't lay a glove on them. Wilson wanted to stage another caper but McGeachie wasn't willing. And then he disappeared.

At around 4.25 p.m. on Tuesday, 30 December, Inspector Andrew Hyslop and Constable John Sellars were leaving the Southern Police Office in Craigie Street via a lane that leads into Allison Street. While they sat in their car waiting for a break in traffic that would allow them to ease out, they saw Howard Wilson and another man in the forecourt of a garage hefting two heavy suitcases. They watched as the two men walked into the close mouth at 51 Allison Street, followed by a third man carrying a black tin box. Inspector Hyslop, 44 years old, knew Wilson and the second man. He also knew that Wilson was having money problems. His copper's nose began to twitch. However, he did not link the men's actions to the bank job earlier that day in far-off Linwood. At this stage, the worst he thought was that they were trading in illicit booze.

Knowing that the men had gone into Wilson's ground-floor flat, he told PC Sellars to wait by the close mouth while he went back to the station to fetch help. When he returned with detective constables Angus MacKenzie and John Campbell and PC Edward Barnett, he saw Wilson coming out of a nearby dairy. They stopped him and asked him about the suitcases and the tin box. Wilson was polite and calm and invited them in to see for themselves.

The other two men were in the living room when they entered and Inspector Hyslop saw that one of the suitcases was filled with money. The police, knowing they'd stumbled across something more serious than resetting stolen booze, began a search. Wilson moved into the bedroom and came back with a gun in his hand. It was a Vistok .22 Russian target pistol and in the wrong hands it could be as deadly as a Magnum. Wilson, who'd been target shooting for years, knew how to use it.

He shot Inspector Hyslop first, the bullet hitting the veteran officer in the left side of his face. He fell to the floor, still conscious but unable to move. All he could do was watch as his friends and colleagues rushed to his aid. The hallway of the flat became a killing ground as Wilson whirled and fired, hitting first DC MacKenzie and then PC Barnett. He placed the gun against DC MacKenzie's head and finished him off. PC Sellars threw himself into the bathroom and pressed his weight against the door as Wilson pushed and clawed on the outside. He was a madman now. His eyes were wild with fear; his only thought was to kill. DC Campbell appeared, then ducked as Wilson loosed off a shot, the bullet splintering the door frame. The cop retreated into a room and slammed the door shut. He and PC Sellars heard Wilson shout, 'We'll have to get this bastard, he's the one with the radio!' PC Sellars knew he meant him, for he was already yelling down his radio for help. The other two men would not help Wilson. They were shocked and horrified at what had happened and one refused to fetch more ammunition. The other fled and was arrested later.

Wilson threw his weight against the bathroom door and felt it give a little. Inside, PC Sellars watched as the gun was jammed into the crack and swivelled round towards him. He pushed harder from his side and trapped Wilson's wrist. Cursing, the gunman snatched his hand away and the door closed firmly again. When he heard Inspector Hyslop groan, he decided to finish him off, just as he had done with DC MacKenzie. He stepped closer, held the gun to the man's head and began to squeeze the trigger. DC Campbell was not about to let that happen and launched himself across the hallway to grab Wilson's arm. The two men struggled in the small space for possession of the weapon and once again Wilson's remaining partner in crime refused to help. He had not signed up for this. Robbery was one thing, murder was quite another. However, it also has to be said that he did not rush to aid the police officers; but then, fear can be paralysing.

DC Campbell managed to wrestle the gun from Wilson's hand and he backed out of the flat, keeping both men covered. The radio calls had been answered and as he stepped into the close mouth, swarms of police officers arrived from the nearby station.

DC MacKenzie was rushed to the Victoria Infirmary but was found to be dead on arrival. PC Barnett later succumbed to his wounds. Inspector Hyslop survived, with fragments of the bullet remaining in his neck. DC Campbell suffered a minor injury to his left hand and PC Sellars was unharmed. Wilson and his two partners were lodged in the cells at Craigie Street. That night, a very big, very tough chief inspector stood guard over them to protect them from vengeful officers. He might have despised them, particularly Wilson, for what they had done, but no harm would befall them, not on his watch.

Inspector Hylsop and DC Campbell each received the George Medal for their bravery. DC MacKenzie and PC Barnett were posthumously awarded the Queen's Police Medal for Gallantry. They each left behind a widow, while PC Barnett had two small children. The flag at Craigie Street flew at half mast as a sign of respect.

The shootings prompted calls for the return of the death penalty, which had been fully abolished earlier that month. Dan Wilson, secretary of the Scottish Police Federation, was quoted as saying:

> I hope this is on the conscience tonight of those MPs, particularly the Scottish members, who did not vote for the retention of capital punishment. I am so angry and sick and fed up with the crimes of violence in this country which culminate in murder . . . All policemen in Glasgow must be feeling sick tonight. We might not yet be as bad as America, but we are certainly catching up with it in murders.

Naturally, the widows of the murdered officers agreed with him. They and 1,000 other police wives staged a rally in Glasgow calling for the reintroduction of capital punishment.

Howard Wilson went on to make legal history twice. He was the first man in Scotland to plead guilty to double murder and he was given the longest sentence yet imposed by a Scottish court: 25 years to life for the murder and 12 years for the robberies. His accomplices were each given 12 years for the bank raids. In 1972, Wilson was one of the inmates who rioted during disturbances in Peterhead Prison. He then joined forces with Jimmy Boyle, whom he had once helped stalk while a police officer, during riots at Inverness's Porterfield Prison. The two men had been in the infamous 'cages', specially constructed cells, designed to hold troublesome prisoners, in the prison's segregation block. The five cells each housed a cage containing a bed nailed to the floor. There was no other furniture, no toilet facilities apart from a pot, and food was pushed through to the prisoner.

If you treat people like animals, they will react like animals, and in December 1972 that's precisely what Boyle, Wilson, Glasgow bank robber William McPherson and murderer Larry Winters did. The authorities said it was a jailbreak and an attempt to kill guards with home-made weapons; the prisoners insisted it had begun as a peaceful protest over the treatment and conditions. Whatever it was, it was violent, and one officer was stabbed repeatedly, while another lost an eye. The prisoners were charged with attempted murder and assault. The jury did not accept the attempted murder charges but the men were given six years each for assault and attempting to escape. Boyle and Winters were sent to the Special Unit in Barlinnie, where Winters would die of a drug overdose, while Wilson and McPherson went back to the welcoming arms of Peterhead.

In 1972, Archibald McGeachie's family went to the Court of Session, Scotland's supreme civil court, to have him declared legally dead. He had left behind £9,000 and a baffling mystery. As far as is known, no word has ever been received of him. Perhaps he legged it knowing that things were about to get too hot for him. But underworld rumour has it that he was murdered back in 1969 and urban legend has it that his body was dropped into the foundations of the M8 motorway or one of the support pillars for the Kingston Bridge. If that is the case, then no one can say for certain who killed him or why. If that is the case, then he obviously fell foul of the wrong man.

The Vistok pistol used in the police murders lay for many years in a safe inside Craigie Street police station. It can now be seen at the Strathclyde Police Museum.

Guns don't kill people. People kill people. Guns just make it easier.

CHAPTER SEVENTEEN

IT'S IN THE BLAG

In 1972, three years after Howard Wilson made criminal history with his sentences, another group of accused made legal history because of their lack of a sentence. The case involved armed robbery, a legal blunder and the fact that it was a leap year.

On Monday, 7 February, the manager of the Stepps Hotel in the East End was in his office awaiting the arrival of a security van to remove the weekend's takings. Early that morning, before the van arrived, three masked men armed with a shotgun and a hammer removed them for him. One held the shotgun to the back of the manager's head and demanded that he hand over the cash. The man bravely refused to tell them where it was being stored. Very few raiders set out to use their weapons; in fact, it was frowned upon because there was a rule of thumb that once a weapon was used in the course of a crime, it would have to be destroyed so that it could not be produced in evidence against either the blagger or the armourer who supplied it. The manager did not know that but he still kept his mouth shut. He could not know whether these raiders were desperate enough to wound him, or worse.

It was while they were trying to terrorise him into giving up the information that a waiter walked in carrying two high towers of plates. The shock of seeing the masked, armed men threatening his boss made him drop them. The noise of the crockery shattering was loud enough to waken the dead at that early hour and the gang knew they would have limited time to find their booty and get away. So one of them fired the shotgun into the ceiling, just to show they meant business.

The explosion of gunfire in the small room prompted the manager to give up the location of the money – hidden in the back of a filing cabinet – and the men got away with £19,000. However, they were spotted dumping the getaway vehicle, so police fairly swiftly lifted two young men from the East End schemes, and a few weeks later a third man. All three were remanded in custody to await trial at the High Court, which was set for June. Whatever happened, the Crown believed they had to have the trial completed by midnight on Wednesday, 7 June, for they had calculated that that was when the magical 110-day rule would come into effect.

The rule had become enshrined in Scots law in 1885, when it was laid down that anyone held in custody awaiting trial must have that trial completed within 110 days of their committal. This was to ensure that accused persons receive a speedy and fair trial. The prosecution could apply for an extension citing extenuating circumstances but such applications were regularly refused by the bench. The 110-day rule was strict, often unbending, and flaunting it would lead to the charges being dropped.

In the Stepps Hotel case, the prosecution team blithely continued with the case until Tuesday, 6 June, leaving Wednesday for final speeches. It would all be over long before the deadline. What they had forgotten was that 1972 was a leap year – and by the Wednesday the first two men arrested had been in custody for 111 days. Their defence had not missed this important fact – in fact, one later admitted that he deliberately employed delaying tactics – and that morning they demanded that their clients be freed.

A Police Federation spokesman later dubbed the oversight 'an incredible blunder'. The Crown could do nothing but agree to the defence submission. The third man was later acquitted and the taxpayer had to stump up £20,000 to pay for the trial.

The law was later changed so that the trial has to begin, rather than be completed, before the 110 days are up.

If the 1960s seemed a murderous decade, then the '70s, although still violent, were marked by larceny. Bank robberies appeared to be the favoured means of making a fast buck and there was no shortage of recruits to the growing band of would-be outlaws. Not all were hardened criminals. Matthew Lygate, for instance, was an idealistic young Communist who idolised John Maclean and sought ways to better the life of the working man. Born in the South Side, he trained as a tailor's cutter before deciding that the life of a radical was for him. He joined the Workers Party of Scotland, became its secretary and ran a Party bookshop in Paisley Road West. He followed in Maclean's footsteps by standing for the Gorbals in a by-election, attracting a mere 72 crosses to his name and finishing last. By the early '70s, he had travelled Scotland trying to rally support to the cause, having some measure of success but recruiting far short of the numbers needed to effect real change. In 1972, he decided, as if in emulation of Joseph Stalin's early life, to become a bank robber.

He and three other men – former soldier William McPherson who was said to be the mastermind, Cockney car salesman on the lam from the London law Ian Doran and former monk Colin Lawson – were charged with a massive 25-count indictment that included armed robbery, assault and forming a criminal conspiracy. Police had raided the bookshop and found guns, ammunition and cash tucked away among the propaganda books and leaflets. They found more incriminating material in Lygate's Albert Road flat.

Lygate claimed that he had been asked to take part in robberies but had refused as he felt it would jeopardise his position as a political organiser. However, he did know a number of activists who were engaged in 'guerrilla tactics on behalf of the working classes'. These were the days of the Red Army Faction in Germany and the Symbionese Liberation Army in America, groups staging robberies and even murders for political reasons. Revolution was in the air across the world. Lygate had connections with an Irish group called Saor Eire, or Free Ireland, which funded its activities by robbing banks. He saw their success and wished to emulate it in Scotland.

He must have known his position was untenable. Even so, he sacked his legal team – Nicolas Fairbairn QC and solicitor Joe Beltrami – in order to go it alone. He wanted to present his own closing argument and plea in mitigation. These amounted to a political attack on society and had very little to do with the case against him. The judge lost patience and had him silenced, although with difficulty. Lygate was a politician, and a politician loves an audience; he was not about to yield the floor without a verbal struggle. Finally, his diatribe against the oppression of the working man came to an end and the judge punished him with a hefty 24 years in jail. It was an astounding sentence for what were mere robberies, albeit with violence, but the judge saw Lygate as a very dangerous man, even though he had no previous convictions. To the bench, he was an insurrectionist who would have continued in his wicked ways. William McPherson, who had a string of previous, was given twenty-six years, Doran twenty-five years and Lawson a mere six. As Lygate and McPherson were being led down to the cells, they raised their clenched fists and yelled, 'Long live the workers of Scotland!'

Matthew Lygate was released on parole in 1983. William McPherson was involved in riots in Peterhead and in the Inverness prison riot of '72. He was eventually paroled but was arrested again in 2003 when he was nabbed in Firhill with £20,000 worth of heroin on his person. He thought he was picking up stolen cigarettes, he claimed. Sentenced to five years, he died shortly after in prison of a heart attack, aged sixty-four.

The brain behind the 1973 British Rail works job was crook Robert Marley. Operating from the Railway Tavern in Cowlairs, he reasoned that if a gang pulled the job on 21 December, the works coffers at the Charles Street depot would be filled with Christmas cheer in the form of festive bonuses. He thought they'd net around fifty grand but in the end they reaped less than ten. The other members of the gang were all out-of-town talent: James Aitken, Jim Murphy and Scots-born Steve Doran, who really should have known better, as his brother Ian had gone down along with Matthew Lygate. Sydney Draper, Alan Brown and William Murray completed the team who would tackle the Townhead works. It was believed that at least some of them were part of a roaming robbery crew that had already pulled jobs in Glasgow, Dundee and Erskine. The gang met in the pub and planned the raid, a show of hands providing the mandate for the scheme to go ahead.

It was a professional heist but it was badly bungled. Armed with automatic pistols, sawn-off shotguns and ammonia, Brown, Murphy, Draper, Doran and Murray piled out of the back of a blue Transit van that had pulled up on the railway lines at Inchbelly crossing. They sprinted the few hundred yards into the works while Marley drove the van to the gates to wait for them to come out with the loot. Aitken walked up to the top of a nearby multi-storey car park with a fine view of the works and used high-powered binoculars and a walkie-talkie to direct operations. The wages were issued from boxes piled onto a forklift truck and when he saw it begin to make its rounds he yelled into the radio, 'Go! Now!'

They blinded the driver and another man with ammonia squirted from plastic lemons and shot two security guards in the arm to bring them down. They grabbed the boxes and made for the front gate, where Marley waited with the van. Security guard James Kennedy had just come on duty and rushed out of the gatehouse to intercept the men. He was battered to the ground and the raiders leaped into the van. But Mr Kennedy was not going to let them get away. He pulled himself to his feet and came after them. Brown poked his shotgun out of the van window and pulled the trigger. The brave security guard, a Jehovah's Witness, was blown back by the force of the blast and died.

As the van screeched away, Brown said, 'That geezer was a right game bastard.'

The 42-year-old father of three had defended other people's money with his life. In 1975, he was posthumously awarded the George Cross, the highest civilian award for gallantry, and the Glasgow Corporation Medal for Bravery. British Rail named a locomotive after him.

Marley and Aitken, the original architects of the caper, were horrified that a man had been killed. That had not been part of their plan. The problem is that people with guns kill people. What had begun as a blag had become murder, and the men knew that the city would be too hot for them. They already had their escape route planned and they split up, the money being handed to one of their wives, who transported it to London by train, the cash in a carrier bag on her lap. Loose lips, though, not only sink ships but they can also scupper criminal gangs. Back in Glasgow, people were talking about the job and the name 'Big Jim' was filtering through to the ears of cops, led by Detective Chief Inspector John McVicar. Soon Aitken and Marley were being fingered for being behind the plan.

Marley was the first to be hoovered up and under pressure named the others. Glasgow cops were with officers from the Met in a series of raids led by the legendary Detective Superintendent Jack Slipper of the Yard. Only Billy Murray evaded capture and was not arrested until after his pals had been tried and sentenced. Marley coughing so easily, and his change of plea midway through the trial to guilty, placed him under threat and he had to be given special protection.

The High Court building was filled with blue serge. According to police, they had been tipped off that heavy underworld figures were going to try to rescue their pals, so security was stepped up several notches. Underworld figures and defence lawyers often view these precautions with some cynicism, believing that they are largely attempts to influence the jury by painting the accused as dangerous men before a word of evidence is even heard.

The men received a total of 119 years in prison. The trial judge, Lord Kissen, singled out DCI McVicar (described by one former colleague as 'a magnificent cop with a well-developed sense of humour'), DCI Fletcher Catchpole of the Glasgow Flying Squad (whose unusual name was often mangled into 'Tadpole' by touts and crooks) and DI David Frew for special thanks for bringing the men in. Billy Murray, collared one week later, faced trial alone and changed his plea on the second day. He was given 16 years to life. The men appealed their sentences but were, perhaps predictably, refused. There was – and is – a school of thought that the Scottish appeal court is there simply to uphold sentences. That is not the case, and in Steve Doran's case the judges expressed some anxiety over the standard of evidence against him, in particular a fingerprint in the getaway van that could have been ten days old. However, their concern was not strong enough to merit his convictions being quashed or his sentence reduced.

On 10 December 1987, Sydney Draper escaped from Gartree Prison in Leicestershire when an accomplice hijacked a helicopter and forced the pilot to set down in the prison sports field. It was around 3.15 p.m. when Draper and London gang boss John Kendall, doing eight years for burglary, sprinted across the field and into the chopper. But it was winter. The light was fading and bad weather meant the chopper had to set down earlier than expected. They chose an industrial estate as their makeshift landing strip and the runners commandeered cars to get away. Kendall remained at large for ten days but Draper was on the run for thirteen months before he was finally nabbed in north London. The escape was the only one in British history to involve a helicopter, although in March 2009 detectives foiled a plot to free nine suspected al-Qaeda terrorists from Full Sutton Prison in east Yorkshire using a similar method.

The year after the works job saw Glasgow crooks break yet another Scottish criminal record, this time for the largest ever haul from a Scottish bank. On 30 April 1974, two men walked into the Whiteinch branch of the Clydesdale Bank, fired two shots into the air and made off with £87,000 of other people's money. No one was hurt in the raid, although another round was fired by accident as they sped off in the getaway car. Police moved swiftly to set up roadblocks around Whiteinch, stopping all cars. However, the thieves had driven to high flats at Broomhill, where they ditched the car and hopped onto bikes they'd already stashed there. The mastermind behind the raid, 37-year-old James Crosbie, waved at officers as they let him through a roadblock without searching his backpack, which was stuffed with cash. Had any of the cops on duty recognised him, it might have been a very different story. But now he was to become the most wanted man in Britain.

Born in Springburn in 1937, Crosbie started thieving at the age of 13. He swiftly graduated to doing post offices, factories and shops. Although no doubt capable of handling himself if necessary, he had no reputation for violence and the discharging of the firearms during the Whiteinch raid troubled him. It enabled the police to paint him as a desperate criminal, a John Dillinger-style robber who was capable of anything. He had periods of going straight and had travelled abroad when younger, getting himself a pilot's licence, and had had spells working in the Glasgow shipyards and even for a time in the RAF. But the pull of crime was always strong. During the '60s, he found himself in London and once worked for the Krays on a forgery scam. But the twins, known for being tight with money, omitted to pay him and he never worked for them again.

By the early '70s, he was, ostensibly at least, straight again. He had a furniture shop in Springburn and a nice house in the douce suburb of Bishopbriggs. He had a wife and a young family. However, crime was in his blood and he could not stay on the straight and narrow for long. One day, he was talking to his neighbour, a 40-year-old bank messenger, about delivery times to banks and his thoughts turned to grand larceny. In May 1972, Crosbie and an accomplice robbed the Hillington branch of the Clydesdale Bank of over £60,000. Crosbie escaped the ensuing dragnet by driving to Glasgow Airport, leaving his car and walking back out again. However, a trip to Las Vegas and some high living soon had Crosbie's thoughts turning to another score. And so the Whiteinch job was pulled.

However, from then on it all went wrong for the daring blagger.

He stashed some of the cash in the house of a young girl with whom he'd become friendly. During a 'teenage pop record party' in her Possilpark home, her friends found the case stuffed with £40,000 in cash. Some of the notes stuck to their fingers and they came back for more, eventually siphoning off £13,000 of Crosbie's ill-gotten gains. Finally, someone decided to drop a word into the law's shell-like about the money, and Crosbie was arrested, charged with the two bank robberies and then, astonishingly given the circumstances, allowed out on bail. A more dangerous man might have decided to take it out on the young people but Crosbie was not of that mould. He did not, however, wish to enjoy Her Majesty's hospitality again, so he decided to take off.

But to do that, he needed some folding green, so he called at the Gorgie Road branch of the Royal Bank of Scotland in Edinburgh to make a withdrawal. Naturally, he didn't have an account there, so instead of presenting a withdrawal slip he showed the teller a shotgun, placed a bag on the counter and said, 'Fill it up.' The first teller looked at the man wearing a motorcycle helmet with the visor down and thought it was a joke. She refused. Again, a tougher customer might have used the shotgun. Instead, he repeated the process at the next stall and made off with £17,000. This time, he selected horsepower rather than pedal power for his getaway, but his luck ran out when his motorbike was intercepted by police officers.

In September 1974, Crosbie put his hands up to all three robbery charges in the hope that the court would treat him gently. The judge heard that he had 14 other convictions dating back to 1950 and declared that he was guilty of crimes of the 'utmost depravity' before sending him down for 20 years. Once inside, he discovered talents as an author and, like Howard Wilson before him, won the Koestler Award for writing by a British prisoner. So far, he's had four books published and once again appears to have gone straight.

Intimidating witnesses was obviously not Crosbie's style, which is more than can be said for the so-called XYY Gang. There are two differing explanations as to how this gang of strong-arm guys and blaggers got their name. The underworld claims it is police code for the most desperate of criminals, while a top policeman involved in tracking them down said it was given to them by the Crown Office during the various trials as a means of identification that would not prejudice other cases. The latter is much more likely, although there was a book called 'Supplement Z' kept by the CID clerk in city offices that listed desperate criminals and street crooks, assigning a number to each for identification.

Whatever the reason behind its name, the mob was extremely active in Glasgow and the west of Scotland during the mid-'70s, carrying out a string of armed robberies. At its head was Walter Norval, a career crook in his late 40s who used his intelligence, his brawn and his ruthless nature to hold together a disparate mob of crooks and hard men and meld them into an organised criminal enterprise.

'Wattie' picked his team from the schemes of the East End and the tough streets of Govan, the Gorbals and Milton. Nowhere was safe from them. They targeted works payrolls, banks, factories, hospitals and post offices. Anywhere there was a sizeable amount of loot to be lifted, they were likely to turn up. Each target was cased and each job meticulously planned and executed. There was brutality involved and threat, for these were not gentle men.

The epidemic of raids saw the creation of a special squad within the Serious Crime Squad, headed by Joe Jackson. These detectives were all armed as a matter of course and ready to fight firepower with firepower. For three years, the blaggers operated throughout the city and beyond without the law coming anywhere near them. There were clues – forensic-based mostly, even a few fingerprints – but without any real suspects, these were not much help.

Meanwhile, Wattie Norval was flashing the cash like it was going out of style, on wine, women and song. He was a brawny battler but he had style, even if his ear had been ruined by a bite from an opponent in a prison squabble. He liked good suits and good food. He liked a punt or two, backing the horses or taking his chances at the gaming tables. He liked to spread his wealth and be the big man. And he had a flat up the West End, where he kept the blonde moll by whom he had a son. His home life was different, though. He lived in a run-of-the-mill council house in Milton. He had a wife, seven kids and six grandkids. Grandpa Norval collected his unemployment money and other government aid on a weekly basis and he supplemented his income, legitimate and otherwise, by collecting rents from the tenants of properties owned by his mum.

But if there's one thing true in the criminal world, it is that people talk. After a time, people started talking about Big Wattie. And the cops were listening. A car belonging to him was spotted near to the location of one robbery. They almost caught him after one dawn raid when they zipped around to his house, but he got there before them and his wife swore blind that he'd been there all morning. When they came back some time later, he was off to Tenerife for a fortnight's jolly with his ladyfriend.

Time, though, was running out for him. He was now well in the frame for the robberies and all the police needed was something to hold him on. He handed that to them on a plate when, after another robbery, they found a shotgun and ammo in the boot of his flash new car. He claimed someone must have planted it there, but the police knew better and held him in custody pending further enquiries. Those enquiries concerned other names that had filtered through to them, including John McDuff and one Philip Henry, who had been lifted with two others pulling an extracurricular heist up north.

Henry, it seems, was sick of the life and felt others in the mob didn't show him the proper respect. He cracked under pressure and took police to where he had buried a shotgun used in one of the robberies and some stolen cash. In his book *The Enforcer*, cop Graeme Pearson records that Henry later told him that as the police tramped the Kilpatrick Hills in their suits and town shoes, Henry had considered giving them the slip and making a run for it. However, the die was cast and he knew he had to see the game out. It was said that a contract on his life had been taken out from inside Barlinnie's remand wing.

Henry survived on a diet of chocolate bars because he feared someone would slip something into his prison food, although someone did manage to scald him with boiling water. Another witness was told that he would be 'filled full of holes' if he said anything.

More arrests followed and thirteen of the gang were due to appear in four different trials – hence the need for Mr X and Mr Y code names – in Glasgow's High Court in November 1977. But someone did not want the proceedings to begin. That someone climbed onto the roof of the Saltmarket building, smashed a skylight and threw petrol bombs into the courtroom below. Firefighters battled to save the historic building but the North Court was too badly damaged for the case to be heard there. No matter, the South Court was swiftly cleaned up and the case of Norval and others was heard. The evidence and productions for the case, the real targets of the firebomber, were untouched by the flames, having been kept safely in the basement.

The High Court once again became the object of increased security. Armed police were everywhere, the judges and prosecuting counsel were guarded, witnesses were spirited in and out. Norval got 14 years, a far more lenient sentence than his underlings, with 22-year-old John McDuff – said to be his second-in-command – being hit with 21 years. Philip Henry, who had turned against his old boss, was given four years for his part in the robberies. Later, Norval's daughter was charged with conspiring to destroy the High Court building in a bid to disrupt her father's trial, but she was cleared. Her husband, though, was to begin a five-year stretch for threatening a witness.

By the end of the 1970s, prisoners were protesting at the brutal treatment they claimed they received inside Scotland's penal establishments. Jimmy Boyle had paved the way. Harsh measures by the authorities had led in turn to even harsher counter-measures by Boyle and others. Prisoners complained about 'mufti squads' of prison officers who rushed into cells and delivered tankings for transgressions. The Prison Service, of course, denied the claims. The vicious cycle of recriminations spread throughout the prison system and culminated in the late '70s and early '80s in a series of rooftop protests and riots. These did not involve Boyle, who by that time was learning new uses for sharp tools, having taken up sculpture.

As the '80s began, three young men were serving time in Barlinnie: Archibald Steen was doing life for murder, Jim Steele 12 years for attempted murder and malicious mischief in relation to a shotgun incident in a Garthamlock pub, and his brother John an identical term for the assault and robbery of a debt collector. They had been among the last prisoners brought down from the roof of Peterhead Prison in August 1979 during a protest over conditions. Afterwards, they claimed, they were stripped naked, handcuffed and beaten up for their part in the protest. They also claimed that urine was poured into their tea. The Prison Service consistently denied any such brutality.

On a sunny Sunday morning in June 1980, they staged an astounding escape from the jail – not to avoid punishment for their crimes, they claimed, but to get away from the brutal treatment they suffered at the hands of prison officers. There were rumours at the time that they had received help not just from outside but from inside too. However, 'Johnny Boy' Steele wrote in his book *The Bird That Never Flew* that the help they received was from other prisoners, not officers. A door to the shower room in B Hall was left unlocked for them and they made their escape through the iron bars of a grille, already partially sawn through for them by fellow cons, and onto the roof. The end of a roll of tape nicked from the prison textile shed was tossed over the wall to pals on the outside, who attached a sturdier rope, which was then hauled up. The three men and their pals had pulled off what underworld figures labelled 'the Great Glasgow Rope Trick'.

It was described as Scotland's most daring escape and the public were warned not to approach any of the men if spotted. They were not free for long. Someone talked and in 1980 they appeared in Glasgow High Court. The three men refused to accept advice from counsel that they should plead guilty, and defended themselves. They wanted to tell the court about the brutality they claimed to have suffered in prison. Earlier, John Steele had cheekily claimed that he had not escaped but had been kidnapped by the other two and forced to leave. The judge, Lord Avonside, told the jury that the prisoners' allegations had nothing to do with the charges against them, and commented that 'it is curious you are all complaining of brutal treatment when one looks at your record of violence'.

Jim Steele, a quietly spoken, unassuming guy, now living a peaceful life and who has not seen the inside of a prison since 1989, later recalled, 'I told him that anyone I'd dished out violence to didn't have handcuffs on.'

It didn't do them any good. At the end of the trial, thirty-two-year-old Steen was given an additional four years, while Jim, twenty-six, and John, twenty-four, got another three each.

On their way back to Peterhead, the van transporting them was involved in a crash on the A9 outside Perth. Given their record, it would have been reasonable to assume that this was the result of planning, yet another escape attempt. However, it was merely an accident on one of Scotland's worst roads.

TC Campbell, a former street-gang member, robber and hard man, was among the men later charged with and acquitted of aiding their escape. He, along with another Steele boy, were destined to become thorns in the side of the legal establishment.

CHAPTER EIGHTEEN

SEX AND THE CITY

Joe 'The Pole' Kotarba was no foreign prince. He had come to Glasgow after the Second World War, on the run from fellow countrymen he had betrayed by working for the Nazis. He was pally with another exiled Pole, Franciszek Gacic, who was jailed in 1958 for what became known as 'The Tricycle Killing'. He had beaten his girlfriend, prostitute Margaret Doyle, to a bloody death in his Hill Street flat with the handlebars of a trike. He also slashed her with a six-inch nail – all because she had spat at him and kicked him. He went down for fifteen years for the murder, although he only served ten.

Both he and Joe the Pole were pimps. They ran girls in the city's sex industry and lived off their earnings. They also liked to sample the merchandise and abuse it whenever possible. Gacic paid the price first when, in 1974, his girlfriend Margaret Cunningham snapped. They had been arguing in his North Woodside Road flat and he came at her. She picked up a kitchen knife – for a long time the most common murder weapon – and killed him. 'I saw red, grabbed the knife and stabbed him,' she said. And she kept stabbing him even as he lay motionless on the floor. She'd had enough of him and she did him in. She was sent down for three years for culpable homicide, but no one mourned Gacic.

No one much cared when Josef Kotarba went the same way, not even his stepson Walter Norval. Wattie never had much time for Joe the Pole and his mother's relationship with the pimp was a cause of friction between them. The crime boss did not care for the older man's lifestyle or his reputation for abusing women. And Joe abused a lot of women over the years. He liked it. He liked to hurt them and he liked people to watch him hurt them. He ran around half a dozen girls in Glasgow's sex lanes, including the main drag between Anderston and Blythswood Square and around Glasgow Green, and he checked on them every night. Heaven help any of them who did not have cash to give him, or whom he spotted going with black men – 'gorillas' he called them. These girls were punished severely. He punched them and he kicked them. He was known to use an iron bar. He even tortured them with broken bottles to give him and his drunken pals some jollies. No one had a good word to say about him, not even the man he shared a flat with in Maryhill, who said he was 'horrible, dangerous and a man who could kill'. And it was said that Joe had killed. A French girl had been beaten to death in one of his brothels; he claimed she had been killed by a punter. He was also implicated in the murder of prostitute Janet Davidson but there was not enough evidence to convict.

In July 1977, the 63-year-old former Nazi collaborator bullied one of his girls for the last time. The woman picked up a knife and stabbed him in his Raeberry Street flat. She plunged the blade into him 21 times but she walked free from court when found not guilty of murder. The public gallery greeted the verdict with a round of applause. 'It was him or me,' she had said. 'I kept my eyes closed all the time. I didn't know if the knife was going into the bed or him.' She made a lot of people happy when she killed him, not least Walter Norval, who was part of the crowd celebrating her release from court. He would soon have his own troubles in the same building, but for now he was a happy man.

The city is seldom free of sex crimes. Gacic and Kotarba were hateful men and no loss to society, but their deaths were exceptions.

Mostly, the victims are women or children. The most notorious Glaswegian sex murders are the three so-called Bible John killings of 1968–9, in which women were picked up at the Barrowland Ballroom in the East End and strangled on the way home. Descriptions of the man seen with the first victim, Patricia Docker, were sketchy. They were a bit better for the second, Jemima McDonald. But for the third, Helen Puttock, they were so detailed that a photofit image was released to the press (for the first time in Scotland) and a celebrated oil painting produced of the suspect.

All three women were menstruating at the time of their deaths and it was speculated that their killer was spurred to murder when his sexual advances were stymied. The hunt was the biggest murder probe Glasgow had ever seen and it haunted many who became involved – cops, reporters and the victims' families. However, the killer was never found. Bible John – so called because the suspect in the final murder quoted from the Bible during a taxi ride from the east side to the west side – stepped into the shadows and into legend. And anytime the city witnesses a similar sex crime, his spectre rises again.

The question is, was there a Bible John? Or were the three murders completely separate? The first killing differed from the others in that Pat Docker was murdered elsewhere and her naked body dumped in a lane near her home. The other two women were strangled and sexually assaulted where they lay. Criticism has also been levelled at the decision to focus on the description of the third suspect and to investigate all three murders under one umbrella. Strathclyde Police claimed that the murders were never linked for the purposes of investigation, but in fact they were – and it is felt that this was a mistake. If the three probes had been conducted independently, then perhaps a vital piece of evidence could have been uncovered. But perhaps not.

Hundreds of people think they know who Bible John was. It was a guy next door who behaved strangely at the time and had a suit similar to the one police described. It was a relative who was later convicted of rape. It was someone else who had very strange material in his attic. But there's seldom anything that resembles proof.

A 1995 police probe concentrated on newfangled DNA profiling. A sample of semen found on Helen Puttock's tights contained the miracle genetic fingerprint and a search was launched to try to match it with any of the suspects. Investigations zeroed in on one man, by that time dead. His relatives agreed to give blood and, according to one forensic scientist, the match was the closest she'd ever seen. Permission was granted in 1996 to exhume his body. Unwisely, it was decided that the information should be leaked to the press, and a Sunday newspaper broke the exclusive. The man was virtually convicted before the results were known and the exhumation became a media circus. Then everything went quiet. What was supposed to take weeks turned into months – until it was somewhat sheepishly revealed that no match could be found.

Cynics believed that the entire affair was merely a bit of PR for DNA profiling, but if that was the case, it failed. The problem lay with the samples. DNA can easily be contaminated and can erode if samples are not stored properly. Genetic fingerprinting was barely a glimmer in a scientist's eye in the late 1960s and although the original sample would have been stored carefully, the precautions taken might not have been sufficient to protect the material to the degree required. In addition, the suspect had been buried in a family lair and the passage of time had seen the coffin break down and the corpse contaminated. In all, the DNA 'breakthrough' in the Bible John case was something of a disaster.

Whenever a new multiple killer is brought to justice, someone tries to link him with the murders of 1968–9. The most recent is Peter Tobin, who was convicted of the brutal murders of Angelika Kluk, a Polish student whose body was found buried beneath a Glasgow church, and of teenager Vicky Hamilton, for many years the subject of one of Scotland's most perplexing missing persons cases. I know of one academic who is busy as I write trying to link Tobin to the Bible John killings. Tobin, it seems, told a prison psychiatrist that he was responsible for other murders and the claim was taken seriously enough for a special UK-wide operation code-named Anagram to be set up to piece together any evidence. In relation to the Bible John killings, Tobin was known to be living in the city at the time of the first two but was resident in Brighton when Helen Puttock was murdered.

However, the claims must be approached with caution. The Bible John victims were older than Tobin's known victims (Angelika Kluk was 23 but she looked much younger). And killers can be egotists, meaning his claim of being responsible for anything between 40 and 48 deaths could be merely bragging, a way to feel important. There is a danger that we might elevate an insignificant little pervert into the answer to a great mystery. He would love that.

Angus Sinclair has also been put forward as a potential suspect in the Bible John killings. Like Tobin, he would have been in his early 20s at the time. Like Tobin, he is a paedophile and killer. He was only sixteen when he killed for the first time, a seven-year-old girl strangled and raped in St Peter's Street, Glasgow. He was treated leniently by the courts and was convicted only of culpable homicide. Then, in 1982, he was arrested by Joe Jackson and his team for a disturbing series of attacks on children over a three-year period. The eldest was fourteen. The youngest was three. On his arrest, he said, 'I've done so many I cannae remember them all. I could have done 50, I just don't know.' At his trial, he requested to be chemically castrated.

One of the 50 was 17-year-old Mary Gallagher in 1979. At 17, she was perhaps out of the usual age range of his victims, but she was only 4 ft 11 in. In 2000, he appeared in court from prison, having been snared by DNA evidence, to receive another life sentence for Mary's murder.

Then his name came into the frame for another series of murders. During 1977 and 1978, three young women were brutally slain in Glasgow and, as in the Bible John case ten years before, the killer or killers were never caught. Anna Kenny, Agnes Cooney and Hilda McAulay were all killed as they left places of entertainment, sexually assaulted, beaten and strangled. In 1977, two Edinburgh girls, Helen Scott and Christine Eadie, were found dead after being seen in the

World's End pub on the High Street. After Sinclair's conviction for the murder of Mary Gallagher, Strathclyde, Lothian and Borders, and Central police forces formed Operation Trinity to study similarities between these and other cold cases and look into whether or not DNA breakthroughs could help solve them. Sinclair's name soon rose to the top and, with DNA samples having been found on ropes binding the two Edinburgh girls, it was decided to proceed against him for that double murder. However, the prosecution collapsed, leading to bitter recriminations between police and lawyers. According to a *News of the World* report in November 2008, Sinclair had already confessed his involvement in the killings to pals in jail. No strong evidence has been produced linking him to the Bible John killings.

Now, though, there is a new wrinkle to the Bible John case. A well-known Glasgow crook has told more than one person in prison that he murdered a man he believed to be the sex killer. This man disappeared late in 1969 and the jailhouse chit-chat says that he had to die because he was 'making life too hot for them all'. Of course, it could simply be that the convicted criminal is trying to justify yet another murder – although he has never been convicted of that particular slaying.

If there was a single killer called Bible John, why did he stop after three victims? Serial sex murderers do not usually just stop, they generally keep going until they are caught or killed, although some may 'mature' – in other words, grow out of their murderous impulses. Others might 'evolve', perfecting their skills, changing their patterns. But they seldom stop. Perhaps our man, if he existed, was killed by a partner. Or perhaps he moved away and continued murdering elsewhere. Perhaps he was jailed and began killing again – and again – when he came out. But, as yet, no firm link between such murders has been established. Glasgow's most notorious serial murderer, if such a killer ever existed, remains a shadowy enigma.

* * *

Such killers are still relatively rare, although women are always at risk, as are children, from violent men. And some young men like to exercise their machismo by beating up gay men. It was at Queen's Park, adjacent to the recreation ground where Henry Senior died in the honey trap and Tony Miller and Denovan killed John Cremin, that Michael Doran was viciously beaten to death in 1995.

The gang of gaybashers knew that the park was a favourite pick-up point for the South Side's gay community and set out on a robbing spree. Their third victim on that June night was 35-year-old Mr Doran. They stabbed him and then stamped on his head as he lay on the ground, breaking every bone in his face and fracturing his skull. Three young men, aged between sixteen and twenty, were sentenced to life for the murder. A fourteen-year-old girl was also sentenced to be detained without limit of time, but the following year her conviction was quashed by the appeal court and labelled a miscarriage of justice.

The park's reputation as one of the city's murder blackspots was sealed in 2007 when 40-year-old sales executive Moira Jones was murdered. A 33-year-old Slovakian man was subsequently convicted.

Of all the city's citizens, however, the most under threat are the prostitutes who nightly sell their services on the streets. You see them on the grid of streets between Anderston Cross and Blythswood Square, standing on corners, legs bare even on the coldest of nights, skirts short to show off the merchandise, faces pinched and drawn, bodies hunched against the cold, waiting for the next customer. In decades past, women were forced into selling their bodies by circumstance or a need for alcohol. Little has changed, except the thirst for booze has been replaced by a hunger for drugs. They are old and they are young. They are married and single. They have families and they are childless. They put themselves out there to service the men who cannot get sex any other way, or whose desires are too exotic for their regular partners. They stand there alone and they go off alone with the men, either by foot or in a car, and they often do not know what they are heading for.

Rape and violence are constant threats, robbery and refusal to pay common. In the 1990s, a number of street girls were murdered in the city. They were only doing their job and someone decided that it might be fun to kill them. The slayings became almost an epidemic, but police insisted that there was no link between them. Arrests were made in a few of the cases, but more often than not the cases resulted in acquittal.

But still the girls are out there, night after night, in the rain, in the cold. Waiting for the next customer. Waiting for the next payment. Waiting for the next battering. Waiting for the wrong man to pick them up.

CHAPTER NINETEEN

TO INFINITY AND BEYOND

On 18 August 1991, Robert Mills was with pals in an East End pub. The 21-year-old man had been soaking up a lot of booze, and he and a friend were both thrown out. Outside, there was trouble and someone stabbed the young soldier. He had lived through the first Gulf War only to die on the streets of home, blood pumping from a knife wound. A man was later charged with his murder and cleared by a not proven verdict. He denied killing Gunner Mills, saying that he had been set up by 'faceless men' to take the fall. He had gone on the run because friends had warned him he was going to be the patsy to prevent others from going down. Mills' death was tragic, senseless and needless. His friends remember him, his family mourn him, but his death is barely remembered outwith that tight circle.

That same weekend, another man died in a hail of bullets on a Provanmill street and we do remember him. The death of Arthur Thompson junior made front-page news while the tit-for-tat slayings of Robert Glover and Joseph Hanlon, and the subsequent trial of gangland enforcer Paul Ferris for Thompson's murder, helped change the way the city viewed its underworld. Ferris, acquitted of the assassination, became the latest in a growing line of criminal media darlings. He penned a number of books, which all sold well. He became the youthful but scarred public face of a world that used to prefer to remain hidden. The murders of Hanlon and Glover were reputedly ordered by a grieving Arthur Thompson and the triggerman, now dead, was never charged.

And the death march played on. It seemed, after Big Arthur's natural death, that the city's gang bosses were vying for supremacy. Gunshots rang out and blades flashed and things seemed to be getting out of hand. One former crook, speaking from his cell, once told me that in the old days the boys used to be careful who they gave guns to but now 'they're letting any idiot have one'. Something had to be done and finally someone took a leaf out of Tarzan Wilson's book and read up on the Mafia. The would-be godfathers came together and announced that they themselves were going to crack down on the violence. From now on, any physical action would have to be cleared by a committee. And they gave this Scotia Nostra a name: 'the Coalition'.

It was doomed to failure. Michael Corleone said that if history has taught us anything it's that 'we can kill anyone'. If Scottish history has taught us anything, it's that we never agree with each other for long.

The death march played on . . . and on . . . The old niceties of not involving families or 'civilians' had been swept away forever as men were gunned down on their doorsteps. Bullets spat from cars and motorbikes. Men were lured away by people they thought were friends to be murdered by men who most assuredly were not.

The shootings, bombings, maimings and intimidation all went hand in hand with the growing profits being amassed by the men at the top. The gentleman's trade of safe-blowing had long since given way to the less refined skills of the armed blagger. Extortion, moneylending and prostitution remained popular money-makers. Drugs have been around for decades, but the boys did not show much interest in the trade until the 1970s, when the snowstorm of powder began to blow north. The old guys did not dip much more than a toe into the trade but the young guns dived in, recognising that fortunes could be made from the veins of the lost and the lonely. And with the growth of the drug racket came the increase in violence. Where someone is making a profit, there are always another two or three other someones wishing to cash in. In the business world, a buy-out or takeover can be unpleasant; in the underworld, it can be lethal.

The growth of illicit earnings also increased the need for legitimate companies to help clean up the dirty money. Gang bosses had been known to own pubs and clubs and restaurants. The Caravel Bar, where Robert Mills was murdered, was owned by Thomas McGraw, aka 'the Craw', aka 'the Licensee'. He was a founder member of the Barlanark Team, a gang of raiders who specialised in tanning post offices and cash-and-carry firms across the country. Former member TC Campbell has said that there were about forty men in the team who worked in squads of six to ten on jobs. They were highly organised, using walkie-talkies to keep in contact and also to warn of any impending interest by local cops.

McGraw rose through the ranks thanks to a mixture of ruthlessness, business acumen and, rumour has it, a tendency to rat on rivals. But he also had fingers in a number of other little pies, including property companies, taxi firms and an ice-cream-van wholesalers. He tried to keep his profile low but with the wind change in the 1990s he was soon outed and he became, after Ferris, the best-known of Glasgow's gangland figures. All sorts of crimes were laid at his doorstep, including the murders of six members of the Doyle family in a horrific fire in 1984 – the so-called Ice Cream Wars murders. There is no evidence linking him to that horror, only an involvement in the ice-cream-van trade and his professional connection with Thomas Campbell, who was convicted of the murders. Joe Steele, the younger brother of Jim and John, also went down for the senseless killings. He and Campbell proved to be far from model prisoners. Although they never resorted to violence, they caused problems for the authorities – Campbell with a series of health-threatening hunger strikes and Steele with a number of high-profile escapes, during one of which he superglued himself to the gates of Buckingham Palace. Eventually, after years of campaigning, both men were cleared on a last-ditch appeal. McGraw was arrested along with the others during police raids and, according to police sources, he named everyone he could after caution. However, he did not see the inside of the courtroom, despite being named in testimony several times.

McGraw was also named several times during testimony in Paul Ferris's trial for the murder of Arthur Thompson junior but again was never called to give evidence. A high-profile drug-smuggling case against him also collapsed, and observers commented that he seemed to lead a charmed life. Perhaps he was too clever for the law. They called him a grass – the 'Licensee' tag was said to be his police informant code name and to relate as much to a licence to commit crime as to his pub ownership. He had enemies – they were the ones putting it about that he was a coppers' tout – and he was known to sport a bulletproof vest under his clothes, while his fancy four-wheel drive was said to be heavily armoured. He also attracted the attention of Her Majesty's Inland Revenue. Gangsters don't like being scrutinised by the taxman. Other mobsters they can deal with, the police they understand, but the Revenue is a different ball game. Police officers hoped that the Government would succeed where they had failed, much like the US Treasury did in the 1930s with Al Capone. However, their hopes were dashed when McGraw reached an understanding with the taxman and coughed up some cash. The Government knew what McGraw was but they seemed more interested in getting their cut than in bringing him to justice.

Tam McGraw was marked for death many times but he surprised them all, like Big Arthur, by dying in his bed of a heart attack. But when one goes, there are always others to take his place.

The old City of Glasgow Police might have amalgamated with other forces under the Strathclyde banner in 1975, but they still have the usual array of murders, rapes, thefts and domestic disputes to deal with. Recessions come and go but Glasgow's underworld thrives. Moneylending, in these recessionary times, is an earner. Armed robbery is not as popular as it once was, what with sophisticated alarm systems, fortress-like armoured cars and electronic transfers taking the place of cash. Now the boys have moved into identity theft and credit-card fraud as a means to supplement their income. But drugs, including the smuggling of cigarettes, still make up the bulk of their income, despite the occasional shortage of supply and raids by law enforcement.

The home-grown lads face a certain amount of incursion from foreign-born gangs. The Triads have been around for decades but they tend to keep very much to the Chinese community. They can trace their origins back to the ancient Tong societies of their homeland and are incredibly violent. Early in 2009, rival Chinese gangs faced off against each other in a Glasgow city-centre street armed with knives, hatchets and machetes. Eastern European thugs and the Russian Mafia, or 'Cossack Nostra', traffic in drugs and people – it's estimated that 6,000 illegal immigrant women work as prostitutes in Scotland – but Glasgow crime in this polyglot age still in the main has a local accent.

There are always calls for the legalisation of certain, if not all, drugs. This, it is proposed, would damage the gangsters' profits at a stroke. Others say that while that may be true, it will not cut down on the number of addicts or the associated crime rate. Addicts, they say, would still turn to crime to feed their habit, whether the smack, hash or coke came from legitimate or illegitimate sources. They also point out that cigarettes and alcohol are legal and yet there is a thriving black market for both. Booze, according to the former head of the Scottish Crime and Drug Enforcement Agency (SCDEA), is 'the biggest drug of concern in Scotland'.

In an interview in *Scotland on Sunday* in November 2007, Graeme Pearson said:

> I talk to prisoners and so many of them tell me that they began at the age of 11 or 12 years old, binge drinking before moving on to drugs, starting with cannabis and then heading into other drugs. They end up skipping school and then, eventually, they are kicked out and they end up without any qualifications and before they know it they are unable to do anything with their lives.

Pearson was a former Strathclyde Police detective who had helped bring Walter Norval's gang down. He quit the Drug Enforcement Agency after three years, claiming that it was understaffed and under-resourced.

There have been successes in the drug war, of course. Raids have been made, collars felt and bodies banged up, while legislation allows the authorities to seize the assets and cash of convicted criminals. In October 2008, almost three-quarters of a million pounds was confiscated from the coffers of James 'the Iceman' Stevenson. The Glasgow crook had been sent down for 12 years for money-laundering offences in relation to drug trafficking. He had cleaned up the dirty money through a fleet of taxis and property development. That same month, Donald Birrell, doing ten years for money-laundering and fraud, had Scotland's first Financial Reporting Order (FRO) slapped on him. This meant that for the next seven years he would have to come clean to the SCDEA about all his financial dealings. Johnny Gwynne, the SCDEA's acting deputy director general, commented:

> An FRO gives us the authority to monitor and investigate the financial activities of convicted criminals and ensure they are not setting up illegal operations. It also means that criminals will no longer be able to enjoy the profits of their criminal activity and sends a clear message to those involved in organised crime that we are serious about dismantling their activities and making it harder for them to operate.

Drugs have now become a constant, along with knife crime. The blade has been cutting a swathe through the city since time immemorial. In every decade from the 1920s, newspapers have carried reports about the rise of knife culture but the truth is that it is has not risen, it has only stayed the same. Tough judges have not wiped knives out, tough laws have not wiped them out, tough cops have not wiped them out. The press can pontificate and politicians can posture, but the blade was, is and probably always will be prevalent in the city streets and schemes.

And hand in hand with the blade goes the gang member. The gangs did not die with Sillitoe and they did not die with Carmont. Frankie Vaughan's much-publicised crusade in Easterhouse made barely a dent. They lived on into the 1970s and the '80s and the '90s. They live on still. It is estimated there are at least 52 different gangs in the city, perhaps even as many as 170. The hairstyles have changed, the clothes have changed, the method of throwing down the gauntlet has changed – it's more likely to be text or email than a message relayed by a female member or a hoarse challenge in the street of 'I'm your man!' Social networking sites such as Bebo and Facebook are also used by gang members, but the cops have got wise to that and they now trawl the millions of pages in the ether in search of tip-offs and intelligence. The reasons for fights are still the same – territory, an insult, revenge or just because there's a 'y' in the day of the week. The weapons remain standard: the steakie, the pickaxe handle, the makeshift chib, the axe, the chain, the broken bottle, the sword, the machete, the knuckleduster. The blood's still the same colour and it still flows freely. And often their fights are filmed, on video, on mobile phone, so that they can enjoy an after-battle movie.

Like their fathers and grandfathers before them, many of the warriors will have got 'tanked up' before the fight. Unlike their forefathers, many will be high as kites. A number of them would not think twice about slicing and dicing anyone who gets in their way, whether it be a police officer or a member of the public. There's been a breakdown in community spirit, they say. But in Glasgow the gangs are a kind of twisted community. Young men join up because they want to belong, because they're bored, because they need the security of numbers, because they like a rammy, because their dad joined up. It's almost like a family business.

Again the police are fighting back. The Violence Reduction Task Force is based in Saracen police station and is designed to crack down on gang violence and knife crime. But it's only got 20 men, and with around 3,000 to 5,000 gang members in the city it's hard not to think about Custer and the Little Big Horn. However, in its first year – from March 2008 to March 2009 – the unit made over 1,000 arrests, seized 2,752 blades and carried out 212,466 stop and searches.

In December 2008, £5 million was pledged to help end street violence. The scheme was based on the Operation Ceasefire project in Boston and was given the less exciting name of the Community Initiative to Reduce Violence (CIRV). Its aim was to bring rival gang members together and warn them that future rammies would not be tolerated. Police showed them what they already knew about their membership and their activities while support workers tried to show them there was a different way to live their lives. The idea was to tell them that they knew who they were and if they did not stop they would come and get them. Although some hardened coppers viewed the scheme with a measure of contempt – believing there was no way that the young thugs would listen – the scheme did show early signs of promise. The first surprise was when the gang members actually turned up for the meetings; the second was when 43 per cent came back for referrals to support agencies to help them get off the streets, off the drugs, out of the violence and into work.

Assistant Chief Constable Campbell Corrigan provided a soundbite to encapsulate the operation, saying, 'If you choose to take part in gang-related violence, chances are we will find you, so be prepared to pay the consequences.'

The gangs will never die and the violence will never end. They are embedded in the city like a dead gangster's body in the Kingston Bridge support. Criminals, like the poor, are always with us. Humanity's dark heart will never be denied. We will kill, steal and destroy until we ourselves are but dust in space.

BIBLIOGRAPHY

Adams, Norman, *Scotland's Chronicles of Blood* (Robert Hale, London, 1996)

Aird, Andrew, *Glimpses of Old Glasgow* (Aird & Coghill, Glasgow, 1894)

Allason, Rupert, *The Branch* (Secker & Warburg, London, 1983)

Bailey, Brian, *Hangmen of England* (W.H. Allen, London, 1989)

Beltrami, Joseph, *The Defender* (W. & R. Chambers, Edinburgh, 1980)

Boyle, Jimmy, *A Sense of Freedom* (Pan, London, 1977)

Campbell, Thomas, and McKay, Reg, *Indictment* (Canongate, Edinburgh, 2001)

Churchill, Sir Winston, *The Island Race* (Cassell, London, 1964)

Clarke, John, *Life and Times of George III* (BCA, London, 1972)

Cleland, James, *Annals of Glasgow* (John Hedderwick, Glasgow, 1816)

Cockburn, Lord Henry, *Cockburn's Memorials* (Robert Grant and Son, Edinburgh, 1946)

Colquhoun, Robert, *Life Begins at Midnight* (John Long, London, 1962)

Corbett, David, *Both Sides of the Fence* (Mainstream, Edinburgh, 2002)

Donald, Colin Duncan, *Collection of Broadsheets* (three volumes, Glasgow, 1890)

Glasser, Ralph, *Growing Up in the Gorbals* (Pan Books, London, 1987)

Jackson, Joe, *Chasing Killers* (Mainstream, Edinburgh, 2008)

Jeffrey, Robert, *Gangs of Glasgow* (B&W, Edinburgh, 2008)

—*Glasgow's Godfather* (B&W, Edinburgh, 2003)

Kay, John, *A Series of Original Portraits and Caricature Etchings with Biographical Sketches* (Hugh Paton, Edinburgh, 1838)

Kenna, Rudolph, and Sutherland, Ian, *In Custody: A Companion to Strathclyde Police Museum* (Strathclyde Police/Clutha Books, Glasgow, 1998)

Kennedy, Ludovic, *A Presumption of Innocence* (Gollancz, London, 1976)

Fido, Martin, *Murder Guide to London* (Weidenfeld & Nicolson, London, 1986)

Galbraith, Russell, *George Square 1919* (Mainstream, Edinburgh, 1988)

Gaute, J.H., and Odell, Robin, *Murderer's Who's Who* (Pan Books, London, 1980)

—*Murder Whatdunit* (Pan Books, London, 1984)

Grant, Douglas, *The Thin Blue Line* (John Long, London, 1973)

Hodge, James H. (ed.), *Famous Trials 4* (Penguin, London, 1954)

—*Famous Trials 10* (Penguin, London, 1964)

Knox, Bill, *Court of Murder* (John Long, London, 1968)

Lane, Brian, *Encyclopaedia of Forensic Science* (Headline, London, 1992)

—*The Murder Guide* (BCA, London, 1991)

Leslie, David, *Crimelord: The Licensee* (Mainstream, Edinburgh, 2005)

Lindsay, Maurice, *Victorian and Edwardian Glasgow* (B.T. Batsford, London, 1987)

Livingstone, Sheila, *Confess and Be Hanged* (Birlinn, Edinburgh, 2000)

MacGregor, George, *History of Glasgow* (Thomas D. Morrison, Glasgow, 1881)

MacKay, James, *Alan Pinkerton: The Eye Who Never Slept* (Mainstream, Edinburgh, 1996)

MacKenzie, Peter, *Old Reminiscences and Remarkable Characters of Glasgow* (James P. Forrester, Glasgow, 1875)

Meehan, Paddy, and Forbes, George, *Such Bad Company* (Paul Harris, Edinburgh, 1982)

Morton, James, *Gangland 2* (Warner, London, 1995)

Munn, Charles W., *Clydesdale Bank: The First 150 Years* (Collins, Glasgow, 1988)

Nicol, A.M., *Manuel: Scotland's First Serial Killer* (B&W, Edinburgh, 2008)

Oakley, C.A., *The Second City* (Blackie, Glasgow/London, 1990)

Old Glasgow Club Transcriptions (Aird & Coghill, Glasgow, 1913)

Palmer, Alan, *Life and Times of George IV* (BCA, London, 1972)

Pierrepoint, Albert, *Executioner: Pierrepoint* (Coronet, London, 1977)

Prebble, John, *John Prebble's Scotland* (Penguin, London, 1986)

—*The Lion in the North* (Secker & Warburg, London, 1971)

Roughead, William, *Malice Domestic* (W. Green and Son, Edinburgh, 1928)

—*Twelve Scots Trials* (Mercat Press, Edinburgh, 1995)

Rumbelow, Donald, *The Triple Tree* (Harrap, London, 1982)

Shinwell, Emanuel, *I've Lived Through It All* (Gollancz, London, 1973)

Sillitoe, Sir Percy, *Cloak Without Dagger* (Cassell & Co, London, 1955)

Smith, Sir Sydney, *Mostly Murder* (Panther, London, 1984)

Steele, John, *The Bird That Never Flew* (Mainstream, Edinburgh, 2002)

Tod, T.M., *The Scots Black Kalendar* (Munro & Scott, Perth, 1938)

Toughill, Thomas, *Oscar Slater: The Mystery Solved* (Canongate, Edinburgh, 1993)

Whittington-Egan, Molly, *Scottish Murder Stories* (Neil Wilson Publishing, Glasgow, 1998)

Whittington-Egan, Richard, *The Oscar Slater Murder Story* (Neil Wilson Publishing, Glasgow, 2001)

Young, Alex F., *Encyclopaedia of Scottish Executions 1750–1963* (Eric Dobbs, Edinburgh, 1998)